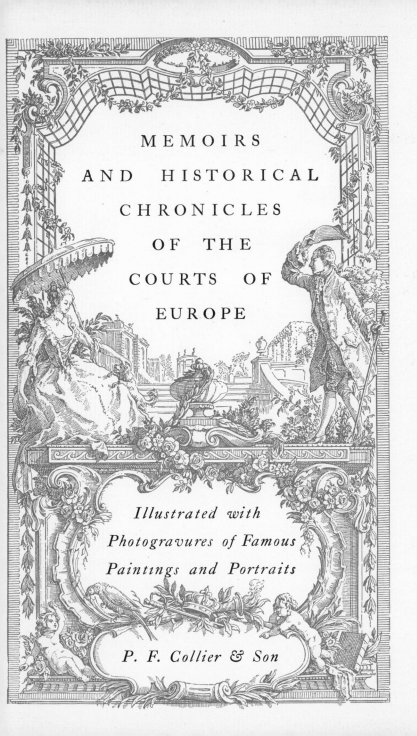

MEMOIRS
AND HISTORICAL
CHRONICLES
OF THE
COURTS OF
EUROPE

Illustrated with
Photogravures of Famous
Paintings and Portraits

P. F. Collier & Son

LOUIS XV
IN THE BOUDOIR OF MADAME DU BARRY

From the original painting by Benozur Gyala

MEMOIRS OF
MADAME DU BARRY
Of the Court of Louis XV

BY H NOEL WILLIAMS

*With a Special Introduction
and Illustrations*

VIGILANS ET AUDAX

NEW YORK
P F COLLIER & SON
PUBLISHERS

CONTENTS

CONTENTS

CONTENTS

INTRODUCTION

A SWEET, ingenuous face, a graceful charm of form, and a kind heart, united to make little Jeanne Bécu—a *fille publique* of unknown fatherhood—Comtesse Du Barry and a "left-hand queen of France."

It is a strange tale, but the marvelous freaks of fortune were never more signally illustrated than in the historical deeds of Louis XV. of France and the experiences of this amiable waif, his favorite.

Madame du Barry is often spoken of as "the profligate mistress of Louis XV." She certainly did dispense the riches of the King's treasury with lavish hand; but H. Noel Williams, in her thorough and conscientious researches into contemporary sources of information— memoirs, correspondence, journals, memoranda—and especially convinced by some more recent monographs upon Du Barry, by M. Charles Vatel, and the brothers De Goncourt—finds much to commend in her career. Without the wit of De Montespan, she was free also from the arrogance and superstition of that lady: not having the refined elegance of De Pompadour, she was also free from her predecessor's ambition to control and her vindictive pursuit of those who balked or offended her. Even the cynical Voltaire conceded that she was "a good-hearted woman."

It is impossible to blink the irregularities and sordidness of the girl's early life in Paris. In the midst of it, she was brought under the notice of Louis XV. by a scheming friend of her mother's, who managed that

the King should see her at supper with a gay company.
Soon after, his majesty caused her to be introduced
into the palace as the Comtesse Du Barry.   Madame
De Gramont, sister of the powerful Duc de Choiseul—
then minister of Foreign Affairs, of the Army and the
Marine, and even considering the assumption of care
of the Finances also—was unappeasably enraged to see
this "little girl of the streets," as she called Du Barry,
quietly pass into the position which she, with all her
aristocratic beauty, influential connections and imperious will, had after many efforts failed to gain.
She enlisted the great ascendency of her brother and
his Court faction in an implacable war of sneers, lampoons and scandals against the new-comer.

But Du Barry was difficult to wound, because she
was light-heartedly above all this.   She bore no malice;
she spoke unkindly of none,—even protecting from
punishment some of her slanderers; she cared so little
about politics and governmental intrigues that accusations of interference with grave affairs dropped, as impossible.   She readily and easily forgave her opponents,
and even made friendly overtures time and again to
Choiseul.   But the minister, urged on by his sister, repulsed all her endeavors for reconciliation, until at last
the long-tried patience gave way, and Du Barry complained of his persistent persecutions to the King.   His
majesty wrote to Choiseul a letter, still preserved,
urging him in kindly fashion to treat her courteously.
It was of no avail.   The minister continued his course,
until he was removed by the King.   Much sympathy
has been expended upon this man for his disgrace at
the hands of a king's mistress; but it has been shown
that Choiseul's ambitions had culminated in secret
attempts "to plunge France into what must have been
a disastrous war, for the sole purpose of maintaining
himself in power."

The extravagant expenditures of Du Barry's life at this time were perhaps no greater than might have been expected in a pleasure-loving woman, suddenly given free access to a royal treasury. Moreover, she was by nature recklessly generous, giving on every hand—to her friends, to her relatives, to every case of distress or need that reached her knowledge, wherever she could express sympathy or relieve trouble. That this was a genuine impulse of heart was evidenced in her later life, when, no longer a royal pensioner, but with greatly reduced resources, she was still a Lady Bountiful to her less fortunate neighbors.

After the death of Louis (May 10, 1774), Madame Du Barry was exiled from the court, and spent most of her life at her château of Louveciennes. However, she did not escape the machinations of the professional friends of "liberty, equality and fraternity" in the revolutionary upheavals. In 1791 a robbery of jewels had been perpetrated at Madame Du Barry's château, and was well known throughout France. In 1791 and 1792 she went to England for the purpose of regaining her lost property. Hereupon, although she had returned to her home, she was denounced as an *emigrée* and an aristocrat, by an Englishman, George Grieve, who had been active in revolutionary France, and boasted that he had brought seventeen heads to the guillotine.

Strong friends interceded for her, and she herself made dignified response to the accusation formulated by the Committee. But in September, 1793, she was arrested, taken to Paris, and imprisoned; on December 7, haled before the Revolutionary Court for the farce of a predetermined trial; and two days later, beheaded by the guillotine.

This story, romantic in its vicissitudes of fact beyond the imaginings of poet or dramatist, is told by the present writer with lucidity, vivacity, and a convincing control of evidences, that lay strong hold on the sympathy of the reader. For beneath all the surface of Du Barry's career is a refreshing sense of the persistence of native sweet-heartedness and generosity, whether amid the scenes of a reckless youth, the intrigues of a court, the friendly hospitalities of a country retiracy, or the terrors of an unjust death.

MADAME DU BARRY

CHAPTER I

AFTER the death of Madame de Pompadour, on April 15, 1764, there was an interregnum of more than four years at Versailles. It must not be supposed, however, that such a condition of affairs was in any way due to lack of enterprise on the part of the ladies of the Court, many of whom ardently coveted the post vacated by the famous marchioness; and, indeed, for some months, Versailles was a perfect hot-bed of intrigue and conspiracy.

Of the numerous candidates, the chances of two were, by common consent, acknowledged to be far superior to those of their competitors, insomuch that, after a while, the latter decided to stand aside and leave them in undisputed possession of the arena.

The two ladies in question were the Duchesse de Gramont,[1] sister of the all-powerful Minister, the Duc de Choiseul, and the Marquise d'Esparbès, both of whom had been intimate friends of Madame de Pompadour, and, therefore, considered that they had special claims to succeed her. The duchess was not beautiful and a little masculine in appearance, proud, overbearing, and "spiteful as the devil," but intelligent, witty,

[1] Béatrix de Choiseul-Stainville, born at Lunéville in 1730, guillotined in 1793. In 1759, she had married the Duc de Gramont, but, three months later, unable to endure the "crapulous" life led by her husband, separated from him and went to live at her brother's house, where scandalous tongues declared that she occupied a somewhat equivocal position.

and (according to Lauzun) "desirable." The marchioness is described as short and red-haired, "with a
somewhat misshapen nose;" but these blemishes were
atoned for by a dazzling complexion and shapely white
hands, of which she was so proud that she was in
the habit of having them bled, in order to preserve
their transparency.

Urged on by her brother, and encouraged by his
clients, who saw in her elevation a sure guarantee of
the continuance of their patron's favour, Madame de
Gramont appears to have underrated the difficulties
of her task, and, believing success assured, to have
conducted her wooing in too masterful a manner. The
result was that Louis XV., whose heart always yielded
more readily to a prolonged siege than a direct assault,
became alarmed, was at pains to avoid dangerous *tête-
à-têtes* with the lady, and, finally, decided to ensure
his escape by accepting the favours which Madame
d'Esparbès was so anxious to bestow upon him—
favours which, it may be mentioned, had already been
enjoyed by several of his subjects, the aged Richelieu
and the youthful Lauzun among the number.

Matters had actually progressed so far that Madame
d'Esparbès was on the point of being "proclaimed"
at Marly, where a splendid suite of apartments had
been allotted her, when Choiseul, who was absolutely
determined, that, if his sister were not to be promoted
to the vacant post, no one else should occupy it, contrived to dash the cup of happiness from her lips.

Meeting her one day on the grand staircase, surrounded by a crowd of courtiers, he took her by the
chin, and exclaimed in a patronising tone: "Well,
little one, how are your affairs progressing?"

Poor Madame d'Esparbès, utterly taken aback by
such extraordinary behaviour, was unable to say a
single word by way of retort, and could only look

supremely foolish; while her enemy walked away, chuckling over her discomfiture, and related the incident to every one whom he chanced to meet.

"The women who do not love the duke (and they are many) are disgusted at the cowardice displayed by Madame d'Esparbès," writes Prince Xavier of Saxony, "and regard her as a simpleton and a prude, protesting that, in her place, they would have applied two good blows to the ministerial cheeks, to teach him to give himself the air of taking ladies by the chin."

This public insult put an end, nevertheless, to the hopes of Madame d'Esparbès. For a *grande maîtresse,* she was sadly deficient in aplomb; and this proved her undoing. Louis disliked scandal and ridicule; and, finding that he must choose between a woman who was the laughing-stock of his Court and a Minister whose services he at that time deemed indispensable, did not hesitate to decide in favour of the latter. And so it happened that the next communication which poor Madame d'Esparbès received from her royal lover was not a *poulet,* but a *lettre de cachet,* coldly informing her that it was his Majesty's pleasure that she should retire to her father-in law's country-seat, near Montauban.

After the departure of Madame d'Esparbès, the King appears to have diverted himself with the inmates of the Parc-aux-Cerfs,[2] varied by an intrigue with a Mademoiselle de Luzy, an actress who excelled in *soubrette* parts, and what is believed to have been a *liaison* of a platonic character with the Comtesse de Seran.

The Comtesse de Seran, who is described by Mar-

[2] For a full account of this mysterious establishment, see *Mémoires de Madame du Hasset* (edit. 1825), p. 91 *et seq.;* M. Le Roi's *Curiosités historiques,* p. 230 *et seq.,* and chapter xi. of the author's "Madame de Pompadour" (London, Harpers; New York, Scribner's 1902).

montel as "beautiful as the goddess of Love, and still more interesting by her kindness and native innocence than by the lustre of her beauty," was a young lady of twenty married to a very worthy gentleman of ancient family, but of an ugliness so appalling ("red-haired, ill-made, with only one eye, and a cataract in that") that, when he was presented to her as her future husband, "she turned pale with horror, and her heart revolted against him with disgust and repugnance."

Madame de Seran aspired to be one of the ladies of the Duchesse de Chartres; but, as there was some little difficulty in the way, owing to a doubt as to the exact length of her pedigree—only those who could trace their nobility back four hundred years were eligible for the post—the matter was referred to Louis XV., who, "after listening with more attention to the praises of her beauty than the proofs of her noble blood," gave his consent, on condition that, after being presented, she should come and thank him in person.

We will let Marmontel, the countess's confidant, relate what followed:

"The rendezvous was in the King's private apartments; the lady went, trembling exceedingly. Her friends were on the tip-toe of expectation; the young countess was to be omnipotent; the King and the Court were to be at her feet; while all her friends would be loaded with favours. The company awaited the young sovereign; they counted every minute; they died with impatience to see her arrive, and yet they were glad at her being so long in arriving.

"At last she does arrive, and gives us an account of all that had passed. A page of the Bedchamber awaited her at the gate of the chapel, and she ascended by a secret staircase into the private apartments. She had not long to wait for the King. He had accosted her with an agreeable air, had taken her hands, had pressed them respectfully, and, observing her apprehension, had encouraged her by gentle words and looks full of kindness. He then made her sit opposite to him, congratulated her upon the success of the appearance she had made, and said that every one was agreed that no one so handsome had ever been seen at his Court."

" 'Then, said she, 'it must be true, Sire, that happiness makes us beautiful, and, in that case, I should be still happier now.'

" 'Accordingly you are so,' said he, taking my hands and gently squeezing them in his, which were then trembling. After a moment's hesitation, in which his looks alone spoke, he asked me what position I should be most ambitious to obtain.

"I answered, 'The place of the Princesse d'Armagnac.' (She was an old friend of the King, who was lately dead.)

" 'Ah!' said he, 'you are very young to supply the place of a friend who was present at my birth, who held me upon her knees, and whom I have loved from my cradle. Time, Madame, is necessary to obtain my confidence. I have been so often deceived.'

" 'Oh!' said I, 'I will not deceive you; and if time only is required to deserve the exalted title of your friend, I have that to give you.'

"This language from a person only twenty surprised, but did not displease him. Changing the subject, he inquired if I thought his private apartments furnished with taste. 'No,' said I, 'I should prefer them blue,' and as blue is his favorite colour, he was flattered by the reply. I added that in every other respect they appeared to me charming.

" 'If you like them,' said he, 'I hope you will sometimes be so good as to come, every Sunday, for instance, at the same hour as now.'

"I assured him that I would avail myself of every opportunity of paying my court to him, upon which he left me and went to sup with his children. He made an appointment for this day week, at the same hour. I give you all warning, therefore, that I shall be the King's friend, and that I will never be anything more."

The expectant friends, we may suppose, did everything possible to turn the lady from her resolution; but, according to Marmontel, she adhered to it firmly, and though she paid the King weekly visits, finding on the first occasion that the salon furniture had been changed to blue, and corresponded with him in the intervals between their meetings, the connection never went beyond the bounds of friendship. "The King at his age," he writes, "was not sorry to have an opportunity of tasting the charms of a sentimental union—the more flattering and agreeable that it was new, and that it sensibly affected him without endangering his vanity." The writer adds that he was "an ocular witness of the purity of this connection," as Madame de Seran was in the habit of communicating to him his Majesty's letters and her replies.

The mystery of the private meetings between the King and the lady did not escape the watchful eyes of the Court, which was naturally but little inclined to share Marmontel's view of the matter. Choiseul was furious, and, in accordance with his determination to keep at a distance from the King every woman who was not devoted to himself, prepared to crush Madame de Seran, as he had crushed Madame d'Esparbès. The countess, however, warned of his designs, hastened to undeceive him. She was acquainted with La Borde, the Court banker, one of Choiseul's staunchest allies, and requested him to arrange for her an interview with the Minister at his house and in his presence.

"Monsieur le Duc," said she, "I have a favour to ask of you. You, I understand, speak very slightingly of me; you believe me to be one of those women who aim at gaining possession of the King's heart and acquiring influence over his mind, which gives you umbrage. I might have punished you for the liberty you have taken, but I prefer to undeceive you. The King expressed a desire to see me, which I did not refuse to gratify; we have had private conversations and have carried on a constant correspondence. You are aware of all this; but the letters of the King will soon inform you of something which you do not know. Read them; you will find an extreme kindness, but as much respect as tenderness, and nothing at which I have cause to blush. I love the King as a father; I would give my life for him, but, King as he is, he will never prevail upon me to deceive him, nor to degrade myself by granting what my heart neither will nor can bestow."

Thereupon, she handed to the duke his Majesty's letters, which contained such expressions as "You are only too admirable"; "Permit me to kiss your hands"; "Permit me, in absence at least, to embrace you," and so forth.

Choiseul read the letters, and, much relieved, "prepared to throw himself at the lady's feet to implore her forgiveness."

"The King is indeed in the right," said he; "you are but too admirable. Now tell me what service can be rendered to you by the new friend you have attached for life?"

The lady accepted an appointment for a M. de la Bathe, a young officer who was about to marry her sister; but would take nothing herself from the King, except a little hôtel situated at the back of the Oratory.[a]

[a] *Mémoires de Marmontel* (edit. 1804), iii. 64, *et seq.*

About this time, Louis XV. would appear to have been seized with one of his periodical fits of remorse. As a rule, these attacks began with Lent, reached their climax in Holy Week, and ended at Easter; but the present one was prolonged until after the death of the Queen in June, 1768. "Advancing in years, worn out with pleasures," writes Mercy-Argenteau, the Austrian Ambassador, "he appeared to seek in the bosom of his family the tranquillity and happiness which disorders would not permit of; he visited the Queen regularly every evening, and this princess, who for a long time had not enjoyed the least credit, obtained then many things which indicated that she would recover a certain ascendency over her husband's mind. At the same time, the King showed on several occasions a desire to put away from him too near temptations to a licentious life; the number of inmates of the Parc-aux-Cerfs was reduced to two, one of whom, Mademoiselle Estain, requested permission to retire, and did, in point of fact, do so. The illness of the Queen supervened, and from the first her state was considered hopeless.

"Then every one believed that the King, already inclining towards a reformation in his morals, would, perhaps, in the event of widowerhood, think of espousing a young and amiable wife, who would be able to assure him repose of conscience and happiness for the remainder of his days; and this idea was firmly established in the public mind."[4]

Vain hope! Scarcely had poor Marie Leczinska been laid in her grave than Louis fell again, and this time lower than he had ever yet descended.

Cheverny says that the "little hotel" was, in reality, *une belle maison*, and scoffs at the idea that the King got nothing in return; but then Cheverny was a scandal-monger.

[4] Mercy to Kaunitz, November 9, 1768.

CHAPTER II

ABOUT the middle of the reign of Louis XIV., there lived in Paris a *rôtisseur*, or roasting cook, named Fabien Bécu. This Bécu, who is said to have been a singularly handsome man, had the good fortune to find favour in the eyes of a certain Dame de Cantigny, or Quantigny, who carried her infatuation so far as to marry him. Their wedded life, however, does not seem to have been of long duration, and, after bearing him a daughter, of whom nothing is known, the countess died, "leaving her affairs in great disorder." Fabien had perforce to return to the kitchen, and entered the service of the beautiful Madame de Ludres, who, for some months in the early part of the year 1677, disputed with Madame de Montespan the possession of the heart of *le Grand Monarque*. Worsted in the unequal contest, and unable to bear the cruel taunts and insults which her "thunderous and triumphant" rival heaped upon her, Madame de Ludres quitted the Court and retired to her country-seat, the Château de Vane, in Lorraine. Fabien accompanied his mistress, and, in 1693, married a fellow servant, a girl called Jeanne Husson, by whom he had seven children, three sons and four daughters. Of the sons, Charles, the eldest, became *valet-de-chambre* to Stanislaus Leczinski, ex-King of Poland, while his two brothers, Jean-Baptiste and Nicolas, took service with noble families in Paris. Of the daughters, two, Marie-Anne and Marguerite, married persons in their own station in life; a third, Hélène,

became *femme-de-chambre* to Madame Bignon, wife of the librarian of the Bibliothèque du Roi; while the fourth Anne, who with her sister Hélène, inherited Fabien Bécu's good looks, settled at Vaudouleurs, a small town on the borders of Champagne and Lorraine, now in the Department of the Meuse.[1]

Anne Bécu was by occupation a sempstress, but inasmuch as she lived in a large and comfortable house, the neighbours entertained a shrewd suspicion that she had a more lucrative source of revenue than her needle—a suspicion which was confirmed when, on August 19, 1743, she gave birth to a natural daughter, who was baptized the same day, the *acte de naissance* being as follows:

"Jeanne, natural daughter of Anne Bécu, otherwise known as Quantigny, was born the nineteenth of August of the year seventeen hundred and forty-three and baptized the same day; having for godfather Joseph Demange, and for godmother Jeanne Birabin, who have signed with me.

"JEANNE BIRABINE. L. GALON,
Vicar of Vaucouleurs.
JOSEPH DEMANGE."[2]

Such was the origin of the future Comtesse du Barry, the last left-hand queen of France.

It will be observed that in the above certificate the name of the father is omitted, nor has the question of the child's paternity been settled to this day, notwithstanding the fact that it has given rise to interminable disputes between historians and a long and costly lawsuit.[3] The majority of encyclopædias and bio-

[1] M. Vatel's *Histoire de Madame du Barry,* i. 1, *et seq.*
[2] E. and J. de Goncourt's *La Du Barry,* p. 6.
[3] See p. 342, *infra.*

graphical dictionaries, including even some of comparatively recent date, agree in giving the little girl for father a certain Gomard de Vaubernier, a clerk in the Excise, an error the origin of which we shall presently explain; but the theory which finds most favour with modern writers is that which ascribes the paternity to a Picpus monk,[4] one Jean Jacques Gomard, in religion Frère Ange, with whom Jeanne Bécu was on very intimate terms in later years in Paris, and who is believed to have been at this time an inmate of a community established at Vaucouleurs, in the Rue de Chaussée, the remains of whose house may still be seen.[5]

Some time between the spring of 1747 and the close of 1749, Anne Bécu, with her little daughter, removed from Vaucouleurs to Paris, where, as we have mentioned, two of her brothers and her sister Hélène were in service. This step was not improbably prompted by the fact that, in February of the former year, Anne had become the mother of a second child, a boy, who was baptized as Claude,[6] and was beginning to find herself regarded with disfavour by her neighbours. Soon after their arrival in the capital, Jeanne, who, even at this early age, showed promise of quite remarkable beauty, attracted the attention of a M. Billard-Dumouceaux,[7] a rich financier and army con-

[4] The Picpus monks, so called from the site of their chief monastery at the village of Picpus, near Paris, were Tertiaries, or members of the Third Order of St. Francis. They were not, strictly speaking, monks at all, but non-conventual members, who continued to live in society without the obligation of celibacy.

[5] M. Vatel's *Histoire de Madame du Barry*, i. 5.

[6] Nothing seems to be known about the subsequent career of this boy.

[7] Pidansat de Mairobert and other contemporary biographers of Madame du Barry assert that this M. Dumouceaux was Jeanne's godfather, having been present at Vaucouleurs at the time of her birth and undertaken the duty at the request of her father, Vaubernier, the Excise clerk, who was one of his subordinates.

tractor, and, according to Grosley, "the most amiable man in Paris," who constituted himself a kind of informal guardian to the child, and took both her and her mother to reside with him, the latter, apparently, in the capacity of cook. M. Dumouceaux was a patron of the arts, and himself a pastelist of some ability, which probably accounts for the fact that in the inventory of the Château of Louveciennes, the residence which Louis XIV. gave to the favourite, mention is made of a portrait of Madame du Barry *as a child*. M. Vatel is of opinion that this is a copy of a work executed for M. Dumouceaux by one of the artists who frequented his house.

When Jeanne was seven years old, through the influence of M. Dumouceaux or one of his friends, very possibly the Abbé Arnaud (who used to boast in after years of having dandled the future favorite of Louis XV. upon his knee), admission was procured for her to the Couvent de Sainte-Aure, in the Rue Neuve Sainte-Geneviève. This was a community which had been founded, about the year 1687, by Père Gardeau, curé of Saint-Etienne-du-Mont, "to provide an asylum for young girls of his parish whom poverty had led into dissipation." But, in 1723, it had been changed to "an establishment for the education of youth, where they are instructed in Christian piety and in arts suitable for women," and thrown open to "all young people, born of honest parents, who may find themselves in circumstances in which they are in danger of ruin."[8]

This is, of course, ridiculous, as we have shown that Joseph Demange was the *parrain* of Jeanne Bécu and that Vaubernier was a myth; and we mention it merely as an instance of the amount of credence to be placed in the testimony of these chroniclers.

[8] Hurtaut's *Dictionnaire de la ville de Paris et ses environs* (Paris, 1777), i. 413. *Tableau de l'humanité et de la bienfaisance*, 1769, by Alletz, cited by M. Vatel.

The nuns, who followed, in a modified form, the regulations of Saint Augustin, and entitled themselves *"adoratrices du sacré cœur de Jésus,"* numbered fifty-three, of whom ten were lay-sisters; they provided accommodation for forty pupils, who paid from 250 to 300 livres a year and certain extras, and also admitted, at an annual charge of 500 livres, ladies who wished to use the convent as a temporary retreat.

On the whole, the life was not austere, but conventual habits were very strictly observed. The pupils rose at five; at seven, they attended mass in a private chapel built for the use of the convent; at eleven, they dined on plain but sufficient food; and at nine, they retired to their dormitories. The costume was severe and simple. On the head each little girl wore a black woolen hood, with a band of coarse cloth bound tightly across the forehead, a plain frock of white Aumale serge, an unstarched veil, and shoes of yellow calf fastened with cords of the same. Playfulness, jesting, raillery, affectation, and even loud laughter were forbidden and punished. The curriculum, besides instruction in religious duties, included reading, writing, drawing, needlework, embroidery, and housekeeping.''*

To this convent, then, Jeanne was sent, "with two pairs of sheets and six towels," and here she remained until she was fifteen; at least we hear no more of her until the early part of 1759. Of her life there nothing is known, except that she would appear to have received a tolerable education. Her spelling and her grammar are ridiculed by writers like Pidansat de Mairobert, but, as M. Vatel very justly points out, in those days few ladies knew how to spell correctly; and the *grandes dames* who reproached Richelieu with

* *Constitution des religieuses de Sainte-Aure, suivant la règle de Saint-Augustin* (Paris, 1786), cited by the Goncourts.

his infidelities wrote *"Vous ne mémé plu."*[10] "With
the exception of the letters addressed to Henry Seymour,"[11] and which appear to have been dictated by
ardent passion," he says, "her style is dull or, as she
called it, *terre-à-terre*. What must be borne in mind
from the letters verified as hers is that she received
and retained a certain amount of intellectual culture,
which could have been acquired only at Sainte-Aure.
We find her expressing an opinion on Nero, whose
cruelties she considered to have been exaggerated; on
Lovelace, &c. She read Cicero and Demosthenes, and
had a great love for Shakespeare, translated, of course,
since she professed herself unacquainted with the
English language. She had learned how to draw, and
founded a prize for the pupils at the School of Drawing opened by M. de Sartines. This little accomplish-
ment ought also to be placed to the credit of the education she received at the convent."[12]

Nor were the years spent at Sainte-Aure without
their effect upon Jeanne's character. The curriculum,
as we have said, included instruction in household
management; and, even in the midst of her greatest
prodigality, when she was squandering the public
money with both hands on an army of jewellers,
dressmakers, milliners, and bric-à-brac dealers, she
never forgot the lessons of her childhood. She kept
a daily account of her expenses; she carefully checked
every item in the bills of her tradesmen; she exercised
as keen a supervision over her household as the wife
of any bourgeois; and when in London, in 1792, we

[10] Madame de Pompadour, who was one of the most accomplished women of her time, never seemed able to distinguish
between the possessive pronoun *se* and the demonstrative *ce*, and,
like Louis XV., was in the habit of adding an *s* to the third
person plural of verbs; while the orthography of Madame Geof-
frin, who kept a literary salon, was a thing to marvel at.
[11] See p. 294, *et sequ., infra.*
[12] *Histoire de Madame du Barry,* i. 27.

find her writing instructions to her steward to make jam of all the fruit grown at Louveciennes.

Again, as with Madame de Montespan, the traces of her early religious education remained ineffaceable, and throughout her life she manifested the most profound respect for the forms and ceremonies of the Church. She built a private chapel in her hôtel at Versailles, another at Saint-Vrain, a third at Louveciennes, where the services were conducted by a Recollect, who came from Saint-Germain expressly for the purpose. She enriched the Church at Louveciennes by gifts of candles, pictures, and ornaments of all kinds. Banished to the Abbey of Pont-aux-Dames after the death of Louis XV., she speedily conciliated the abbess, Madame de Fontenille, who had been strongly prejudiced against her, and made so many friends among the nuns that her enemies accused her of a hypocritical simulation of devotion. Finally, in 1792, she gave shelter, at no small risk to herself, to the Abbé de Jorre, the Abbé de Roche-Fontenille, nephew of the Abbess of Pont-aux-Dames, and a number of other persecuted ecclesiastics.

On leaving the convent, Jeanne went to live with her mother, who had some years previously married a man named Nicolas Rançon, described in the marriage certificate as "a domestic," and now resided in the Rue Neuve Saint-Etienne. If we are to believe the Goncourts, the family were in great poverty, and the little girl was compelled to earn a precarious livelihood by peddling haberdashery, sham jewellery, and other trifles "that people buy for the sake of the *beaux yeux* of the seller," about the streets, and that, while engaged in this occupation, she fell a victim to the Comte de Genlis, "one of the most fascinating libertines of the age," who, in after years, was profoundly aston-

ished to recognize in the mistress of Louis XV. a little girl of the streets whom his *valet-de-chambre* had once brought him.[13]

The account, however, which the Goncourts give of Jeanne's early life is, for the most part, based on very untrustworthy evidence, and must be regarded with suspicion, and the earliest authentic information which we have of the future favourite after her admission to Sainte-Aure is in the spring of 1759, when she makes her appearance in a somewhat singular connection.

On April 18, 1759, Anne Bécu, or Rançon, as she now was, accompanied by her daughter, who, it may be mentioned, also called herself Rançon, and gave her age as fourteen and a half, though she was within four months of completing her sixteenth year, presented herself before Charpentier, the commissary of police for their quarter, to lodge a complaint, and demand protection, against the widow Lametz, or Lameth, dressmaker, of the Rue Neuve des Petits-Champs. It appeared that Madame Rançon and Jeanne had made the acquaintance of the widow's son, who was a *coiffeur de dames* at the house of a Madame Peugevin, where Hélène Bécu, Anne's sister, was employed as *femme-de-chambre,* and which young Lametz used to visit in his professional capacity. Madame Rançon suggested that Lametz should give a few lessons in his art to her daughter, which, as may be supposed, he was willing enough to do, and henceforth seems to have spent the greater part of his time at the Rançons' house.

After the lessons had continued for some months, with great satisfaction to all parties concerned, the young man's frequent absences from home began to arouse the suspicions of his mother, who caused in-

[3] E. and J. de Goncourt's *La Du Barry,* p. 12.

quiries to be made, with the result that one fine day she called upon Madame Rançon, overwhelmed her with reproaches and insults, and concluded by threatening to denounce both her and Jeanne to the curé of the parish for compassing the moral and material ruin of her son. This was a menace not to be treated lightly, as in those days the parochial clergy were invested with considerable powers, and the police were in the habit of committing persons to prison on their application,[14] and, consequently, Madame Rançon lost no time in invoking the protection of the commissary of her quarter.

The affair does not appear to have proceeded any further, though a lengthy *procès-verbal* was drawn up, which, in later years, was brought to light and furnished the enemies of the future Comtesse du Barry with one of their favourite weapons.

Shortly after the Lametz episode, Jeanne became lady's companion, or *femme-de-chambre,* to the widow of a farmer-general named La Garde, who resided at a villa called the Cour-Neuve, in the suburbs of Paris. Pidansat de Mairobert, the chronicler in whom the Goncourts repose such misplaced confidence, asserts that she was indebted for this post to the Picpus monk, Gomard, whom most writers now believe to be the father of Jeanne, but whom he metamorphoses into her paternal uncle. Gomard had now entered the priesthood, and, according to Pidansat, had been appointed private chaplain to Madame de la Garde; but M. Vatel, who carefully examined the papers of the La Garde family, declares that he was never in any way connected with it.

[14] On the other hand, the police appear to have exercised a very strict supervision over the conduct of the clergy, both regular and secular, and to have promptly brought any irregularities which they discovered to the notice of the ecclesiastical authorities.

M. Vatel's researches enabled him to demolish another fiction, which had long obtained credence. The story went that Madame de la Garde had two sons, both young men, residing with her, that the lads fell in love with Jeanne and quarrelled violently about her, and that, in order to restore tranquillity, their mother was compelled to turn her out of the house.

M. Vatel says that Madame de la Garde certainly had two sons, Nicolas and François Pierre, but they were not romantic youths, but middle-aged and married men, occupying responsible positions, Nicolas being, like his father before him, a farmer-general, and François Pierre a *maître des requêtes*. Moreover, they did not reside with their mother, but had separate establishments of their own, the elder living in the Place Louis-le-Grand and the younger in the Rue Neuve du Luxembourg.[15]

From *demoiselle de compagnie* Jeanne became *demoiselle de boutique*. Towards the close of the year 1760, or at the beginning of 1761, she left Madame de la Garde, and was apprenticed by her parents—apparently under the name of Mademoiselle Lange, or l'Ange—to a man-milliner called Labille, in the Rue Neuve des Petits-Champs.[16] In establishments of this kind pretty girls were exposed to endless temptations, and it would have needed one of much more austere virtue than poor Jeanne to have successfully resisted the assaults of the gilded youths, who, under the pretext of purchasing lace ruffles, cravats, and so forth, frequented the shop and "ogled the demoiselles from morn till eve." That she had several lovers at this

---

[15] *Histoire de Madame du Barry,* i. 41, *et seq.*

[16] And not in the Rue Saint-Honoré, where so many writers have located it. The account given by the Goncourts of Madame du Barry passing the shop on her way to the scaffold in 1793, and gazing pathetically up at the girls crowding to the windows to catch a glimpse of the ex-milliner, is a myth.

time is not disputed, though none of them seem to
have been of sufficient social importance to call for the
attention of contemporary writers.

Jeanne does not appear to have remained long at
Labille's shop, and little is known of her life during the
next two or three years, in which some writers assert
that she sank so low as to become a woman of the
town, and even for a time an inmate of an establishment kept by a notorious *entremetteuse* called La
Gourdan. M. Vatel discusses this very unpleasant
question at considerable length, and his conclusion is
that the charge is devoid of foundation and was a
mere invention of the Choiseul party, about whose
methods of warfare we shall have occasion to speak
hereafter.[17] The register of loose women, he says,
was kept by the police with minute exactitude, but
it contains no name resembling any of those by which
Jeanne Bécu was at different periods known. Moreover when in 1776 the woman Gourdan, having been
indiscreet enough to allow the wife of a magistrate
to make assignations at her house, was haled before
the Tournelle, or Criminal Court of the Parliament
of Paris, the ledger containing the names of all her
pensionnaires for many years past was impounded.
M. Vatel is of opinion that if Madame du Barry's
had appeared therein, it would have been made known,
as she was then in disgrace, and no one was interested
in defending her.[18]

Upon so very delicate a subject we naturally prefer

[17] Sara Goudard, in her *Remarques sur les Anecdotes concernant
Madame du Barry,* relates that in the early days of Jeanne's
favour, when the Choiseul party were making desperate efforts
to prevent her presentation at Court, a stranger came to La
Gourdan and offered her a large sum of money if she would
publicly attest that the new favourite had been one of her *pen-
sionaires,* but that the woman refused, " as she would not consent to publish such a lie."
[18] *Histoire de Madame du Barry,* i. 57, *et seq.*

not to dwell, and will, therefore, merely remark that
M. Vatel, in his zealous championship of Madame du
Barry, appears to entirely ignore the possibility that a
person who is known to have lost at least three *aliases*
might very well have had others which have escaped
the notice of historians.

But if, for lack of evidence, we must acquit Jeanne
Bécu of having been a woman of the town, there can be
no possible doubt that during these years she had become one of those who, as M. Vatel delicately expresses it, "ignore the obligations of virtue without
having the excuse of passion"; in other words, that
she was a *femme entretenue* in the very fullest accep-
tation of the term. According to Soulavie—not, however, a writer in whom much confidence is now reposed—a M. Lavauvenardière was the first *amant
en tître* of the lady; while other chroniclers mention
an Abbé de Bonnac, a Colonel de Marcieu, and a M.
Duval, a clerk in the Marine, as among her pro-
tectors.

Towards the close of 1763, Jeanne, who now called
herself Mademoiselle Beauvarnier, or Beauvernier,
seems to have been in the habit of frequenting a
gambling-house in the Rue de Bourbon, kept by a
"Marquise" Duquesnoy—gambling-houses were the
favourite haunt of the *filles galantes* of those days—
and it was here apparently that she encountered Jean
du Barry, the man with whose assistance she was
one day to rise "from the dregs to the zenith of her
profession."

Jean du Barry, who was at this time in his fortieth
year, was a member of an old family in Languedoc,
which traced its descent back to the beginning of the
fifteenth century. His father, Antoine du Barry, had
been a brave soldier, who had served with distinction
in the War of the Spanish Succession and retired from

the army with the Cross of Saint-Louis. Married in 1748 to a Mademoiselle de Verongrèse, "a handsome and honest person, who had nothing to say to the shameful conduct of her husband," Jean speedily wearied of his wife and the monotony of provincial life, and, two years later, came to Paris, calling himself the Comte du Barry-Cérès, though he had no claim whatever to any title. Endowed with a handsome presence, imperturbable assurance, a ready wit,[19] and an amusing Gascon accent, he succeeded in making a favourable impression on the Marquis de Rouillé, then Minister for Foreign Affairs, and was despatched on secret missions to England, Germany, and Russia. Rouillé, however, resigned office in 1757, and his successors, Bernis and Choiseul, turned a deaf ear to Du Barry's applications for further employment, though, as some compensation for the forced abandonment of his diplomatic ambitions, he contrived to obtain contracts both for the army and navy, and an interest in the supply of provisions to the troops of Corsica.

With the profits of his contracts he plunged into all kinds of debauchery and dissipation, and the infamy of his life was such as to astonish even the depraved society amid which he moved and earn for him the sobriquet of the "Roué." From the police reports of the time it would appear that he was in the habit of introducing young beauties of humble station —generally unfortunate girls whom he had himself seduced and then grown weary of—to the haunts of

[19] One day at Spa, Jean du Barry was keeping a faro bank and watching very closely to avoid being cheated. He appeared to entertain some suspicion of the Electress Dowager of Saxony, who was one of the players, and the princess expressed her amazement that he should believe her capable of any irregularity. "A thousand pardons, Madame," exclaimed Du Barry. " My suspicions could not possibly refer to you. You royal personages never cheat for anything but crowns."

fashionable vice, in the expectation of their attracting
the attention of some wealthy libertine, in which event
Du Barry seldom failed to reap a substantial profit
from his speculation. Madame du Hausset tells us that
on one occasion, during the *régime* of Madame de Pompadour, he had aspired to provide Louis XV. with a
mistress, in return for which service he had the impertinence to demand the post of Minister to Cologne.

"I went one day to the comedy at Compiègne," she
says, "and Madame (de Pompadour) having put some
questions to me about the play, inquired if there were
many people present, and whether I had not remarked
a very pretty young lady. I replied that there was,
in fact, in a box near mine, a young woman who was
surrounded by all the young gentlemen of the Court.
She smiled and said: 'That was Mademoiselle Dorothée; she has been this evening to sup with the King,
and will go to-morrow to the chase. You are astonished to see me so well informed, but I know still
more. She was brought here by a Gascon, whose
name is Du Barré or Du Barry, and who is the greatest
scoundrel in France. He founds his hopes on the
charms of Mademoiselle Dorothée, which he imagines
the King will not be able to resist. She is really very
pretty. I have had an opportunity of seeing her in
my garden, to which they brought her under pretext
of taking a stroll. She is the daughter of a water-
carrier at Strasburg, and her adorer demands, to begin
with, to be made Minister at Cologne.' "[20]

This intrigue was promptly nipped in the bud by
Lebel, the King's confidential *valet-de-chambre,* who
had the management of his royal master's love-affairs,
and had no mind to allow a stranger to usurp his
functions; and M. du Barry and his *protégée* were
compelled to return to Paris empty-handed.

[20] *Mémoires de Madame du Hausset* (edit. 1891), p. 62.

The *"Roué,"* struck by Jeanne's beauty, "invited
her to take charge of his house and do the honours
of it," as he himself euphemistically expresses it.[21] She,
on her part, we may well believe, was ready enough
to entertain his proposal, as he enjoyed the reputation
of being exceedingly liberal to the ladies whom he
honoured with his attentions, and was said to "cover
them with gold and diamonds";[22] and Jeanne's partiality
for jewellery amounted to an absolute passion—a
passion which was one day to bring her to the guillotine.

Mademoiselle Beauvarnier and her mother accordingly took up their residence with Du Barry, at his
house in the Rue Neuve Saint-Eustache, whence they
subsequently removed to one in the Rue de Jussieu.
The presence of Madame Rançon was presumably intended to disguise the nature of the relations which
existed between her daughter and the "count," but, if
such were the object in view, it would not appear to
have been attained, as the following entry in the
Journal de la Police will testify:

"December 14, 1764.—The Marquis du Barry, who
was responsible for having brought *la belle Dorothée*[23]
from Strasburg to Paris, and for having given the
demoiselle Beauvoisin her start in life, exhibited last
Monday, in his box at the Comédie Italienne, the
demoiselle Veauvernier (*sic*), his mistress. She is a
person nineteen years old, tall, well-made, and of distinguished appearance, with a very pretty face. No
doubt he intends to dispose of her (*brocanter*) advan-
tageously. When he begins to weary of a woman, he
invariably has recourse to this expedient. But, at the
same time, it must be admitted that he is a connoisseur,
and that his merchandise is always salable."

[21] Letter of Jean du Barry *to* Malesherbes.
[22] Manuel's *La Police dévoilée,* i. 231.   [23] See p. 24, *supra.*

Soon after Jeanne became Du Barry's mistress her
name underwent a third modification. The *"Roué"*
considered that Beauvarnier was not a sufficiently aristocratic patronymic, so he transformed it into Vaubernier, with a territorial prefix, and the young lady
became Mademoiselle de Vaubernier.[24]

Of Jeanne's life with the *"Roué"* we have few details. Montigny tells us that she never went out on
foot, but drove about in a coach, accompanied by two
children, "who were not her own," but whom all the
tradesmen with whom she dealt declared *"qu'elle tenoit
dans la plus grande décence."*[25] From the police reports
we learn that she was on terms of great intimacy with a
certain Comtesse La Rena, described as "a married
woman living apart from her husband, and enjoying
an income of about 25,000 livres, the proceeds of her
galanteries, principally with Milord Marche,[26] who had
conceived so violent a passion for her that he had lived
with her seven years in England";[27] while she also frequented the house of a Mademoiselle Legrand, a
courtesan who affected literary society, and whom
Dumouriez, in his *Mémoires,* compares to Ninon de

[24] She also appears to have been known as Mademoiselle l'Ange,
" on account of her celestial face," says Lauzun, and, on occasion, to have masqueraded as her protector's wife. Thus, in
May 1767, we find her laying a complaint before a police-com-
missary against a dressmaker named Etienne, who had appro-
priated a piece of Indian muslin which had been sent her to make
into a gown, and used abusive language and threats towards the
" *Roué's* " son, Adolphe, who had been deputed to remonstrate
with her. In this document we find the lady styling herself
" Dame Jeanne de Vaubernier, *spouse* of Messire Jean Comte du
Barry."

[25] *Les illustres victimes vengées.*

[26] William Douglas, Earl of Marche, afterwards fourth Duke
of Queensberry, the notorious " Old Q."

[27] " I have had Lord Marche and the Rena here for one night,
which does not raise my reputation in the neighbourhood."—
Horace Walpole *to* Conway, September 9, 1762.

l'Enclos. Here she was in the habit of meeting a
circle of wits and men of letters: Crébillon *fils*—the
author of some of the most licentious romances ever
penned, one of which, *Le Sopha,* so shocked Madame
de Pompadour's sense of propriety that she caused
him to be banished from Paris—Collé, Guibert, and
Favier.

At Du Barry's own house, too, Jeanne became acquainted with several of the most celebrated personages of her time, for the *"Roué,"* consummate scoundrel though he was, was, notwithstanding, a man of
considerable attainments and charm of manner, and
an admirable host. Among his visitors were that ever-
green sinner, the Duc de Richelieu, the Duc de Duras,
his *alter ego* the Duc de Nivernais, whom Lord Ches-
terfield held up as a model for his son to form himself
upon,[28] and the Prince de Ligne, whose connection
with the lady is interesting, if only for the striking
portrait which he has left us of her:

"She is tall, well-made, ravishingly fair, with an
open forehead, fine eyes, pretty lashes, an oval face
with little moles upon her cheeks, which only serve to
enhance her beauty, an aquiline nose, a laughing
mouth, a clear skin, and a bosom with which most
would be wise to shun comparison."[29]

Another celebrity whose acquaintance "Mademoiselle de Vaubernier" made at this time was that senti-

[28] " I send you here enclosed a letter of recommendation to the
Duke of Nivernais, the French Ambassador at Rome, who is, in
my opinion, one of the prettiest men I ever knew in my life.
I do not know a better model for you to form yourself upon;
pray observe and frequent him as much as you can. He will
show you what manners and graces are."—Letter of July 6, 1749.

[29] Here is another contemporary portrait of the lady: " Madame
du Barry was truly pretty; beautiful head, beautiful eyes, beautiful hair of an ashen grey hue; beautiful, rounded arms and
divine hands; her enchanting smile charmed every one."—
Souvenirs de Jeanne Etienne Despréaux, p. 14.

mental libertine, the Duc de Lauzun. Lauzun, who
was then in quest of consolation for his rejection at
the hands of the beautiful Lady Sarah Bunbury, met
Jeanne at one of the Opera balls and accepted an invitation from the *"Roué"* to sup at his house, where
his host, who was suffering from inflammation of the
eyes, received him in a superb *robe-de-chambre,* with
his hat on his head, to keep in place two baked apples,
which some quack had recommended as a remedy for
his complaint. The house was in good taste, and
among the guests were several very pretty women,
one of whom, a Madame de Fontanelle, "had come
from Lyons with the design of becoming the mistress
of the King, and of the first person who might ask
her in the interim." Mademoiselle de Vaubernier was
very gracious to Lauzun, who expresses his conviction
that she would have been "more than willing" to consider any proposal he might have cared to make.
However, the affair went no further than a flirtation.[30]

Scandal, indeed, attributes several lovers to Jeanne
during this period—the Comte de Fitz-James, a M.
d'Arcambal, a rich financier, and Radix de Sainte-Foy,
Treasurer of the Marine,[31] are among those upon
whom she is reported to have bestowed her favours;
while Senac de Meilhan says that it soon became quite
le bon air "to have supped at least with her." These

[30] *Mémoires du Duc de Lauzun* (edit. 1858), p. 78.

[31] *"January* 29, 1768.—. . . The demoiselle Beauvarnier, mistress, or rather *vache à lait,* of the sieur du Barry. It is M. de
Sainte-Foy, Treasurer of the Marine, whom this last-named
person is at present engaged in 'fleecing,' under the good pleasure
of the sieur du Barry."—*Etat des femmes et filles galantes,* cited
by M. Vatel.

When Madame du Barry became the mistress of Louis XV.,
that monarch is said to have remarked to the Duc de Noailles,
"I am told that I have succeeded M. de Sainte-Foy." To which
the witty courtier retorted, "Just as your Majesty succeeded
Pharamond," implying that there had been a good many others
in between.—Sismondi's *Histoire des Français,* xxix. 401.

suppers, with a little game of lansquenet, brélan, or *passe-passe* to follow, must, we fear, have proved somewhat costly experiences for the lady's admirers, and the *"Roué"* had, no doubt, good reason to congratulate himself upon his bargain. However, as the next chapter will show, the time was not far distant when Jeanne was to establish infinitely greater claims upon the gratitude of her scoundrelly protector.

CHAPTER III

A GREAT deal of conflicting evidence exists in regard to the first meeting of Louis XV. and Jeanne Bécu. The general opinion of their contemporaries appears to have been that the lady's charms were brought to his Majesty's notice by the *valet-de-chambre* Lebel, the indefatigable purveyor of the Parc-aux-Cerfs, at the solicitation of the *"Roué."* According to one story, Lebel invited Jeanne, Radix de Sainte-Foy, her lover of the moment, and some other persons to sup with him in his apartments at Versailles, where the King, who had been an unseen spectator of the banquet, "through a secret window made in the dining-room wall," was so enraptured with her beauty and vivacity that he ordered her to be brought to him the following day, or, according to other versions, the same evening.[1]

A more probable solution of the question, however, which attributes the meeting to accident, is to be found in a letter written by Jean du Barry, in 1776, to Malesherbes, then Minister of the Household to Louis XVI. The *"Roué,"* who on the death of Louis XV. had been promptly exiled, was desirous of visiting Paris, "in order to see his doctor, his oculist, and his creditors"; and, in the hope of securing permission to do so, enters into a sort of justification of his life, including an explanation of his share in the introduction of "Mademoiselle de Vaubernier" to the late King. Here is what he says on the matter:

[1] Dutens's *Mémoires d'un voyageur qui se repose* (edit. 1806), ii. 36.

"Having at that time no other care than that of
watching over the education of my son, page to the
King, who possessed but indifferent health, I withdrew into a very limited circle of acquaintances. And
it was then that I begged Madame Rançon and her
daughter, Mademoiselle Vaubernier, to take charge of
my house and do the honours of it, a task which they
performed for several years with kindness and intelligence.

"Moved by gratitude, and with a view to providing
for their future, I then surrendered to them my interest in the provisioning of Corsica, which they enjoyed for some months.

"The new arrangements made by M. de Choiseul
having deprived them of this, they solicited from him
its continuance; and it was in the course of the different journeys which he required them to make to
Versailles that Mademoiselle Vaubernier attracted the
attention of the late King.   M. Lebel received his
orders, and the latter, with whom neither she nor myself had any acquaintance, arranged matters with her
alone . . . ."[2]

Although the above version of the affair is quite in
accordance with the habits of his Most Christian
Majesty, who, d'Argenson tells us, was accustomed
to "throw the handkerchief" to any pretty young girl
or woman he might chance to see at Mass or elsewhere,[3] we should hesitate to accept it, since it was
so obviously to the writer's interest to minimise his

[2] *Revue de Paris*, November 1836.
[3] " *February* 13, 1753.—The King is indulging in *passades;* he
throws the handkerchief to young girls and women whom he
perceives at Mass or at the *grand couvert*. Bachelier, his old
prime minister (Lebel's predecessor), brings them to him. A
young beauty of Montpellier, daughter of the Président Nicquet,
with whom I am acquainted, has lately 'taken the leap' (*sautée
le pas*), and is still at Versailles; she expects to become *maîtresse
déclarée*."

part in the transaction. But, as it happens, his account is confirmed by two independent chroniclers, Sara Goudard and Montigny; while we learn from the unpublished Memoirs of Choiseul[*] that Jeanne did actually visit the Minister at Versailles, on two occasions, in reference to the matter mentioned by Du Barry.

But whether it was accident or design which threw Jeanne across the path of Louis XV., it is beyond question that the old King's subjugation was immediate and complete.

The secret of the extraordinary fascination which she exercised over him, and continued to exercise to the day of his death, lay not so much in her physical charms, great as these undoubtedly were, but in her high spirits, her unfailing good-humour, and, above all, in her absolute freedom from affectation. "Instead of imitating the great ladies who bored the King, she showed herself just as she was, under the aspect of a veritable courtesan, with all the cynicism, animation, and refinements of her trade. Louis XV. felt his jaded senses revive as if by a miracle. He was enchanted by it. The new favourite seemed to him an exceptional being. He determined to cover her with a rain of gold and

[*] These memoirs, which must not be confused with the *Mémoires de M. le duc de Choiseul, écrits par lui-même,* printed at Choiseul's private press at Chanteloup in 1773, and published in 1790, are declared by M. Vatel to be " as authentic as important," and such would appear to be the opinion of most historians, including, among recent writers, M. Pierre de Nolhac. On the other hand, Ritter von Arneth and M. Flammermont, in a note to their *Correspondance secrète du Comte de Mercy-Argenteau avec l'Empereur Joseph II. et le Prince von Kaunitz* (Paris, 1896), assert that they are spurious. Whether the memoirs are genuine or not, however, there can be no question that they are the work of some one intimately acquainted with the Court of Louis XV., and, if not written by Choiseul, largely inspired by him.

jewels, and make her the first *femme entretenue* in
France—in all Europe."[5]

It was in the early days of July 1768, that the events
of which we have just spoken occurred, and the Court
was on the point of setting out on its annual visit to
Compiègne. Louis XV. was naturally desirous that
his new conquest should follow him thither. But,
as a demoiselle, particularly one of humble birth,
could not well perform the functions of a royal
mistress without risk of grave scandal—it was a sort
of unwritten law that the favourite must be a married
and titled woman—he decided that a husband with the
necessary qualifications must be found for her without delay, and communicated his wishes to Jeanne du
Barry, through the medium of Lebel.[6]

So lucrative a rôle as that of honorary consort to
the King's new mistress would have suited the *"Roué"*
admirably, but, unfortunately, he was debarred from
playing it, his neglected wife being still in the flesh.
However, there was no necessity to let the post pass out
of his sphere of influence, as he had a bachelor brother,
Guillaume by name, a needy officer or ex-officer of
Marines, who lived with his widowed mother and
his two sisters at the family-seat of the Du Barrys, at
Lévignac, near Toulouse, and who seemed expressly
made for the occasion.[7]

[5] Imbert de Saint-Amand's *Les Femmes de Versailles*: *Les
dernières années de Louis XV.*, p. 23.

[6] The monarch's infatuation for Mademoiselle de Vaubernier
by no means commended itself to this worthy, to whose interest
it was to keep his royal master supplied with a constant succession of charmers. So angry was he that he took upon himself to
remonstrate vehemently with his Majesty, who, highly incensed
at his presumption, threatened to strike him with the fire-irons
if he did not at once desist. This threat, we are told, affected M.
Lebel so deeply as to bring on an attack of colic, whereof he died
two days later.

[7] Jeanne du Barry had another brother Nicolas, called Elie,

The good folk at Lévignac had not seen their relative for years, and were, in consequence, not a little astonished when one day he descended upon them, informed them that he had come to make all their fortunes, and carried the whole family off to Toulouse, where, before a notary named Sens, the old lady signed a procuration authorising Guillaume du Barry "to contract a marriage with any person whom he should judge suitable, on the express understanding that the said dame should not be required to make any provision for her son on the occasion of the said marriage."

This formality completed, Jean, the intended bridegroom, and their two sisters, all set out for Paris, travelling in such frantic haste as to suggest the possibility of there being some other candidate for Mademoiselle de Vaubernier's hand in the field; and, on July 23, the day after their arrival in the capital, the marriage contract was duly executed.[8]

A more amazing piece of impudence than this contract it would be difficult to conceive.

The future husband, who had been plain Guillaume du Barry in the procuration signed at Toulouse, becomes "high and puissant seigneur, messire Guillaume, Comte du Barry, son of the deceased messire Antoine, Comte du Barry, and of the dame Catherine Delacaze, his spouse."

The *"Roué"* arrogates to himself even more imposing qualifications, and is not only a high and puissant seigneur, but the holder of a presumably important

and a third sister who had married a peasant of Lévignac, named Filieuse. The two sisters who lived with their mother had been baptized respectively Françoise and Marthe, but were known by the sobriquets of *"Chon"* and *"Bitschi."* The elder, *"Chon,"* was a young woman of considerable intelligence, and, according to Pidansat de Mairobert, contributed to the *Mercure.*

[8] M. Lenôtre's *Vieilles maisons, vieux papiers,* 197 *et seq.*

office under the Crown, Governor of Lévignac, to wit.
Lévignac, it may be mentioned, was a little village,
which probably did not contain a single house of any
size apart from the château of the Du Barrys.

But the most startling transformation is reserved
for the future bride, who not only changes her name
for the fourth time, but invents, or has invented for
her, a father to bear it, and styles herself "the demoiselle Jeanne Gomard de Vaubernier, a minor, daughter
of the dame Rançon and of the *sieur Jean Jacques
Gomard de Vaubernier,* interested in the affairs of the
King, *her first husband."*

As may be anticipated, the body of this precious
document is in keeping with the preamble.

It provides that there should be no community of
goods between the parties, but that the wife should
charge herself with all the expenses of the *ménage:*
food, rent, table-linen, household utensils, keep of
horses, and so forth, and with the maintenance and
education of the children born of the marriage! In
return for this, the husband was to make her an annual allowance of 6000 livres, payable half-yearly and
in advance, in addition to a sum of 1000 livres per
annum which he is declared to have already settled
upon her.

A paper annexed to the contract reveals the lady's
fondness for jewellery and fine raiment. It states that
she possesses diamonds (collar, aigrette earings, &c.)
to the value of 16,000 livres; English, Brussels, and
Valenciennes lace worth 6000 livres; thirty silk
gowns, two dozen corsets, and other articles of apparel
in proportion. Altogether her property is valued at
30,000 livres, which is declared to be "the result of
her earnings and economies."

In order to sustain the titles and dignities which the
Du Barrys had bestowed upon themselves, a coat-of-

arms was, of course, required; but the inventive genius
of the *"Roué"* was fully equal to the occasion. He
instituted researches into his genealogy, and quickly
discovered that his family was a branch of the old
Irish house of Barrymore, the arms and motto of
which—*Boutez-en-avant*—the "Comtesse" du Barry
forthwith assumed and retained for the rest of her
life.[9]

The religious ceremony, indispensable at this period
to the validity of a marriage, was postponed until
September 1—M. Vatel thinks on account of the illness and death of Lebel, who had died on August 17—
when it took place at the Church of Saint-Laurent, at
five o'clock in the morning, in order to avoid undesirable publicity. The mysterious Gomard, the ex-Pic-
pus, the *soi-disant* uncle and presumed father of
Jeanne,[10] appeared to represent the stepfather and
mother of the bride, resplendent in "a frock of maroon

[9] The family of Barry of Barry's Court, Viscounts Buttevant
and Earls of Barrymore, traced their descent back to one William
de Barri, of Norman origin. William de Barri's eldest son,
Robert, accompanied Robert Fitz-Stephen to Ireland in 1169,
to assist Dermot, King of Leinster, to regain his throne, and,
after a series of exploits which earned for him the name of
Barrymore, was slain at Lismore, about the year 1185. He was
succeeded by his brother, Philip de Barry, whose son, David,
became Viscount Buttevant. One of David's lineal descendants,
another David de Barri, was created Earl of Barrymore in 1628,
as a reward for his fidelity to English interests. The title became extinct on the death of the eighth earl without issue in
1824.—Burke's "Dormant and Extinct Peerages," p. 24, *et seq.*

It is worth noting that the then Earl of Barrymore, Richard
Barry, the sixth holder of the title, acknowledged Madame du
Barry's claim, but, according to Mr. J. B. Robinson ("The Last
Earls of Barrymore," p. 146), he was wrong in so doing, though
his supposition that he had collateral relatives in France was
correct. "The French branch," says the author, "is another
family altogether, the present (1894) representative of which is
the Comte Barry de Mervel (Château de Mervel, Seine-In-
férieure), whose ancestor accompanied James II. into exile."

[10] He seems to have been now known as the Abbé Gomard and
to have been assistant-priest at Saint-Eustache.

bouracan with gold buttons, coat, vest, and breeches of Lille camelot, and a cassock and cloak of Saint-Maur cloth,"[11] and, not to be outdone by the Du Barrys, gave a false Christian name—he had lent his own to the mythical brother, Gomard de Vaubernier —and had the impudence to style himself "Almoner to the King."

The marriage contract had been, as we have seen, a tissue of lies; the documents connected with the religious ceremony were infinitely worse. Proofs of Jeanne's claim to be the legitimate daughter of the aforementioned Gomard de Vaubernier "interested in the affairs of the King, were, of course, required; and to furnish these wholesale forgery was resorted to. Two certificates were produced. The first, which purported to be signed by the vicar of Vaucouleurs and witnessed by the provost of the town, stated that Jeanne had been born on August 19, 1746, instead of 1743, from the marriage of Jeanne Bécu, otherwise known as Quantigny, and Jean Jacques Gomard de Vaubernier. (It is upon this document that the erroneous information in regard to Madame du Barry's origin to be found in so many works of reference is based.) The second declared that the said Vaubernier had died in September, 1749, at Vaucouleurs, in the presence of his "father-in-law," Fabian Bécu, who had, as a matter of fact, died himself four years earlier.

Falsification of documents in those days was punished by the galleys, and, in cases where the intention was to deceive the King, by death. Why then, it may be asked, were the *"Roué"* and his accomplices so ready to brave the terrors of the law, and who was

[11] Apparently the gift of the bride, as these articles figure in an account rendered to Madame du Barry about this time by Carlier, the tailor who made her servants' liveries.

the instigator of these shameful frauds? It is, in our opinion, absurd to ascribe them, as some writers do, to the impudence of Jean du Barry, who was far too astute a personage to commit such an act, unless he were well assured of absolute impunity. The matter, we fear, must always remain obscure, but there is grave reason to believe that Louis XV. himself was an accessory; in other words, that when he had insisted on his mistress's marriage he had given her to understand that if her friends saw fit to exercise their inventive talents on her behalf it would not be altogether displeasing to him.

Madame du Barry and her *de jure* husband parted at the church door, and do not appear to have ever set eyes on one another again. The latter, who immediately after the nuptial ceremony had received, as the price of his complaisance, a brevet conferring a pension of 5000 livres upon him, did not, as the Goncourts, M. Vatel and Mr. Douglas all state, return the same day to Toulouse. He remained in Paris, installed himself in a fine apartment in the Rue de Bourgogne, and proceeded to enjoy life. To console himself for the loss of his wife, he formed a *liaison* with a damsel of nineteen, named Madeleine Lemoine, who lived on the other side of the street, and is described by a contemporary as "a piquant brunette, with magnificent eyes, a pretty mouth, and teeth of dazzling whiteness,"[12] and who, in the course of the following year, presented him with a son. To Guillaume's credit it should be added that he seems to have been genuinely attached to Mademoiselle Lemoine, as he remained faithful to her for the rest of his life, and soon after his wife's death, in 1793, married her, "in order to assure his name to the

[12] *Souvenirs d'une actrice,* Louise Fusil, cited by M. Lenôtre in *Vieilles maisons, vieux papiers,* p. 205.

woman to whom he was united by ties of gratitude
and esteem."[13]

At Compiègne, whither Madame du Barry had
followed the Court after the signing of the marriage
contract, her relations with the King appear to have
been conducted with a certain amount of discretion,
and to have aroused but little comment. But when, at
the beginning of October, the Court migrated, as usual,
to Fontainebleau, the new favourite was given a suite
of apartments in the château itself, and his Majesty's
attentions to her became so very marked that nothing
else was spoken of, and the Austrian Ambassador,
Mercy-Argenteau, deemed it advisable to send the following report of the affair to his Government:

MERCY *to* KAUNITZ.
Fontainebleau, November 1, 1768.

"Monseigneur,—I believe I ought to render to your
Highness a full account of certain circumstances
which have arisen at this Court, and which appear to
me likely to effect objects too important not to merit
your attention. A person named Du Barry, Breton[14]
gentleman, great intriguer, broker of the pleasures of
M. de Richelieu and several others, lived for some
years with a creature whom he delivered over to his
acquaintances for a pecuniary consideration, when
the state of his finances obliged him to have recourse
to such expedients. This Du Barry, at length, after
having married his concubine to one of his brothers,
found means, through the instrumentality of the
first *valet-de-chambre,* named Lebel, to introduce her
to the King shortly before the last visit to Compiègne, whither this woman followed the Court, and

[13] *Ibid.* p. 215.
[14] Mercy was, of course, misinformed; Jean du Barry was a
Languedocien.

was lodged in a private house. This first appearance occasioned but little sensation, but, shortly afterwards, one saw the new favourite in possession of a very elegant equipage and a very handsomely furnished lodging. Then some young gentlemen of the Court sought to introduce themselves to her, in order to pay their respects. The Sieur du Barry made, in the meanwhile, researches into his genealogy, and discovered that he was descended from the ancient Irish family of Barrymore, whereof he assumed the arms, which one sees displayed on the carriage of Madame du Barry and on a very handsome sedan-chair, which she makes use of in the interior of the château. She is lodged in the court called *des Fontaines,* near the apartment which Madame de Pompadour used to occupy; she has a number of servants and brilliant liveries, and on fête-days and Sundays one sees her at the King's Mass, in one of the chapels on the *rez-de-chaussée,* which is reserved for her.

"A treatment so different to that which would be accorded a simple girl augmented from day to day the attention of the courtiers. On my side, I took measures to inform myself of the tone which this woman adopts among her intimates. I ascertained that she was beginning to give herself airs of importance; that she spoke of the Government and the Ministers, and of the great services which a favourite rendered the State by enlightening the King in regard to the vices of the administration. I ascertained further that this woman expected to be publicly presented at Court, and that a subordinate cabal, supported by some persons of more exalted rank, favoured this project; that they had even sounded *Mesdames de France,*[15] and that one of the *Mesdames* was of opinion

[15] The four unmarried daughters of Louis XV. Adélaïde, Victorie, Sophie, and Louise.

that, however objectionable so indecent a presentation might be, it was, nevertheless, better to support it than to expose themselves to the danger of the King's re-marriage.[16]

"The serious turn this affair was taking finally determined me to speak of it to the Spanish Ambassador, who was but imperfectly informed in regard to it. We agreed that he should explain his views to M. de Choiseul, and he did so forthwith. But, to our profound astonishment, the Minister appeared, or wished to appear, ignorant of a great part of the circumstances of this intrigue, and M. de Fuentes experienced considerable difficulty in convincing him of it. He represented to M. de Choiseul how greatly the person of the King would be degraded by such a scandal; he enlarged upon all the grievous consequences which would result from the re-establishment of a *maitresse-en-titre;* finally, he succeeded in fixing the attention of M. de Choiseul upon this matter, and they deliberated on the means of averting the danger. M. de Fuentes proposed to compose a letter, which he should write to his Court, and which, having been intercepted, should be brought to the notice of his Most Christian Majesty. This expedient has been adopted and will be carried out. Independently of that, M. de Choiseul is resolved to seize an opportunity of speaking to the King about his new mistress; to disclose to Him the true character of this creature; to represent to Him how greatly the dignity of the monarchy will be injured in the public estimation if He gives publicity to the favour of a woman who cannot, or ought not, reasonably to serve any but the most secret pleasures.

[16] Mercy was mistaken; *Mesdames* do not appear to have learned of their father's intrigue till later. Moreover, they opposed it strongly as soon as they found that it was something more than a *galanterie.* See p. 61, *infra.*

"Now, Monseigneur, you are in possession of this strange story, which I still flatter myself will prove but a transient affair. I am endeavouring to utilise it, through the medium of the Ambassador of Spain, in order to make M. de Choiseul understand how greatly it would be to the advantage both of the State and the King himself that this prince, who still clings to pleasures of the senses, should procure legitimate means, and liberate himself by a marriage from all these disorders, which are such a bad example for the Royal Family, a source of intrigues so disturbing to the Ministers, and so injurious to the proper conduct of affairs. I cannot too highly praise the good will and zeal with which M. de Fuentes lends himself to the execution of all the measures which I suggest to him in regard to this matter, and which would be almost impossible, or, at any rate, very dangerous for me to employ myself.

" Since writing my letter I have had a long conference with M. le Duc de Choiseul on the matters of which my despatches treat to-day, and our conversation has taken so favourable a turn that I ended by speaking to him of Madame du Barry, under the pretext of friendship and attachment to his person. I repeated to him all that I had ascertained about this woman, and he professed himself much indebted to me for this overture. He permitted himself to speak very freely to me of this intrigue, with which I perceive he is now much occupied, and even begged me to communicate to him everything that I may learn about it in the future, though he did not confide to me the measures which he proposes to take, and which, thanks to the Spanish Ambassador, I am acquainted with. I have come to an understanding with the latter that we should act in concert, without allowing M. de

Choiseul to become aware of it, and I hope, Monseigneur, that we shall succeed in co-operating in this way to good purpose. I shall exercise great care to avoid all imprudence in a matter so delicate."[17]

[17] *Correspondance secrète du Comte de Mercy-Argenteau avec l'Empereur Joseph II. et le Prince von Kaunitz*, par le Chevalier d'Arnett et M. Jules Flammermont (Paris, 1896, ii. 338, *et seq.*

CHAPTER IV

HISTORY affords us few instances of a states-man who with the aid of only moderate abilities has attained to such a position as the Duc de Choiseul.[1] From the day on which he first entered the Council, as the nominee of Madame de Pompadour, at the close of 1757, his influence, thanks to his own self-confidence and resolution, the inca-pacity of his colleagues, and the indolence and apathy of the King had gone on steadily increasing, until he had become, to all intents and purposes, master of France. He combined in his own person the func-tions of three departments, Foreign Affairs, the Army, and the Marine,[2] and even talked of taking charge of the Finances as well. He held the *surintendance des postes,* an office which placed in his hands great and much-dreaded powers, as it enabled him to violate at will the sanctity of private correspondence.[3] He was colonel-general of the Gardes Suisses, a command usually reserved for Princes of the Blood, governor of the Invalides, governor-general of Touraine, and *grand bailli* of Hagueneau, and he also held several minor

[1] We are aware that some French historians regard Choiseul as a great Minister, and such was undoubtedly the opinion of many of his contemporaries. But his qualities were more showy than solid, and, compared with the illustrious statesmen of the two preceding reigns, his record is poor indeed.

[2] The Marine was nominally held by Choiseul's cousin, the Duc de Choiseul-Praslin, but he was a nonentity, and historians invariably speak of it as one of Choiseul's departments.

[3] See on this subject the *Mémoires de Madame de Hausset* (edit. 1825), p. 105, and the author's " Madame de Pompadour," p. 291, *et seq.*

posts. His relatives and *protégés* filled all the most lucrative positions in the Army, the Diplomatic Service and the Church; he lived in almost royal state, and enormous as was his official income,[4] his household expenses alone were believed to exceed it.

Moreover, his credit abroad was immense. The foreign policy of Spain was conducted entirely on his advice; Turkey looked to him for support against Russian aggression; at Vienna he was regarded as the mainstay of the Franco-Austrian alliance, and he had but recently concluded the arrangements for a marriage between the Dauphin and the Archduchess Marie Antionette.

A Minister so circumstanced, one would suppose, could have afforded to regard the advent of a new mistress with equanimity; but such was very far from being the case. Whether from genuine concern for the dignity of the Monarchy, which he believed would be irremediably degraded by association with a woman of so humble an origin and so unenviable a reputation,[5] or because he was apprehensive that Madame du Barry might develop a taste for political intrigue to his own detriment, or merely because his vanity was wounded by the King's omission to consult him in the matter, Choiseul from the very first evinced the bitterest hostility towards the lady.

It may be doubted, however, if the Minister would have carried his enmity to the lengths which he did had it not been for the influence of his sister, Madame de Gramont.

[4] Senac de Meilhan computes the income which Choiseul derived from his various offices at upwards of 700,000 livres.

[5] This was the popular view. " People imagined that it was on moral and public grounds that the Duc de Choiseul was opposed to Madame du Barry, and owing to this belief, *devoid of foundation,* he became the idol of the magistrates, their numerous partisans, and, finally, of the entire public."—Senac de Meilhan's *Portraits et Caractères du xviii Siècle,* p. 32.

This haughty, ambitious, and intriguing woman, undeterred by Louis XV.'s insensibility to her charms, had never ceased to persevere in her efforts to effect his subjugation, and, aware that the feebleness of the monarch's character rendered it improbable that he would be for long able to withstand the resolution and daring with which she conducted her operations, had believed herself within measurable distance of success. Her fury and mortification, therefore, on seeing the prize for which she had so long striven snatched from her grasp by "a little girl of the streets," knew no bounds, and she and all the coterie which followed her inspirations pronounced against the favourite with the utmost violence. "She entreated her brother to show no yielding to the ignominy of this new power, and she braved the King and his mistress with an assured arrogance which was hardly justified by her own long-compromised virtue."[6] This gentle little Duchesse de Choiseul, jealous of her sister-in-law and fearful of being thought less severe or less ardent against the enemies of her husband, made common cause with Madame de Gramont, while the haughty and high-tempered Princesse de Beauvau, "who always knew how to proportion her efforts to the obstacles which stood in the way of her desires," declared that any one who did not openly side with them would forfeit her regard.[7]

[6] M. Gaston Maugras's *Le Duc et la Duchesse de Choiseul.*
[7] The following anecdote, related by Chamfort, will show the real motive of the feminine opposition to the new favourite:

"Madame du Barry, being at Luciennes, had a fancy to see Le Val, the residence of M. de Beauvau. She inquired of the latter if it would not displease Madame de Beauvau, and Madame de Beauvau professed that she would be delighted to receive her and do the honours. There was some talk of events which had happened in the time of Louis XV., and Madame du Barry complained of various things which seemed to indicate that she had been the object of hatred. 'Not at all,' said Madame de Beau-

Madame du Barry, conscious of the weakness of her position, would have been ready to make almost any concession to avoid a struggle with such redoubtable antagonists; but Choiseul, urged on by the angry women who surrounded him, would hear of no compromise, and the war began, as was the custom in those days, by a campaign of calumny—a storm of epigrams, pamphlets, and *chansons*.

A song called *La Bourbonnaise* had at this time a great vogue both in Paris and the provinces. One of the scribes employed by Choiseul conceived the idea of writing a fresh set of verses, describing the career of Madame du Barry, and the new version, copies of which were distributed broadcast, soon ousted the old, and became so popular that, according to Grimm, there was no street or corner of the city where one did not hear it sung.

> " La Bourbonnaise
> Arrivant à Paris,
> A gagné des *Louis*.
> La Bourbonnaise
> A gagné des *Louis*.
> Chez un marquis.
>
> " Pour apanage
> Elle avait la beauté !
> Elle avait la beauté
> Pour apanage.
> Mais ce petit trésor
> Lui vaut de l'or."

From a peasant she blossoms into a *grande dame,* who rides in her coach, and at length, one fine day, finds herself at Versailles:

> " Elle est allée
> Se faire voir en cour,
> Se faire voir en cour

vau, ' *we only wanted your place.*' "—Chamfort's *Maximes, pensées, caractères, et anecdotes* (edit. 1796), p. 179.

> Elle est allée.
> On dit qu'elle a, ma foi,
> Plu même au roi."

Later, some additional verses, by no means conplimentary to the King and his new enchantress, appeared:

> " Quelle nouvelle!
> Une fille de rien;
> Une fille de rien,
> Quelle nouvelle!
> Donne au roi de l'amour
> Est à la cour.

> " Elle est gentille,
> Elle a les yeux fripons;
> Elle a les yeux fripons,
> Elle est gentille.
> Elle excite avec art
> Un vieux paillard."

The stage likewise lent its aid to the enmity of the Minister. Plays were written round the adventures of the new favourite, and performed at the booths and fairs in and around Paris. On October 30, Gaudon's troop of actors[8] gave a representation of a burlesque called *La Bourbonnaise à la guinguette,* the action of which is supposed to take place at the *Cadran bleu,* a well-known tavern in the Faubourg des Porcherons. The heroine is represented as a course virago, using the *argot* of the slums, indulging in scandalous *liaisons,* and tossing off bumpers of wine and brandy. A cook, a coiffeur, a Government clerk, and the keeper of a gambling-house, characters intended to represent Anne Bécu, Lametz, Saint-Foy, and the *"Roué,"* were allotted leading parts in this precious

---

[8] Founded by an actor named Restier in 1735, under the name of *" la grande troupe étrangère."* It performed at the fairs of Saint-Laurent and Saint-Germain, and it is probably at the latter, which was held in October, that the *Bourbonnaise à la guinguette* was played.

production, which was afterwards printed to ensure
greater publicity.

A few days later, a second *Bourbonnaise,* "an
operetta with dialogues in prose," was performed by
Nicolet's troupe.[9] In this piece, which was the work
of Beaunoir, a playwright of some merit, the satire
is more refined than in *La Bourbonnaise à la guinguette,* but it is not less mordant, and "the most
critical period of Madame du Barry's life is laid
bare, with exaggerations no doubt, but with a sub-
stratum of truth." The operetta turns upon the
Bourbonnaise's relations with a *coiffeur de dames*
named Retappe, who is, of course, Lametz. The
Bourbonnaise is about to espouse Retappe when a
neighbour interferes and urges her to exploit her
beauty. The maiden and Ratappe take counsel together; at first they are inclined to reject such an odious
proposition, but eventually avarice proves stronger
than virtue. The scene thereupon changes to a gambling-house, to which Retappe brings gilded youths to
pay their court to the Bourbonnaise. She invites them
to join her in a game of cards, with results which may
be anticipated. Then a peddling jeweller arrives, and
the gilded youths expend more of their money in load-
ing their hostess with presents. Further sums are
extracted from them, when the Bourbonnaise's creditors, previously invited by the lady, make a sudden
descent and refuse to leave till their claims are satisfied. The play concludes with a duel between two of
the heroine's admirers, the arrival of the watch, and
the hurried break-up of the company.[10]

The movement once launched went merrily on.
Two other plays, one satirizing the favourite and the

[9] "This troupe is the only one which has a successful existence
to-day (1779)."—Hurtaut and Magny's *Dictionnaire de la ville de
Paris et ses environs,* iv. 705.

[10] Vatel's *Histoire de Madame du Barry,* i. 144, *et seq.*

other the *"Roué,"* a manuscript pamphlet, called *L'Apprentissage d'une fille de modes,* in which Madame du Barry figures under the name of Agnes Pompon, and a biting satire, *L'Apothéose du Roi Pétaud,* which was attributed, though, it would seem, without foundation, to Voltaire, followed one another in quick succession; and, at the beginning of December, the Austrian Ambassador informs his Government that nothing is talked of in the theatres and the streets but the scandalous conduct of the King, and that the popular exasperation is becoming so great that placards are being affixed to the walls, "which, among expressions of the most terrifying description, prognosticate that France is still able to produce Ravaillacs and Damiens."[11]

M. Vatel, in his *Histoire de Madame du Barry,* expresses surprise that Choiseul should have condescended to such methods of warfare, since it would have been easy for him, with the Lieutenant of Police and his numerous agents under his orders, to have procured documentary proofs of the new favourite's humble origin and discreditable past, and also of the impudent frauds perpetrated on the occasion of her marriage, and to have laid them before the King. Had this course been adopted, he argues, all danger of Madame du Barry becoming *maîtresse en titre* would have been averted, as, though the monarch's infatuation might have been strong enough to induce him to overlook her quasi-criminal complicity in the Du Barrys' forgeries, he would certainly never have dared to force her upon his Court.

M. Vatel, however, was unacquainted with the correspondence between Mercy and Kaunitz, published some years ago, from which it appears that Choiseul had fully intended to take this step, but was dissuaded

[11] Letter of Mercy *to* Kaunitz, December 9, 1768.

therefrom by the representations of the Ambassadors of Austria and Spain, to both of which Powers it was a matter of the most vital importance that Choiseul's credit with his royal master should remain unimpaired. Mercy and Fuentes pointed out that an open remonstrance, which could not fail to humiliate the King, might very well do the Minister irreparable injury, and should, at all costs, be avoided. The scandal was a public one; all France deplored it. It would be wiser to allow the echo of the rumours concerning the favourite's past to reach the ears of the monarch; and a Minister so powerful as Choiseul could easily find means of ensuring this, without committing himself.[12]

Unfortunately for Choiseul and his advisers, the campaign of calumny had the very opposite effect to that which they had anticipated. The pamphleteers and playwrights whom the Minister employed did their work but too well. Not content with bringing accusations against the favourite which had some foundation in fact, their zeal led them to charge her with vices and faults of which she was wholly guiltless, such as drunkenness, vulgarity, and ignorance. What chivalry remained to Louis XV. was aroused by these shameful attacks upon a defenceless woman. His reply was to redouble his attentions to his mistress, to load her with favours, and, finally, to order apartments to be prepared for her at Versailles.

[12] Despatch of Mercy *to* Kaunitz, December 9, 1768.

CHAPTER V

IT would appear to have been in the closing weeks of 1768 or the first of the following year that Madame du Barry was installed at Versailles. The apartments allotted to her were those of the deceased *valet-de-chambre* Lebel, situated on the *rez-de-chaussée* of the Cour Royale, and here she remained until the spring of 1770, when she removed to the suite which had formerly been occupied by the deceased Dauphiness, Marie Josèphe of Saxony, on the second floor of the château, immediately above the King's private apartments.[1]

A little court soon gathered about her: ambitious young noblemen, eager to worship at the shrine of the rising sun; foreigners of rank, like the Prince de Ligne, who came thither curious to see how the little courtesan he had known in the Rue de Jussien comported herself amid her new surroundings, and some of Jeanne's old literary acquaintances, like Robbé de Beauveset[2] and Cailhava.[3] In the afternoons, a stream

[1] The Goncourts (who also assert that the new favourite was installed at Versailles immediately after her marriage), M. Vatel, and Mr. Douglas all say that the apartments to which Madame du Barry removed were those of Madame Adélaïde, Louis XV.'s eldest daughter, who was given those of the Dauphiness in exchange. This, as M. de Nolhac points out in his interesting work, *Le Château de Versailles sous Louis XV.*, is an error.

[2] Pierre Honoré Robbé de Beauveset (1712-1792), a poet celebrated, or at least known, for his profane and licentious verses. Madame du Hausset says: "This same Archbishop of Paris (Christophe de Beaumont) gave a pension of 1200 livres to the greatest scoundrel in Paris (Robbé de Beauveset), who writes abominable verses; this pension being granted on condition that his poems were never printed. I was informed of this

of visitors might be seen wending its way towards the apartments of the new divinity; and Madame de Gramont, whose windows overlooked the Cour Royale, compelled to witness the triumph of her rival, was beside herself with mortification and jealousy, and urged her brother to prosecute the campaign of slander with renewed vigour.

As soon as Madame du Barry was installed at Versailles, the question of her presentation to the King was raised. The Goncourts assert that Jean du Barry was the prime mover in this affair, but, in our opinion, there can be little doubt that the responsibility rests with the Duc de Richelieu, who, on January 1, 1769, had entered upon his term of office as First Gentleman of the Bedchamber, in which capacity he had charge of the presentations for the ensuing year.

This hero of gallantry was now in his seventy-third year, but age had not diminished his predilection for the fair sex nor his love of intrigue. Bitterly jealous of Choiseul's ascendency over the King, and incensed by the Minister's refusal to allow him scope for the exercise of the meddlesome activity which he mistook for genius, he had viewed with unalloyed satisfaction the advent of a rival influence. At first, having no great confidence in the permanency of the

by M. de Marigny, to whom he recited some of his shocking verses one evening when he supped with him, in company with some persons of quality. He chinked the money in his pocket and said, laughing: 'This is my good archbishop's; I keep my word with him; my poem will never be printed so long as I live, but I read it. What would the worthy prelate say if he knew that I had shared my last quarter's allowance with a charming little dancer from the Opera?'"

[3] Jean François Cailhava d'Estandoux (1731-1813), author of a number of comedies, including *Le Mariage impromptu*, *L'Egoïsme*, and *Le Journaliste Anglais*, in the last of which he revenged himself upon La Harpe, who had severely criticised his productions in the *Mercure*, by making him appear in a most odious rôle.

monarch's latest passion, he had hesitated to commit himself too deeply; but once assured that the affair was something more than a caprice, he resolved to lend his support to Madame du Barry, hoping thereby to ensure the undoing of his enemy and the realisation of certain political ambitions of his own, to which his reputation for levity had hitherto opposed an insurmountable barrier.

Richelieu's office of First Gentleman of the Bedchamber afforded him ample opportunity for private conversation with his royal master, and it is probable that he experienced but little difficulty in inducing the King to lend a willing ear to his suggestion.

There is, indeed, some reason to suppose that Louis already entertained the idea of having his mistress presented, and that the marriage on which he had insisted had had no other object than to pave the way for this ceremony. The nature of his senile passion rendered it imperative that its object should be always near him; but until the lady had been presented it was impossible for her to ride in the royal carriages, to be admitted to his Majesty's *petits soupers,* to pay her court to the Dauphin or the King's daughters (*Mesdames*), to be present at the ceremonies or festivities of the Court, to enjoy, in a word, any of those privileges "without which the mistress was nothing but a mistress, with which the mistress was the favourite."[4] For the King to keep her at Versailles or in the other royal châteaux without acknowledging her was to tacitly admit that he was in the wrong, to recognise limits to his power, and Louis XV. had always believed, as Choiseul observes, that "the *éclat* he threw into his amours was a proof of his authority."

The presentation was then decided on, but before it

[4] E. and J. de Goncourt's *La Du Barry,* p. 45.

could take place two obstacles had to be surmounted. The first of these, by a singular coincidence, the King had himself created. The right of presentation solicited by so many ladies was accorded to comparatively few. By a decree of April 1760, Louis XV. had very strictly defined the conditions upon which this favour was to be accorded. No lady was henceforth to be eligible who could not satisfy the Court genealogist that both she and her husband were of noble birth.

To the claim of Madame du Barry's titular husband no objection was likely to be raised; indeed, it had already been conceded when his younger brother, Elie du Barry, had been admitted as a pupil to the Ecole Militaire, and his nephew Adolphe, the *"Roué's"* son, appointed page to the King, for both of which positions proofs of noble birth were rigorously insisted on. But the favourite herself was in a very different case. How was she to get rid of the Bécus and find a genealogy for the Vauberniers?

Although Louis XV. firmly believed that his kingly dignity placed him above all laws, moral and religious, he shared the general prejudice of his age, and entertained the deepest veneration for the rules of etiquette; and the difficulty with which he now found himself confronted appears to have occasioned him the keenest embarrassment. According to Belleval, he approached the Princesse de Tingry, with the idea of purchasing for Madame du Barry the principality of Lus in Bigorre,[5] and allowing her to masquerade as a foreign princess, in which event, of course, no proofs of nobility would be required. If such were the case, the negotiations fell through, for when the

⁵ Lus in Bigorre was a little town in Gascony, situated on the River Gave, in the valley of Baréges, three leagues from the Spanish frontier. It had been united to the royal domain in the time of Philippe le Bel, but still enjoyed a nominal independence. It is now known as Luz-Saint-Sauveur.

lady was presented it was certainly not as a foreign princess.[6] How the difficulty was finally overcome does not appear to be known. Some writers are of opinion that the proofs were dispensed with altogether, while there is a more than remote possibility that Jean du Barry was again called upon to exercise his inventive talent.

The second obstacle was less serious, but not less embarrassing. It was necessary to find a lady who had already been presented to act as *marraine* to the new postulant. This was no easy task. The resentment of the feminine portion of the Court against the favourite was far from being confined to the coterie dominated by Madame de Gramont; it was well-nigh universal. It was felt that for a woman of exalted position to undertake so unenviable a duty would mean degradation; while for one of lower rank to do so would be to court social ostracism. Every lady who was applied to indignantly refused, or took refuge in specious excuses.[7] The Baronne de Montmorency, who it was thought might be willing to play the part "in return for money and many favours," set so exorbitant a price upon her services that the King found it impossible to comply with her demands, and the friends of Madame du Barry were in despair. Finally, however, a *marraine* was found in the person of the Comtesse de Béarn, a lady of very ancient but impoverished family,[8] who since the death of her

<hr>

[6] *Souvenirs d'un Chevau-léger*, p. 117.

[7] One lady did consent, but, finding that the King's daughters turned their backs upon her next time she went to Court, she took to her bed and gave out that she was stricken with a mortal disease.

[8] Angélique Gabrielle Joumard des Achards, married in 1738 to François Alexandre Galard, Vicomte de Béarn, Seigneur d'Argentines. The Galards of Béarn claimed descent from the Mérovingiens, through Eude of Aquitaine. They had enjoyed at one time a quasi-princely rank.

husband had resided entirely upon her estates, and
cared little for the opinion of a Court which she had
ceased to adorn. The countess had come to Paris to
prosecute a lawsuit, in which she herself had been engaged for some years and her family for more than
two centuries. This lawsuit had at length been decided in her favour, but in the interim she had incurred large debts, which she was totally unable to
settle. When, therefore, one fine day, Richelieu, who
was a distant connection of her own, waited upon her,
and suggested a way out of the difficulty, she readily
agreed to do what was required of her, and the duke
at once fixed the presentation of Madame du Barry
for January 25.

Meanwhile the war of *chansons,* pamphlets, and
plays continued with unabated vigour, but whatever
effect it may have produced upon the Court and the
city it had little or none upon the amorous old
monarch, unless to excite his resentment at such un-
warrantable interference in his private affairs. Cha-
grined at his want of success, Choiseul had recourse
to other measures; he cast about for a rival beauty who
might be capable of weaning the King from Madame
du Barry, and fixed upon the wife of a Paris doctor, a
Madame Millin, "young and charming and devoted to
his interests."

"I have seen her," writes Belleval, "but, though
very pretty, she is not to be compared with the
favourite. No one seems to think that M. de Choiseul
will succeed in this affair, for the King is too infatuated."[9]

[9] *Souvenirs d'un Chevau-léger,* p. 118.

Writing under date January 15, Hardy confirms Belleval's account of this incident, and describes Madame Mellin in much
the same terms: "Young and pretty, but less beautiful than
the countess (du Barry)." Some time afterwards, Choiseul put

Such, indeed, proved to be the case; his Majesty would have nothing to say to Madame Millin, and, in despair, the Minister decided to seek the assistance of *Mesdames.*

The four unmarried daughters of Louis XV., Mesdames Adélaïde, Victoire, Sophie, and Louise, lived a very retired and uneventful life, and had little influence or credit; but the King, in his selfish way, was much attached to them, and, in accordance with an old habit, which dated from the time when the princesses were young and agreeable companions, paid them daily visits, always at the same hour. The strict seclusion into which they had withdrawn since the death of the Queen, and the rigorous discretion they imposed upon their ladies and little circle of intimates, had hitherto prevented them from learning of their royal father's latest conquest, and they were ignorant even of the existence of such a person as Madame du Barry. Choiseul, however, having decided that the time had come to enlighten them, adroitly contrived that a copy of the following verses, which satirised the favourite without overstepping the bounds of propriety, should be brought under the notice of the princesses:

> "Lisette ta beauté séduit
>   Et charme tout le monde.
> En vain la Duchesse en rougit,
>   Et la princesse en gronde.
> Chacun sait qui Vénus naquit
>   De l'écume de l'onde.
>
> "En vit-elle moins tous les Dieux
>   Lui rendre un juste hommage,
> Et Pâris, ce berger fameux,
>   Lui donner l'avantage,
> Même sur la reine des Cieux
>   Et Minerve le Sage.

forward another lady, his cousin, the Vicomte de Choiseul's wife, a beautiful Creole; but the King was insensible to her charms.

"Dans le Serrail (*sic*) du Grand Seigneur
  Quelle est la Favorite?
C'est la plus belle au gré du cœur
  Du Maître qui l'habite.
C'est le seul titre en sa faveur
  Et c'est le vrai mérite." [10]

After perusing these verses, *Mesdames* very
naturally asked for an explanation, and were
astonished to find that not only was the King engaged in a fresh *liaison,* but that it was viewed with
complacence by not a few of their devout friends, who
seemed to regard Madame du Barry as destined to repair the evil which Madame de Pompadour and Choiseul had brought upon the Church by their anti-Jesuit
policy. The preceptor of the Dauphin and his brothers, the Duke de La Vauguyon, and Madame de
Marsan, *gouvernante* of the princesses, did not hesitate to assert their conviction that Providence had
chosen this instrument, all unworthy though it was, to
chasten the haughty Minister and bring about his
fall.[11]

[10] These pretty verses have been ascribed to several persons: to
the Duc de Nivernais, the Chevalier de Boufflers, and the Abbé de
Lattaignan, canon of Rheims. At the time when they were
written the duke was generally believed to be the author; but
M. Vatel is inclined to give the credit to the abbé. However
that may be, the Choiseul party appear to have been of opinion
that the irony was a little difficult to detect, and, accordingly,
employed one of their scribes to parody the first verse:

"De deux Vénus on parle dans le monde,
  De toutes deux gouverner fut le lot.
L'une naquit de l'écume de l'onde,
  L'autre naquit de l'écume du pot."

The "scum of the pot" is, of course, an allusion to the occupation of the favorite's mother, who had at one time been a cook.
[11] Hardy, in his *Journal,* relates that on the evening of February
1, 1769, a priest of his acquaintance was dining with a friend.
At dessert, another priest who was present invited the company
to drink to "the presentation." Hardy's friend inquired his
meaning, and was told: "It is that which took place yesterday,
or will take place to-day, the presentation of the new Esther,

Now, *Mesdames* detested Choiseul. The eldest, Madame Adélaïde, a haughty and vindictive woman, saw in him only the ally of Austria and the creature of Madame de Pompadour; the youngest, Madame Louise, the most intelligent of the family, could not pardon his expulsion of the Jesuits and his sympathy with the philosophers. However, they were too sincere in their desire for their royal father's spiritual welfare—they had since the Queen's death cherished the illusion that the King was "sincerely converted and resolved to live like a good Christian"—to be deceived by the specious arguments of La Vauguyon and Madame de Marsan; and no sooner had they made themselves acquainted with the details of the affair, than they determined to sacrifice their personal feelings and make common cause with the Minister.

But, unfortunately for Choiseul, the princesses could not bring themselves to adopt the course which would, in all likelihood, have at least prevented the presentation of Madame du Barry, even if it had had no further results—that of openly remonstrating with the King. They preferred to attack the new favourite by indirect methods, namely, by using their influence to promote their father's marriage with the Archduchess Elizabeth. In this, as the following letter from Mercy to Kaunitz clearly indicates, they were unconsciously permitting themselves to be made the agents of the Austrian Ambassador, who, eager to turn the affair to the advantage of his Court, had contrived to gain over Madame Victor's *dame d'atours* (Mistress of the Robes) and confidante, the Comtesse de Durfort,

who is to supplant Haman and deliver the Jewish people from oppression." The new Esther was Madame du Barry, Haman was Choiseul, and the Jewish people, the clerical party.—*Journal des événements tels qu'ils parviennent à ma connaissance.* (Bibliothèque Nationale.)

and, through her, was pulling the strings with considerable adroitness:

MERCY *to* KAUNITZ.
"Paris, December 29, 1768.

"Monseigneur,—Some very interesting circumstances have lately arisen relative to the matter of which I had the honour to render an account to your Highness in my letter of November 1. I acquainted you on that occasion with the first details of the intrigue of Madame du Barry, and I added that I was endeavouring to turn this conjuncture to account—to make it understood how important it was to the tranquillity of the Ministers and the glory of the King that this prince should extricate himself by means of a second marriage from the irregularities to which he does not cease to abandon himself.

"As soon as this could be done without exciting suspicion, I insinuated my views into every quarter where I judged them capable of producing some effect, and I found occasion to speak of them, amongst others, to Madame de Durfort, *dame d'atours* to *Madame de France* (Madame Victor). This lady spoke to me with considerable frankness about Madame du Barry; she confided to me that, at the outset, *Mesdames* had not imagined that this adventure was likely to have serious consequences, but that, alarmed by the public clamour and by the results which are only too easy to foresee, they were in despair about it, and were seeking means to put an end to the intrigue.

"A week after the first overtures of Madame de Durfort, she informed me that *Mesdames,* still full of this project, were at length convinced that there was no other way to establish tranquillity at Court and in the Royal Family, and that to effect it they were prepared to use every means of persuasion and to endeavour that the choice of the King should fall upon the Archduchess Elizabeth. Madame de Durfort added that in supporting this project she had at the same time suggested the language which *Mesdames* should employ towards the monarch, in order to prevail upon him to comply with their wishes.

"In response, I said everything that the circumstances required; I enlarged upon the personal advantages which *Mesdames* would derive from securing in the archduchess a sure friend, who, constantly associated with them, would be in a position to assure the happiness of the Royal Family by the natural influence which she would have over the mind of the King and over that of the Dauphin and future Dauphiness.[12] I did not forget to speak of matters likely to interest Madame de Durfort, and I left her persuaded to my view of the affair and very pleased with the conversation which I had had with her. . . ."[13]

Madame de Durfort faithfully carried out her employer's instructions, and, a few days later, *Mesdames,* summoning up their courage, astonished the King by a request that he should give them a queen, and that the queen should be the Archduchess Elizabeth of Austria. The monarch seemed at first much embarrassed, affected to believe that his daughters spoke in jest, and enlarged upon the inconveniences inseparable from second marriages; but ended by laughing good-humouredly and agreeing to give the matter his consideration. *Mesdames* returned to the charge each time their father came to visit them, with the result

[12] Marie Antoinette, the Archduchess Elizabeth's younger sister.

[13] *Correspondance secrète du Comte de Mercy-Argenteau avec l'Empereur Joseph II. et le Prince von Kaunitz,* par le Chevalier d'Arneth et M. Jules Flammermont (Paris, 1896), ii. 347.

that one day they succeeded in extracting from him
a definite promise to demand the archduchess in marriage, "provided that her person did not displease
him"; whereupon the princesses, delighted at the suc-
of their scheme, immediately proposed that an artist
should be sent to Vienna to paint the archduchess.
The King consented, and it was decided to offer the
commission to Drouais.

Things seemed to promise well, though Drouais declined the proffered commission, or rather placed a
prohibitive price on his services,[14] no doubt because,
unknown to *Mesdames,* he was at that time engaged
on two portraits of the favourite, to which we shall
have occasion to refer later.[15] And we are inclined to
think that it is highly probable that Louis would have
kept the promise he had made his daughters, had the
efforts of the latter but been seconded by Choiseul.
This, however, the Minister seemed unwilling to do,
though Mercy lost no opportunity of "reminding him
of all the reasons which ought to render such a project
(the King's marriage) eminently agreeable and desirable to him."

The truth is that the idea of Louis XV.'s union
with a young princess was very far from commending
itself to the Minister or his sister, Madame de Gramont. To rid themselves of Madame du Barry by such
means seemed to them as unwise as for a person to
submit to a dangerous operation for a disease which
might conceivably never reach an acute stage. "Persons in power," wrote Mercy to Kaunitz, "imagine
that a queen, judicious and amiable, who would succeed in gaining the affection of her husband, might
open his eyes to the irregularities and the enormous
abuses which exist in all departments here, and cause
much embarrassment to those who direct them. They

[14] 80,000 livres.   [15] See p. 103, *infra.*

are consequently of opinion that it behoves them to divert the mind of the King from ideas of marriage; and I have very strong proofs that Madame de Gramont, more interested than any one in the maintenance of the present abuses, has succeeded in persuading M. de Choiseul to renounce his own predilections in this affair."[16]

Thus, blinded by ambition and cupidity, the Choiseuls prepared the way for their own fall, by rejecting that which would, in all probability, have proved their salvation.

Nevertheless, for several weeks the question of the King's re-marriage continued to be a frequent subject of conversation between Louis XV. and his daughters, and *Mesdames* occupied themselves in seeking a painter to take the place of Drouais, and ended by recommending Ducrest. The princesses entertained no doubt whatever as to their father's sincerity; but such was not the opinion of the watchful Mercy, who sorrowfully admits to Kaunitz that the delay in sending a painter to Vienna "renders the intentions of the King so doubtful that he cannot bring himself to hope for a favourable issue." He adds that Choiseul is so much incensed against Madame du Barry that he and the Spanish Ambassador have experienced the greatest difficulty in prevailing upon him to renounce "the rash and violent measures on which he appeared determined"; but that, on the other hand, the Minister still clings to the belief that the favourite will not, after all, be presented,[17] and, in

[16] Despatch of November 1, 1768.
[17] Madame du Deffand was of the same opinion. On January 14 she wrote to Horace Walpole: "I suppose you know all about the divinity in question (Madame du Barry); a nymph brought out from the most famous retreats of Cythera and Paphos. No, no; I cannot believe in all that folks foresee; the greatest obstacles may be overcome, and one may yet be checked by shame, by mere decency."

consequence, cannot be persuaded to urge upon the King the advisability of marrying the Austrian archduchess. From the same letter we learn that his Most Christian Majesty is passing the greater part of his time with his new enchantress, that the public is murmuring and "permitting itself the utmost freedom of speech," that the revenue for the past year shows a deficit of 38,000 million livres, that the Comptroller-General is at his wits' end, and that France seems bankrupt in both money and morals.[18]

Choiseul's belief that the presentation of Madame du Barry would, after all, be abandoned seemed not unlikely to be justified, for January 25 passed without the dreaded event taking place. Madame de Béarn's courage, it appeared, had failed her at the last moment; the icy reception she had encountered on the occasion of a recent visit to Court had given her a sprained ankle, and she sent word that it was impossible for her to leave her room.

The enemies of the favourite could hardly restrain their elation, and, indeed, Fate seemed to be playing into their hands, for ere Madame de Béarn had had time to regain her courage and the use of her ankle, another accident—a genuine one this time—intervened to postpone the evil day a second time.

On February 4, Louis XV., while hunting in the Forest of Saint-Germain, was thrown from his horse, falling heavily on his right shoulder. The pain was so severe that he believed that his arm was broken, and, according to one account, "behaved with a weakness which would have been ridiculous in a little girl ten years old." A litter was hastily improvised on which the monarch was conveyed to his carriage, and orders were given to return to Versailles, where, the news having preceded his arrival, and a report hav-

[18] Despatch of January 24, 1769.

ing spread that the accident was of an alarming character, the Court was in a ferment of excitement,
every one speculating as to how his or her position
would be affected in the event of the King succumbing
to his supposed injuries.

On reaching the château, it was found that Louis's
arm had swollen to such an extent as to render it
necessary to cut away the sleeve of his coat; but an
examination revealed that beyond a slight dislocation
of the shoulder no harm had been done, and the excitement of the selfish courtiers speedily subsided.
However, having regard to the King's age, the accident was a rather severe one, and obliged him to keep
his apartments for some time, as a result of which
confinement he developed so alarming an attack of
ennui that Sénac, his first physician, confided to
Mercy his fear that if his Majesty were to be much
longer deprived of violent exercise, his mind would
become affected, "a danger with which he had long
been threatened."[19]

Illness invariably had the effect of temporarily de-
taching Louis from his mistresses, and for several
days Madame du Barry did not see the King. On
the other hand, *Mesdames* were constant in their attendance upon their royal father, while the Dauphin
and his brothers and sisters, by his Majesty's request,
also paid several visits to the sick-room. The impression was general that this return to family life
could hardly fail to make for virtue, or, at least, for
decency; and when it was announced that the King
had given orders for the apartments of Madame
Adélaïde, which adjoined his own, to be renovated,
few doubted that the object was to prepare for a
future queen, the Archduchess Elizabeth.

The monarch recovered and resumed his visits to

[19] Mercy *to* Kaunitz, March 14, 1769.

his new mistress, but the weeks went by and nothing further was heard of the dreaded presentation. Gradually the opponents of the lady permitted their apprehensions to be lulled to rest. The interest of the Court was transferred to other matters: the marriage of the Duc de Chartres and Mademoiselle de Penthièvre, the completion of the *grande salle* of the Opera at Versailles, the magnificent fêtes which were to celebrate the approaching union of the Dauphin and Marie Antoinette; people ceased to talk of the "Bourbonnaise."

The astonishment and indignation, therefore, may be imagined when towards the middle of April the announcement was made that on the 22nd of the month his Majesty would hold a presentation, and that among the ladies who were to participate in the honour would be the Comtesse du Barry.

The long-deferred ceremony duly took place, and Madame du Barry appears to have acquitted herself well, and to have shown commendable *sang-froid* in what the following account, given by Madame de Genlis, an eye-witness, will show must have been exceedingly trying circumstances.

"I went to the presentation of my aunt, and was highly diverted, for it was the very same day on which Madame du Barry was presented. It was recognised on all sides that she was splendidly and tastefully attired. By daylight, her face was *passée,* and her complexion spoiled by freckles. Her bearing was revoltingly impudent, and her features far from handsome, but she had fair hair of a charming colour, pretty teeth, and a pleasing expression. She looked

[20] The Marquise de Montesson. The other ladies presented with Madame du Barry were the Marquise de Gouffier, the Comtesse de Boisgelin, and the Comtesse de Lusignan.

extremely well at night. We reached the card-tables in the evening a few minutes before her. At her entrance, all the ladies who were near the door rushed tumultuously forward in the opposite direction, in order to avoid being seated near her, so that between her and the last lady in the room there was an interval of four or five empty places. She regarded this marked and singular movement with the utmost coolness; nothing affected her imperturbable effrontery. When the King appeared at the conclusion of play, she looked at him and smiled. The King at once cast his eyes round the room in search of her; he appeared in an ill-humour, and almost instantly retired. The indignation at Versailles was unbounded;[21] for never had anything so scandalous been seen, not even the triumphs of Madame de Pompadour. It was certainly very strange to see at Court *Madame la Marquise de Pompadour,* while her husband, M. Lenormant d'Etioles, was only a farmer-general, but it was still more odious to see a *fille publique* presented with pomp to the whole of the Royal Family. This and many other instances of unparalleled indecency cruelly degraded royalty, and, consequently, contributed to bring about the Revolution."[22]

The day following her presentation, which was a Sunday, Madame du Barry assisted at the King's

[21] Hardy, who may be considered the mouthpiece of Paris, says: "This event aroused great murmuring both in Paris and Versailles. Some interested persons rejoiced over it, but the greater number were in consternation."

[22] *Mémoires de Madame de Genlis* (edit. 1825), p. 89. A newssheet of the time, which, however, was not improbably inspired by the *"Roué,"* or some other ally of the favourite, is far more indulgent in its criticism: "Madame du Barry has been very well received by *Mesdames,* and even with marked graciousness. All the spectators admired the dignity of her bearing and the ease of her attitudes. The rôle of a lady of the Court is not an easy one to play at first, but Madame du Barry played it as if she had been long accustomed to it."

Mass, and occupied in the chapel the place which had formerly been reserved for Madame de Pompadour. The attendance of noblemen and ladies of the Court, it was remarked, was unusually small, but, as a set-off against this, there were a number of high ecclesiastics in his Majesty's suite, at the head of whom was the Archbishop of Rheims. At the conclusion of the ceremony, Madame du Barry presented herself at the dinner of *Mesdames* and at that of the Dauphin, with the performance of which duties her installation as *maîtresse en titre* may be said to have been accomplished.

CHAPTER VI

MADAME DU BARRY had then realised her ambition: the post of *maîtresse en titre*, this "glorious dishonour" so ardently desired by so many haughty and highborn dames was hers; but her triumph was not yet absolute. It remained for her to overcome the hostility of a Court which had taxed the resources of her brilliant predecessor to the utmost before it had allowed itself to be coerced or cajoled into complacence; and Madame de Pompadour, though at the outset of her career she was even more friendless than Madame du Barry, had had to encounter no such powerful Minister as Choiseul, no such bitter antagonists of her own sex as the Duchesses de Gramont and de Choiseul and the Princesse de Beauvau.

The three ladies in question lost not a moment in proclaiming, or rather reasserting, their inflexible hostility to the new *régime*. Immediately after the presentation, they intimated to the King that, owing to the changes that had recently taken place at Court, they feared that their company was less agreeable to him than formerly, for which reason they begged to be excused from attendance at the suppers of the Petits Cabinets. Thus was dispersed that intimate society which Madame de Pompadour had so skillfully gathered round her, and in which Louis XV. had lived happily for so many years.

Such an example was not likely to be lost upon the feminine portion of the Court, and during a visit to

Marly which followed close upon the presentation, the ladies showed their disapproval of his Majesty's choice in a manner so unmistakable that a general feeling of uneasiness and constraint prevailed, the card-tables—the visits to Marly were noted for the high play which took place[1]—were well-nigh deserted, and every one was relieved when the time came to return to Versailles.

Shunned and slighted on all sides, Madame du Barry was forced to take refuge in the society of Madame de Béarn; but opposition seemed only to render the passion of Louis XV. the more stubborn. "He regards resistance to the object of his caprice," wrote Choiseul, "as a want of respect to his royal person; he recognises in this connection neither decency, nor rank, nor reputation; he believes that every one ought to bow before his mistress, because he honours her with his intimacy; he is bold in setting at defiance all the rules of decorum, though in nothing else. Then he imagines that he has shown his power, and proved to his Court, to his people, to Europe, that he is in very truth a monarch to inspire respect." This is, perhaps, the only occasion on which, bearing up against all difficulties, Louis showed a degree of firmness and perseverance which failed him in matters of the first importance.

A few days after the return of the Court to Versailles, Louis XV., "as some consolation to Madame du Barry, who had made bitter complaints to the King about the contempt that the ladies of the Court manifested towards her,"[2] gave a supper at Bellevue,

[1] And had been so for nearly a century. In 1686, the Duc du Maine wrote to Madame de Maintenon: "As it is impossible to be at Marly without playing, or to find any one willing to play for small stakes, I lost yesterday fifty pistoles to M. de Richelieu and as much to the Comte de Grammont."

[2] Hardy's *Journal.*

the beautiful château which Madame de Pompadour had built on the banks of the Seine, between Sèvres and Meudon, in 1750, and sold to the monarch seven years later. The presence of eight of the haughtiest dames to be found at Versailles was requested, who, of course, had no option but to obey, though, as may be imagined, they did so with the worst possible grace; while invitations were also sent to a number of noble-men, amongst whom, to the general astonishment, Choiseul was included.

"One would imagine," writes Belleval, "that his Majesty derived amusement from seeing the cat and dog together;"[8] but though this view of the matter is quite in keeping with the singular character of Louis XV., we are inclined to think that the invitation was inspired by a very different motive, namely, that the King desired to show the Minister that he was firmly resolved to support his new mistress, and to afford him an opportunity of becoming reconciled to her. A dinner *au grand couvert* would not have suited his purpose so well, while Choiseul would have declined an invitation to Madame du Barry's apart-ments. Bellevue, however, was neutral ground, on which both parties might meet without embarrass-ment.

If such was the King's intention his scheme came to nothing. Choiseul accepted the invitation—he could not well refuse—took his place at table with Louis and the favourite, and treated the latter with punctilious courtesy. But, at the same time, he con-trived to convey the impression that he was doing violence to his feelings by joining the party, and that nothing but the respect he owed his sovereign would have induced him thus to compromise his dignity.

In pursuance of his resolution to compel the Court

[8] *Souvenirs d'un Chevau-léger*, p. 120.

to accept his mistress, Louis now bestirred himself, with an activity very unusual in one of his indolent temperament, to rally people to the standard of Madame du Barry and give her something more than a nominal footing at Versailles. This, as may be supposed, was no pleasant task. The men were complacent enough. The King's personal friends, Richelieu, Soubise, Chauvelin, Villeroi, and others, had no scruples about paying homage to the new divinity; it was all in the day's work, so to speak. But, in an affair of this nature, the masculine attitude was of very secondary importance indeed; it was the women who ruled the Court, and, in the absence of a queen or a dauphiness, the women followed the lead of Madame de Gramont and her coterie and remained obdurate.

To break through the quarantine to which his mistress was subjected the King perceived that the first step must be to secure for her the countenance and support of some great lady—Madame de Béarn had "too much the air of an aunt on hire" to command any following at Court—and, accordingly, turned his eyes towards the old Maréchale de Mirepoix, whose necessities, he thought, might incline her to undertake the rôle, if it carried with it a sufficiently tempting emolument. In this he was not mistaken. The Maréchale de Mirepoix, who was the sister of the Prince de Beauvau, and had been the bosom friend of Madame de Pompadour, belonged to the Choiseul party, though her reluctance to compromise herself with the King had prevented her from taking an active part in the campaign against Madame du Barry. She enjoyed a very considerable income, but, owing to her extravagance and her passion for play, was continually in pecuniary difficulties, and estimated that her expenditure exceeded her receipts by

nearly 20,000 livres, "which occasioned constant disorder in her affairs, and subjected her daily to writs,
executions, and all sorts of humiliations." For some
years past, Louis, who was very fond of the old lady
—she was one of the few persons who possessed the
secret of relieving his *ennui*—had been in the habit of
making her an annual *gratification* of 12,000 livres, to
enable her to pacify the most importunate of her
creditors; and the promise that this sum should be
materially increased sufficed to secure her *chaperon-
nage* for Madame du Barry.

All the partisans of Choiseul were highly indignant
at the defection of Madame de Mirepoix, and were
loud in their denunciation of her conduct, declaring
that it seemed as if she were an appanage of the post
of favourite, to be passed on from one mistress to
another like a piece of furniture. But, though Madame du Deffand wrote that the maréchale appeared
"very sad and troubled, and, for the first time in her
life, unable to disguise her embarrassment," the latter
stood to her guns, and Madame du Barry, either from
inclination or gratitude, soon became so attached to
"la petite maressale," as she called her new ally, that
she could not endure to be separated from her.

The reasons which had prompted *"la petite maressale"* to cast in her lot with the despised favourite
were too generally understood for her to find many
followers. However, the hope of procuring some advantage for themselves or their relatives brought,
after a while, several welcome recruits to the Du
Barry party, prominent amongst whom were the
Princesse de Montmorency and the Comtesse de
Valentinois; while the Marquise de l'Hôpital was
persuaded by Soubise, whose mistress she was, to
throw what little influence she possessed into the same
scale. Thus Madame du Barry found herself the

centre of a group of ladies, which, whatever claim it may have had to consideration, could at least boast great names.

One of the attributes of a *maîtresse en titre* was to receive the homage of men of letters, and, in return, to bestow upon them her patronage and protection. This homage frequently took the form of flattering, not to say fulsome, dedications prefaced to their works. Thus La Fontaine had dedicated the second collection of his fables to Madame de Montespan,[*] Crébillon *père* his *Catilina* to Madame de Pompadour, and Voltaire his *Tancrède* to the same lady. Madame du Barry had not long to wait for Literature to begin burning incense at her shrine. A few weeks after her presentation, a certain Chevalier de la Morlière sent her a copy of a work entitled, *Le Fatalisme, ou collection d'anecdotes pour prouver l'influence du sort sur l'histoire du cœur humaine,* preceded by a most complimentary dedication, wherein he assured her that "Nature had lavished upon her her rarest gifts," that "kindness, benevolence, and sweetness of disposition" were hers, and that, "inspired by these estimable qualities," it would be her destiny to honour the arts and sciences and "all that would appear to her worthy of marked distinction."

Unfortunately for Madame du Barry, the author of *Le Fatalisme* was very far from being a Voltaire, a La Fontaine, or even a Crébillon. Bachaumont describes him as "an author better known by his knavery, impudence, and baseness than by his works," and indeed he appears to have been a most undesirable *protégé*. A man of some talent, he had commenced

[*] Two years later, La Fontaine celebrated the charms of Madame de Montespan's youthful rival, Mademoiselle de Fontanges, whom he apostrophised as "*charmant objet, digne présent des cieux.*"

his literary career by the production of several romances, one of which, called *Angola,* which was published anonymously, had so great a vogue that it was attributed to Crébillon *fils.*[5] The profits of these works, however, failed to accord with the writer's expectations, and he therefore sought to augment them by becoming a "dramatic critic" and levying blackmail upon the luckless playwrights of his time. The *claque* of which he was the head was so numerous and noisy that it was able to secure the success or failure of all but the productions of dramatists of established reputation, and managers trembled at the chevalier's nod.

Emboldened by his success, he imagined that it would be an easy matter to secure the triumph of any work of his own. But in this he was mistaken, as, though the poor actors did not dare to refuse his plays, they failed lamentably, notwithstanding the skilful manœuvres of his friends, "sustained by the zealous efforts of his creditors." After this his influence declined rapidly, and he became an object of ridicule and contempt to those who had formerly solicited his suffrages. Finding himself compelled to seek a fresh field for the exercise of his talents, he established a sort of academy for embryo actresses, and cheated his pupils so outrageously that his relatives were forced to shut him up, on the plea of insanity, to save him from a worse fate. On his release, he resumed his literary pursuits, and when Madame du Barry rose to favour, hastened to make a bid for her patronage.

La Morlière's dedication secured him a ready sale

[5] He was also the author of a work entitled, *Les Lauriers ecclésiastiques, ou campagnes de l'Abbé de T. . . .,* which bears the distinction of being one of the most obscene in the French language. It was suppressed, and the few copies which escaped the vigilance of the police now command a very high price, and are *"très récherchés par les libertins."*

for his book and an invitation to sup with the countess, who accorded him "a gracious reception," and a present of one hundred louis. Here, however, his connection with Madame du Barry seems to have ended, very probably because the lady was annoyed by the ridicule to which the adulation of a person of such chequered antecedents exposed her.

Other men of letters followed La Morlière's example, and among the volumes in the Versailles Library bearing the arms and device of Madame du Barry are four works prefaced by dedications to the favourite.

The first of these is entitled: *Le Royalisme, ou Mémoires de du Barry de Saint-Aunet et de Constance de Cezelli, sa femme, anecdotes héroïques sous Henry IV., par M. de Limairac.* The author in his dedication announces that heroism is the heritage of every Du Barry.

The second is an almanac for the year 1774, called the *Almanach de Flore,* printed in red, with a portrait of Madame du Barry as a sunflower turned to the sun, numerous illustrations, horoscopes, and so forth. It was the work of a certain M. Douin, "captain of cavalry," assisted by a M. Chevalier, "lieutenant of infantry," and one Douin, "formerly soldier of infantry."

The remaining works are by writers of considerable reputation, at least in their own day. One, a translation from the *Idyllen* of Salomon Gessner, is from the pen of Jacques Henri Meister, the friend of Diderot and Grimm, who addresses the new mistress of Louis XV. in the following terms:

> " De la beauté, les talents et les arts
> Chérissent tous l'aimable empire.
> Que l'églogue au naïf sourire
> Arrête un instant vos regards!

Comme vous, belle sans parure,
Elle doit tout aux mains de la nature.
Comme vous, elle a quelquefois
Sous l'air d'une simple bergère,
Charmé les héros et les rois.
. . . ."

The other, a poetical *recueil* containing two comic operas, *Les Etrennes de l' Amour,* and *Le Nouveau Marié,* is by Madame du Barry's friend, Cailhava; and the favourite finds herself apostrophised on the first page as "beautiful Cytherea" and "amiable Hebe."[6]

[6] E. and J. de Goncourt's *La Du Barry,* p. 65 *note.* *Quérard's La France littéraire, passim.*

CHAPTER VII

THE new favourite was soon afforded an opportunity of using her influence in a more worthy manner than in patronising sycophantic men of letters.

Although the punishments meted out to evil-doers in the eighteenth century were still reminiscent of the dark ages, the right of pardon possessed by the Crown was very rarely exercised. Louis XV., so indulgent towards his own follies and vices, was far from being so towards those of others, and was but little inclined to interfere with the course of the law, even in cases where a manifest injustice had been perpetrated; the Queen never had any influence with her husband or his Ministers after the first few years of her married life; Madame de Mailly, charitable and kind-hearted though she was, could never be persuaded to meddle with matters which did not immediately concern her; Madame de Châteauroux's reign was, of course, too short for her to have much opportunity for deeds of mercy; while Madame de Pompadour, who could have dictated her will to the Chancellor as to the other Ministers, was far more ready to people the dungeons than to open them.

The condemned criminal had, therefore, up to the present, lacked an intercessor, but in Madame du Barry he was to find a very efficient one. Whatever may have been the faults of the new mistress—and, apart from her unchastity, prodigality and love of display are, after all, the only charges which can be truthfully brought against her—there can be no question that she was a woman of genuine kindness of disposition in whose heart the sight of suffering never failed to awaken a responsive echo; and on several occasions during her favour we find her intervening with success on behalf of those who would otherwise have suffered the extreme penalty of the law.

Two of these cases occurred in the summer of 1769, only a few weeks after her recognition as Madame de Pompadour's successor.

Harsh as was the old French law, it was particularly so in regard to infanticide. An edict of Henri II., bearing date February 1556, prescribed that a woman convicted of concealing her pregnancy should, in the event of her child's death, be adjudged guilty of homicide and punished accordingly. This law was still in force, and in virtue of it, in June 1769, a girl named Appoline Gregéois, of the parish of Liancourt, in the Vexin, whose offence had been aggravated by several petty thefts, committed, apparently, with the view of providing for her accouchement, was brought to trial and condemned to death.

The case, in some way, was brought to the notice of Madame du Barry, who, touched with compassion, at once interested herself on the unhappy young woman's behalf. At her solicitation the *procureur-général* granted a respite, and, a week later, she had the satisfaction of learning that the capital sentence had been commuted to one of three years' imprisonment.

A fortnight after the favourite's successful intervention on behalf of Appoline Gregéois, her good offices were again requisitioned, on this occasion to save a high and puissant *seigneur* and his lady from the consequences of armed resistance to the officers of the law, which in those days was construed into rebellion against the King. As this case, besides being one of the most sensational of the reign, contributed not a little towards reconciling the nobility to the new *régime*, it is deserving of something more than passing mention.

On the borders of Champagne and the Orléanais stood an old, ruinous château called Parc-Vieil, the seat of a certain Comte and Comtesse de Loüesme. Like the château, the family of Loüesme had fallen on evil times; their estates had been sequestrated and their personal property as well; but, as they had proclaimed their determination of resisting *vi et armis* any attempt to seize the latter, they were, for some time, left in undisturbed possession of their old home.

As ill-luck would have it, however, in the summer of 1768, the bailiwick in which the château of Parc-Vieil was situated passed into the hands of a certain Dorcy, "a man of resolute character and an astute practitioner," who had no sooner been informed of the facts of the case than he determined to bring the Comte and Comtesse de Loüesme to reason without a moment's delay. Accordingly, on July 1, between three and four o'clock in the morning, he arrived at Parc-Vieil, accompanied by two bailiffs named Jolivet and Chamon and the *maréchaussée*, or mounted gendarmerie, of Saint-Fargeau and Courtenay.

Although not precisely a stronghold, Parc-Vieil was far from an easy place to take by storm, as it was surrounded by a deep moat, the place of the drawbridge, which had long since broken down, being supplied by planks, which were removed at night. Dorcy summoned the garrison to surrender; the count and countess appeared on the battlements, and defied him to do his worst, upon which, perceiving that further argument would be useless, the besiegers threw a bridge across the moat and advanced to the assault.

The Comte de Loüesme's threats of armed resistance,

however, had been no idle talk. Hurrying down to the door, he thrust the barrel of a gun through a loophole, and threatened to fire upon the enemy if they approached a step nearer. The bailiff Jolivet seized the gun by the muzzle and attempted to wrest it from the grasp of the infuriated nobleman, with the result that it went off, and a general engagement ensued, in the course of which the Comtesse de Loüesme, who had come to her husband's assistance, fired at Jolivet, wounding him mortally. Another of the attacking party was also fatally injured, and, in the end, Dorcy was compelled to raise the siege.

Two days passed, which were utilised by the garrison in strengthening their defences, and by Dorcy in collecting reinforcements, and, on the night of July 3, quite an army appeared before the château, composed of the *maréchaussée* of Saint-Fargeau, Courtenay, and Montargis, and a number of armed peasants, who had been called upon to support the majesty of the law. A second engagement followed, in which Godard, the coachman of the Loüesmes and an old retainer of the family, was killed, and the countess herself slightly wounded, whereupon the count yielded to the entreaties of his terrified servants and surrendered.

The affair caused an immense sensation, for though such incidents had been common enough during the anarchy of the Fronde, they had since been of very rare occurrence.[1] As the persons implicated were of high rank, it was deemed inexpedient to leave the matter to the jurisdiction of the local courts, and, accordingly,

[1] There had, however, been a somewhat similar affair fourteen years earlier, when the Marquis de Pleumartin, a nobleman of Poitou, for whose arrest a warrant had been *issued, not* the commander of the *maréchaussée* who had come to arrest him. He was condemned to be beheaded, but, in order to spare his family the ignominy of a public execution, he was strangled in prison.— *Journal du Marquis d'Argenson,* January 1755, cited by M. Vatel.

the King issued letters patent directing that the case should be tried by the Parliament of Paris. For some reason, however, the trial was postponed for a year, and it was not until July 4, 1769, that the count and countess were arraigned before the Grande Chambre and Tournelle sitting together.

The prisoners had practically no defence, and the only plea that their advocate could find to put forward was that the first execution had been irregular, inasmuch as Dorcy and his followers had commenced hostilities before sunrise. This was promptly overruled, and five witnesses having deposed that the Comtesse de Loüesme had fired the shot which had been responsible for the death of the unfortunate Jolivet, both she and her husband were condemned to be beheaded, the sentence to be carried out on the following day.[2]

The rank of the condemned, their connection with several persons high in favour at Court, and particularly the fact that they were related to the Chancellor, Maupeou, combined to induce the belief that the capital sentence would be immediately commuted. The astonishment, therefore, was profound when it became known that the Chancellor had refused to take any steps on their behalf, declaring that the crime was one which the King's oath forbade him to pardon; and that Louis XV., acting doubtless on his Minister's advice, had turned a deaf ear to the entreaties of the Comtesse de Moyon, the daughter of the Loüesmes, and replied that the law must take its course.

It was then that a friend of the unhappy pair determined to address himself to the Comtesse de Béarn and, through her, to Madame du Barry, in the hope

[2] Occasionally when the sentence was pronounced in the morning, it was executed the same day. Thus, in November 1746, the *procureur-général* sent a *placet* ordering the release of one Guillaume Cor, to which the reply was: "Remission. Affair concluded. Guillaume Cor has been hanged."

that the latter, whose sympathy had been so readily
aroused by the misfortunes of a poor peasant-girl,
might not be unwilling to interest herself in those of
offenders of a more exalted station.

The favourite at once promised to use her influence
on the side of mercy, and, hastening to the King, threw
herself on her knees before him and announced her
intention of remaining in that position until his
Majesty accorded her prayer. Louis, who had remained unmoved by the tears and supplications of the
Comtesse de Moyon, was not proof against the entreaties of his beautiful mistress, and, raising her
up, exclaimed: " Madame, I am enchanted that the
first favour you obtain from me should be an act of
humanity."

The sentence on the Comte and Comtesse de
Loüesme was commuted to imprisonment, and they
were confined in the Château of Saumur, their relatives being charged with the expense of their maintenance. In 1778, their detention, in its turn, was
commuted to banishment; Louis XV., at the same
time, granting them a small pension.

Not even the bitterest critic of Madame du Barry
has ever ventured to suggest that the countess's conduct in this affair was prompted by any other motive
than humanity; nevertheless, it had all the results of a
most skilful political move. Not only did it afford a
striking proof of the lady's influence over the King,
and thus decide many waverers to accord her their support, but, by inspiring a belief that this influence
would be exercised in no unworthy manner, it conciliated not a few of those who had hitherto opposed
her from disinterested motives. Outside the Court,
too, it produced a strong reaction in her favour; Voltaire, in a letter to the Comtesse de Rochefort, expresses his conviction that Madame du Barry was "a

kind-hearted woman" (*une bonne femme*), and this opinion appears to have been widespread. "No one, unless he had personal motives for enmity to the favourite," writes Pidansat, in one of his rare excursions into the truth, "could fail to like her, and to reject the impressions that prejudiced people and her enemies had spread abroad about her; she was so courteous, affable, and gentle. She had the virtue, rare, especially among her own sex, of never speaking ill of any one, and never permitting herself complaints and reproaches against those who envied her and those who had not only published abroad the not too creditable stories of her life, but had embroidered them with infamies and enormities."[3]

Madame de Montespan had had her Clagny, Madame de Pompadour her Bellevue, her Crécy, and her La Celle; it was, therefore, only in accordance with precedent that Madame du Barry should possess a country-seat befitting her high position; and on July 24, a fortnight after the arrival of the Court on its annual visit to Compiègne, Louis XV. presented his new favourite with a brevet conferring upon her the tenancy for life of the beautiful château and estate of Louveciennes, situated a short distance from the left bank of the Seine and adjoining the park of Marly.[4]

[3] *Anecdotes*, i. 152.
[4] Here is the brevet:
"*Brevet of the gift of the pavilion of Louvetiennes in favour of madame la comtesse du Barri,*
"*Of July 24, 1769.*
"To-day, twenty-fourth of July, seventeen hundred and sixty-nine, the King being at Compiègne, and being desirous of giving to the dame comtesse du Barry a mark of the consideration with which his Majesty honours her, has accorded and made to her a gift of the pavilion of Louvetiennes, its gardens, and dependencies, the enjoyment of which has already been accorded by his Majesty to the comtesse de Toulouse, and after her to Mgr. le duc de Penthièvre, who has surrendered it, in order that the

The estate of Louveciennes, frequently abbreviated into Luciennes, originally belonged to a Marquis de Beringhen, who, in the year 1690, sold it to Louis XIV., or, to speak more precisely, exchanged it for another property, that of Châtellenie-de-Tournan, in Brie. At this period there was no house upon the estate, but Louis XIV. built one as a residence for Baron Deville, the Flemish engineer, who designed the famous hydraulic machine at Marly. Deville left France in 1708, whereupon the house was transformed into a little château and presented for life to Mademoiselle de Clermont, daughter of the Prince de Condé and Mademoiselle de Nantes, upon whose death in 1741, Louis XV. gave it to the Comtesse de Toulouse, in recognition, it is believed, of her services in the King's amours with the sisters de Nesle.[5] The countess died in January 1766, and was succeeded as tenant by her only son, the Duc de Penthièvre. But, a year later, the duke's heir, the young Prince de Lamballe, who had recently married Marie Thérèse de Savoie, Princesse de Carignan, the beautiful and unfortunate lady who met so horrible a fate during the Revolution, died there also, the victim of a painful disease; and his father, unwilling to reside any longer in a house which possessed for him such painful associations, gave the property back to the King.[6]

said dame comtesse du Barry may enjoy during her life the said pavilion and such dependencies as belong and appertain to it, in conformity with the plan deposed at the office of Director-General of his Majesty's Board of Works. . . . And, in assurance of his will, his Majesty has signed with his own hand the present brevet, and caused it to be countersigned by me, under-secretary of State and his orders. (Signed) LOUIS (and, lower down,) PHELY-PEAUX."—*Archives nationales, Registre des Brevets,* cited by E. and J. de Goncourt, *La Du Barry,* p. 64 note.

[5] The Duc de Luynes, who describes the view from Louveciennes as charming and the house as very beautiful, says that the Queen had asked for it, but had been refused.

[6] *Histoire de Madame du Barry,* i. 254.

It is somewhat difficult to understand why Louveciennes should have been chosen as the country-seat of a royal favourite, as the enjoyment to be derived from the beautiful view which its windows commanded must have been largely discounted by the fact that the hydraulic machine, with its unceasing clang, was situated immediately below the house; while the building itself was far too small to accommodate even Madame du Barry's retinue of servants, to say nothing of the numerous *entourage* which etiquette demanded should accompany the King whenever he honoured one of his subjects by a visit.

The hydraulic machine, unfortunately, could not well be removed even to gratify Madame du Barry, but everything that money could effect towards remedying the architectural deficiencies was done, and extensive additions and alterations were designed by Jacques Ange Gabriel, first architect to the King, and carried out by his son, the Comptroller of Buildings at Marly.

These additions and alterations, which included the restoration of part of the château and the making of a bath-room and an orangery, were commonly reported to have involved the expenditure of enormous sums, but, according to a memoir of Gabriel, the total cost of the work was under 139,000 livres.

"The principal dispositions of the building having remained unchanged," says M. Vatel, "one is still able to give a description of this residence. It consisted, on the ground floor, of an entrance-hall or vestibule 20 feet by 18, the lofty ceiling of which is decorated by a frieze, delicately sculptured, representing children at play. Then comes the dining-room, adorned with a beautiful old wainscot, ornamented with all the attributes of the country and the chase. Harvesters' rakes and hats, hunting horns and cymbals, arrows and quivers, all indicate the pleasures of the fields. In the centre of one side of the room is a magnificent marble chimney-piece.

"The salon is decorated in the same style. Its length is 4 toises, its height $2\frac{1}{2}$ toises; it is lighted by two large windows, and is approached by a glass door giving on to a flight of steps. The wainscot shows the same intersections as the dining-room, violins and shepherds' pipes, bagpipes and guitars, phœnix and peacock, and all around a frieze representing figures of women and children.

"Above, on the first floor, was situated the apartment of Madame du Barry, which faced north, while on the south side was that of the King; later, the Duc de Brissac's.[7]

"The main building was prolonged by a gallery of considerable length, which was used as an orangery, and at the end of this was a chapel."[8]

The visit of the Court to Compiègne did not terminate without an unpleasant incident, occasioned by the continued hostility of Choiseul to the new favourite.

For the purpose of giving the Dauphin and his brothers some instruction in military matters, a "pleasure camp" was formed at Verberie, in the plain of Royal-Lieu, under the command of Baron Würmser, Lieutenant-General and Chief-Inspector of the German infantry regiments in the French service. The manœuvres, which lasted three days, were witnessed by Louis XV., his three grandsons, *Mesdames* —and Madame du Barry; and Dumouriez, who had known the lady in the days when she presided over the

[7] Louis Hercule Timoléon de Cossé, Duc de Brissac (1734-1792), the penultimate lover of Madame du Barry.
[8] *Histoire de Madame du Barry*, i. 264.

ménage of the "Roué," and had lately returned from Germany, was profoundly shocked at "the sight of the old King of France degrading himself by standing with doffed hat beside a magnificent phaeton, in which the Du Barry was reclining."[9]

Among the troops assembled at Verberie was the Régiment de Beauce, in which Elie du Barry, younger brother of Jean and Guillaume, held a commission. An exchange of civilities took place between the favourite and the officers of her brother-in-law's regiment; the officers invited Madame du Barry to dine in the camp, and she, in her turn, entertained them to a magnificent banquet. Indeed, so excellent an understanding prevailed that when, on the last day of the manœuvres, the favourite's carriage passed down the line, the Chevalier de la Tour-du-Pin, the colonel of the Régiment de Beauce, thought that he could do no less than order his men to present arms, an honour hitherto expressly reserved on these occasions for the King and members of the Royal Family.

Choiseul, who, in his capacity as Minister of War, had also attended the manœuvres, was highly incensed at the unprecedented marks of distinction accorded to his enemy, and severely reprimanded all concerned. His action was duly reported to Louis XV., who thereupon wrote him the following letter:

LOUIS XV. *to* THE DUC DE CHOISEUL.

"As I have promised to tell you all that occurs to me concerning you, I now acquit myself of that task.

"It is said that you rated Würmser, for what reason I know not, but that you let fall a good round *oath.*[10]

"It is said that you rated the Chevalier de la Tour-

---

[9] *La Vie et les mémoires du Général Dumouriez* (edit. **Berville** and Barrière), i. 141.

[10] The word in the original is too coarse for modern print.

du-Pin, because Madame du Barry dined in the camp, and because the majority of the officers dined with her on the day of the review.

"You also reprimanded Foulon,[11] in his turn.

"You promised that I should hear no more from you about her.[12]

"I speak to you in confidence and friendship. You may be inveighed against in public; it is the fate of Ministers, especially when they are believed to be antagonist to the friends of the master; but, for all that, the master is always very satisfied with their work, and with yours in particular."

Choiseul replies at great length, endeavouring to justify his conduct; which, he maintains, has been grossly, and purposely, misrepresented, and expressly disclaiming all hostilities to Madame du Barry.

After acknowledging, in suitable terms, the expressions of kindness and confidence which the King's letter contained, he declares that his Majesty must know, "in the bottom of his soul," that he (Choiseul) is the particular object of the hatred of those about Madame du Barry. These he divides into two classes: "persons of seventy years of age and upwards"[13] and "young persons." His Majesty, he says, will know how much credit to attach to the statements and motives of the former; as for the latter, "who imagine that they are doing something wonderful in deriding and braving your Minister," they merely excite contempt.

[11] Joseph François Foulon de Doué, who said, or was reported to have said, that if the poor lacked bread, they could eat grass, and was hanged by the mob of Paris, July 22, 1789. He was at this time *commissaire des guerres*.

[12] From this it would appear that Choiseul had at length attempted some remonstrance with the King in regard to Madame du Barry, very probably after the supper at Bellevue.

[13] The Duc de Richelieu.

He denies that he rated Baron Würmser, for it is not rating to say, "My dear Würmser, hasten; the King has been waiting half an hour." Never had he used improper language towards any officer. "Würmser is here and can speak the truth."

He continues:

"As regards the Régiment de Beauce, there is no more truth in that, though there is more appearance of truth. I never rated the Chevalier de la Tour-du-Pin; I never spoke to him about either giving or accepting a dinner. I am, Sire, a thousand leagues above such wretched trifles. The day on which your Majesty witnessed the manœuvres of the forty-two battalions, word was brought me that the Régiment de Beauce, after your Majesty had passed down the line, had saluted and rendered the same honours to Madame du Barry as to yourself. I did not say a word to the person who brought me the information. In the evening, in my apartments, the same thing was repeated, but I appeared to pay no attention to it. The following day, on going to see this brigade manœuvre, I told M. de Rochambeau that it had been reported to me that the Régiment de Beauce had saluted other carriages than those of the Royal Family while his Majesty was in front of the line; that that was not right; and I charged him to warn M. de la Tour-du-Pin that he ought not to salute any one else when the King was in camp."

The Minister then points out that La Tour-du-Pin has been promoted to the rank of brigadier, and that all the requests made by the officers of his regiment (presumably for leave) have been granted, "which proves that there is no ill-humour on my part."

As for Foulon, "who is what is called an intriguer, with boundless ambition," he had not even so much as spoken to him since coming to Compiègne, and if he asserted that he had been reprimanded at any time, "under any circumstances whatever," in reference to Madame du Barry or anything which could possibly concern her, then "M. Foulon is an impudent liar."

He concludes:

"These details are a trifle long, Sire, for which I crave your indulgence; but it behoves me to tell you the truth in regard to these small matters, in order that you may be able to appreciate in future the reports which may reach you. You will be told, Sire, that I have faults; I earnestly desire to correct myself of them, and I reproach myself, in private, with them as bitterly as my enemies can do. They will add that I have committed mistakes as Minister; that is only too true; when I have been aware of them I have avowed them, and I am more sensible than any one can be of my imperfections and the limitation of my talents. But, Sire, I beg you to be persuaded that I fear neither the intriguers nor the results of criticism. I have two objects only, that of serving you well and of pleasing you. It is impossible for me not to believe that I serve your Majesty well, because I serve you to the best of my endeavour. It is difficult, Sire, for you to entertain any doubt as to my desire to please you, if you condescend to reflect that I hold everything from you; that I neither hold nor have ever desired to hold anything except from you; that you unite for me all the sentiments of duty, of personal attachment, and of gratitude, and that I serve you by affection, and by affection the most zealous, which is better than ambition and talents."[14]

Although Jean du Barry could not, of course, appear at Court, he was none the less an important fac-

[14] *Revue de Paris,* 1829, vol. iv. p. 49 *et seq.* The letters were communicated to this journal by Gabriel, Duc de Choiseul, the Minister's nephew and successor, who possessed the originals.

tor in the political situation. He had persuaded the
favourite to obtain for his ugly, but keen-witted,
sister "Chon" apartments in the château at Versailles
and, through her, contrived to keep himself in constant
communication with his former mistress, who entertained a high opinion of his astuteness and never
failed to apply to him for advice whenever she found
herself in any difficulty.

In consequence of the incident at the review, the
"Roué" came to Compiègne, charged by Madame du
Barry with a mission of conciliation. Being somewhat doubtful as to the reception which his overtures might meet with were he to seek a personal interview with Choiseul, he addressed himself to the
Minister's nephew, the Duc de Lauzun,[15] and begged
him to meet him the following morning in the forest,
as he had something of the utmost importance to
communicate. Not a little mystified, Lauzun consented, and found that Du Barry was desirous that he
should take upon himself the rôle of peacemaker between his uncle and the favourite.

"He complained to me," says the duke, "of the
bitterness which the Duc de Choiseul evinced towards
Madame du Barry and himself; said that she was willing to do justice to so great a Minister and desired
ardently to live on good terms with him, and that he
would not force her to become his enemy; that she had
more influence with the King than Madame de Pompadour had ever had, and that she would be very
grieved if he compelled her to use it to his detriment.
He begged me to relate this conversation to M. de
Choiseul and to convey to him all sorts of protesta-
tions of attachment."

Lauzun good-naturedly promised to do all in his

[15] Choiseul and Lauzun's father, the Duc de Gontaut, had married two sisters, the demoiselles Crozat.

power to promote a better understanding; but, alas! his efforts were vain. When he reached Choiseul's apartments, he found Madame de Gramont there, concerting with her brother new schemes for the discomfiture of her hated rival. With the eyes of his vindictive sister upon him, the duke received the favourite's overtures "with all the haughtiness of a Minister who is harassed by women and believes that he has nothing to fear," and declared that there was "war to the knife" between him and Madame du Barry; while Madame de Gramont "made some outrageous remarks, in which she did not spare even the King."[16]

In order to show his contempt for the favourite and her supporters, Choiseul, a few days later, quitted Compiègne and spent some weeks in visiting his country-seat at Chanteloup and various military stations in Lorraine, thus leaving the field clear for his adversaries.

On the return of the Court from Compiègne, towards the end of August, Louis XV. paid a visit to the Prince de Condé, at Chantilly, and Madame du Barry was officially invited to accompany him. The descendant of the hero of Rocroix had long since decided to bow to the royal will, and had the new mistress been a foreign princess she could hardly have been received with greater honours, her host placing his own *calèche* at her disposal when she wished to follow the chase, seating her beside him at table, and "seeming, in short, to dedicate to her the flowers, the illuminations, and the fanfares of his *fêtes*."

[16] *Mémoires* du Duc de Lauzun (edit. 1858), p. 95 *et seq*.

CHAPTER VIII

IN September, the Salon of the Louvre, which at this period was held every alternate year, opened its doors. The centre of attraction proved to be two portraits of the new favourite, both by Drouais, who had painted the last portrait of Madame de Pompadour, now at Hampton Court. "The better to ensure success," says Pidansat, "he had conceived the idea of representing Madame du Barry in two styles, that is to say, in both masculine and feminine attire." In the first, she is wearing a kind of hunting-coat and a waistcoat with military facings. "She has a flat coiffure, and two or three patches placed here and there relieve the mischievousness of this charming and saucy little face."[1] In the second, she appears "fresh and laughing, with the innocence of a young Flora," in a white gown adorned with a wreath of flowers, and with a string of pearls on her shoulder.

The former portrait, we are told, appealed most to the ladies, and the latter to the men, which gave rise to the following verses:

> " Quels yeux ! que d'attraits ! qu'elle est belle !
>   Est-ce une divinité?
> Non, c'est une simple mortelle,
>   Qui le dispute à la Beauté.
>   Entre vous qui décidera.
>   Beau cavalier, aimable Flore !
>   L'Olympe jaloux se taira,
> Et l'univers surpris admire et doute encore."

Diderot criticises these portraits very severely, expressing his opinion that the painter had ruined his

---

[1] E. and J. de Goncourt's *La Du Barry*, p. 74.
[2] *Mémoires de Favrolle*, ii. 47.

work by over-anxiety to do himself justice, and even going so far as to insinuate that, but for the fact that the original happened to be the talk of the town, they would be unworthy even of passing mention; but the majority of frequenters of the Salon cared little for artistic merit, and the crowd which surrounded them was so great that Horace Walpole, who was then in Paris, renounced his intention of visiting the exhibition.

Both portraits have been several times engraved. The best engraving of Madame du Barry *en habit de chasse* is Beauvarlet's; that of the portrait *à la guirlande,* as it is generally called, by Gaucher.

The homage paid to Madame du Barry by the Prince de Condé was a happy augury for the future. When the Court returned to Versailles, it soon became apparent that the quarantine to which the favourite had hitherto been subjected was steadily relaxing; scarcely a day now passed on which some nobleman or *grande dame* did not come to the conclusion that the claims of loyalty, or self-interest, demanded the sacrifice of personal feelings; scarcely a day now passed on which fresh faces did not appear at the new mistress's toilette, fresh voices whisper compliments in her ear. And Madame du Barry, even her enemies were compelled to admit, conducted herself, in these early days of her reign, with exemplary discretion, and used her newly acquired power with the strictest moderation. Foreigners, like Horace Walpole, were surprised to find in her neither boldness, nor arrogance, nor affectation.[3] She seemed to shun publicity, was at pains to avoid exciting the jealousy of her own sex, and gave

[3] "Thence to the Chapel, where a first row in the balconies was kept for us. Madame du Barri arrived over against us below, without rouge, without powder, and indeed *sans avoir fait sa toilette;* an odd appearance, as she was so conspicuous, close

as yet no indication of the absurd ostentation and wild
extravagance which were to mark the coming years.

But if the growing belief that the King's passion
was a lasting one, and the skilful self-effacement of
the favourite cost the opposition many of its adherents, there was no diminution in the hostility of
those who remained; indeed, with each fresh desertion
from their cause, Choiseul and his partisans seemed
only to become more rancorous, more resolute than
ever to prosecute the campaign until one or other
party was driven from the field.

Madame du Barry did not seek to play a political
rôle; she had not the smallest desire to make and un-
make Ministers, select Ambassadors, appoint generals,
and confer pensions and places, as her predecessor had
done. All she asked was to live in peace and quiet as
the King's mistress, to wear ravishing toilettes and
costly jewels, to take the air in a gilded coach, to have
a retinue of servants at her beck and call, and generally to enjoy the good things of life. Easy and pacific
by nature, she would never have dreamed of injuring
Choiseul had he not been the first to commence hostilities. She showed, indeed, as M. Maugras, the
duke's latest biographer freely admits, the most meri-
torious patience and long-suffering under great provo-
cation, and on several occasions made advances which
plainly showed her desire for a better understanding.[a]

Left to himself, it is probable that Choiseul would
have ended by becoming reconciled to the favourite.

to the altar and amidst both Court and people. She is pretty
when you consider her; yet so little striking, that I should never
have asked who she was. There is nothing bold, assuming, or
affected in her manner. Her husband's sister was along with her.
In the tribune above, surrounded by prelates, was the amorous
and still handsome King. One could not help smiling at the
mixture of piety, pomp, and carnality."—Horace Walpole *to*
George Montagu, September 17, 1769.
[a] *Le Duc et la Duchesse de Choiseul.*

Like most powerful Ministers, he had made many and bitter enemies, and could hardly fail to perceive the danger of adding to their number a person whose influence was increasing daily. Moreover, Madame du Barry asked nothing which he could not have conceded without loss of dignity. She did not demand his friendship, much less his homage; she would have been well content had he only been willing to remain neutral.

But Madame de Gramont and the Princesse de Beauvau had committed themselves far too deeply to draw back now, or allow their relative to do so. Peace with the favourite, they considered, would have involved a sacrifice of their pride, an intolerable humiliation in the eyes of all the ladies of the Court, whose leaders they aspired to be, and was not to be thought of for a moment; and Choiseul, yielding to the influence of his *entourage*, turned a deaf ear to the counsels of prudence, and marched steadily to his fall.[5]

In appearance, the relations between the Minister and the mistress were courteous, as had been the case between Madame de Pompadour and the most implacable of her enemies, the Comte d'Argenson, though in that instance neither party had had the least desire for a reconciliation. Madame du Barry wrote frequently to Choiseul, and always in very gracious terms. There were also several lengthy interviews between them, one of which lasted for three hours. But nothing could overcome the antipathy of the duke, who almost invariably refused the requests which the countess made to him. "A fortnight ago," writes Walpole, "the mistress sent for him (Choiseul) to ask a favour for a dependant. He replied that she might come to him. She insisted, and he went, and stayed above an hour, and yet did not grant what she asked." The writer expresses his opinion that "it was

[5] Walpole *to* Mann, October 9, 1769.

a thousand to one that some *éclat* would happen"
during the approaching visit to Fontainebleau, when
Madame de Gramont and the Princesse de Beauvau
("the Choiseul-women"), who were then visiting
friends abroad, would have returned.[6]

Louis XV., who detested changing his Ministers,
and was, besides, genuinely attached to Choiseul, who,
like Maurepas in days gone by, had the gift of rendering business "amusing," made every effort to bring
about a *rapprochement* between the duke and the
favourite, even going the length of writing the Minister a curious letter entreating him to abandon his attitude of hostility to Madame du Barry.

LOUIS XV. *to* THE DUC DE CHOISEUL

" . . . You manage my affairs very well, and I am
satisfied with you, but be on your guard against those
about you and the givers of advice (*donneurs d'avis*);
that is what I have always hated and what I detest
more than ever. You know Madame du Barry . . .
she is pretty, I am content with her, and I recommend
her every day to beware of those about her and the
givers of advice, for you can well believe that she does
not want for them; she has no bitter feeling against
you, she appreciates your talents, and wishes you no
evil. The exasperation against her has been frightful, without justification for the most part; they would
be at her feet if . . . that is the way of the world.
She is very pretty, she pleases me, that ought to suffice. Do you want me to take a girl of rank? If the
archduchess were such as I should desire her to be,
I would take her to wife with great pleasure,[7] for

[6]*Ibid.*
[7]At the beginning of June 1770, Louis wrote to the Comte de
Broglie, the conductor of his secret correspondence with foreign
Courts, instructing him to obtain private information about the

there must be an end of this, otherwise the *beau sexe* will always trouble me, for very surely, you will not see on my part a dame de Maintenon. And that, I think, is enough for the present. I have no need to recommend secrecy to you about this: my writing is no better than yours."[8]

"Does not this billet, which I have seen," observes Choiseul's friend, Baron de Gleichen, "express the desire for an arrangement, a prayer to lend himself to it, and the avowal, strange enough from a King, that the simple suffrage of his Ministers would do more than all that lay in his royal power? It is most astonishing that the sensitive heart of M. de Choiseul should have resisted so much kindness, the desire to play a trick on his enemies, and the certainty of reigning more comfortably by the aid of a woman who would have been entirely at his orders.'"[9]

The intervention of the King was of no avail; Choiseul, spurred on by Madame de Gramont and her coterie, remained inflexible, and Madame du Barry, having exhausted every means of conciliation, resigned herself to the struggle.

While awaiting a favourable opportunity of ridding herself of her adversary, the weapons to which the lady had recourse were those which Madame de Pompadour had employed with success on more than one occasion, notably against Maurepas; that is to say, she tormented her royal adorer with unceasing complaints about his Minister, until the unfortunate monarch began to detest the very name of Choiseul. Did she happen to be in an ill-humour: how could one be other-

Archduchess Elizabeth, "her person, from head to foot, her disposition," and so forth.
[8]*Revue de Paris,* 1829, vol. iv. p. 43. The letter was one of those which, as already mentioned, were contributed to the journal by Gabriel, Duc de Choiseul, who possessed the originals.
[9]*Souvenirs du Baron de Gleichen,* p. 38.

wise when M. de Choiseul refused to grant the very smallest favour that she asked of him? Were she pale and tearful: what could his Majesty expect when M. de Choiseul's friends were permitted to say such cruel things about her?[10] Nor did she any longer attempt to disguise her resentment against the Minister, and the harmony of the royal card and supper-parties was disturbed, whenever the duke happened to be present, by the contempt and dislike which the favourite never failed to exhibit towards him. "The grandpapa (Choiseul)," writes Madame du Deffand to Horace Walpole, "appears in very good spirits; nevertheless, he is not free from uneasiness. The lady does not conceal her hatred of him any longer. He receives every day little annoyances, such as not being nominated or invited to the *soupers des cabinets,* and, in her apartments, grimaces when he happens to be her partner at whist; mockeries, the shrugging of shoulders—in a word, all the little spiteful tricks of the schoolgirl. . . . Up to the present nothing has happened to injure his credit so far as regards his Ministry."[11]

Contrary to the confident anticipation of Horace Walpole, the visit of the Court to Fontainebleau passed off without any scandal, at least so far as the Choiseuls were concerned, though some unpleasantness arose in another quarter.

The Duc de Lauraguais, a nobleman with a predilection for indifferent verses and practical jokes, brought a courtesan of the baser sort from Paris, installed her in a suite of apartments in the town, and introduced her to all his friends as "Madame la Comtesse de Tonneau"—*tonneau* being synonymous with *baril* (cask), the pronunciation of which is the same as "Barry."[12]

[10]*Le Duc et la Duchesse de Choiseul.*
[11]Letter of November 22, 1769.
[12]An engraving of the time represents Madame du Barry

Had this pleasantry, clumsy though it was, been perpetrated at the expense of Madame de Pompadour, the Duc de Lauraguais would probably have had cause to rue it for the rest of his life. But that haughty dame's successor in the royal affections seems to have been rather amused than otherwise, and the only punishment which the duke received was an intimation that a few months' residence abroad might benefit his health;[13] while the King gave orders to the police to drive all the *femmes galantes* they could find out of the town, a step which, Pidansat de Mairobert tells us, occasioned great annoyance and inconvenience to many gentlemen of the Court.

As compensation for the impertinence of the Duc de Lauraguais, Madame du Barry, while at Fontainebleau, was the recipient of a most charming compliment.

It happened that Louis XV. was in the habit of paying a visit every autumn to a beautiful pavilion which the wealthy farmer-general Bouret had erected, at enormous cost, at Croix-Fontaine, in the forest of Senart. Bouret would appear to have built this pavilion, over which he is said to have nearly ruined himself, as a speculation, with the idea of selling it to Madame de Pompadour, who had a perfect mania for acquiring costly country-seats; but the death of that lady occurred before his project was realised. His

seated in a cask, as was the custom of the *ravaudeuses,* mending stockings and shoes. M. Vatel is of opinion that this caricature inspired the jest, or possibly the jest the caricature.

[13] About the same time, Lauraguais's former mistress, the beautiful and witty actress, Sophie Arnould, with whom the duke was still on friendly terms, displayed such "unexampled audacity" and "essential want of respect" towards Madame du Barry—in what way we are not told—that the King ordered her to be incarcerated in the "Hospital" for six months. The favourite, however, interceded for the popular *prima donna* and obtained her pardon.—Mr. R. B. Douglas' "Sophie Arnould," p. 102.

hopes of finding a purchaser, however, had revived
with the advent of Madame du Barry, and he, accordingly, resolved to leave no stone unturned to ingratiate
himself with the new divinity.

The royal visit this year was paid on September 28,
Madame du Barry accompanying the monarch dressed
in a *habit de chasse* similar to the one she had worn in
Drouais's portrait. After the day's hunting, at which
the killing of two stags had put the King into an excellent humour, Bouret entertained his distinguished
guests to a sumptuous repast, which concluded, he
begged them to step into an adjoining room, where,
he said, he had prepared a surprise for them. It was
a statue of Venus, modelled after that of Guillaume
Coustou *fils,* which had been sent to Potsdam the
previous June, together with a Mars, commissioned
by Frederick the Great at the same time. But the
head of the goddess had been changed—to an admirable likeness of Madame du Barry.

The favourite was, of course, enraptured, while
Louis XV. was highly flattered at such a delicate
tribute to his taste.[14] Nevertheless, Bouret did not
succeed in inducing Madame du Barry to become the
purchaser of his pavilion, and, some years later, having squandered the remainder of his fortune, he was
found dead, under circumstances which pointed to
suicide.

[14] Bouret was certainly a born courtier. On another of his
visits, Louis XV. perceived, on a table in the salon, a magnifi-
cently bound folio entitled, *Le Vrai Bonheur.* He opened it,
and found on each page the words, *" Le Roi est venu chez
Bouret,"* with the date, by anticipation, up to the year 1800.

CHAPTER IX

SHORTLY after the return of the Court from Fontainebleau, Madame du Barry was afforded another opportunity of giving proof of that kindness of heart and sympathy for misfortune which goes so far to efface the memory of her faults.

A young man of Aumale, named Charpentier, having quarrelled with his relatives, left his native town and enlisted in the Régiment du Mestre de Camp-Général, a cavalry corps stationed at Provins. Here his conduct was very satisfactory, until one fine day he was, according to his own account, seized with homesickness and deserted, taking with him his horse and uniform, with the intention apparently of returning them when he had gone two or three posts. This, however, he had no opportunity of doing, as his absence was discovered almost immediately, and he was promptly pursued and brought back. A court-martial followed, and the prisoner's offence being greatly aggravated by the fact of his having carried off his horse and uniform, the officers who tried him had no option but to pass sentence of death.

Fortunately for Charpentier, the commander of his regiment, the Chevalier d'Abense, took compassion upon the unhappy young man, and not only postponed the execution of the sentence to the farthest possible date, but wrote to his friend, the Comte de Belleval, who held a commission in the *Chevau-légers* of the King's Household, explaining the circumstances of the case, and begging him to use what influence he possessed to obtain a pardon from the King.

On receiving the chevalier's letter, Belleval laid the matter before his commanding officer, the Duc d'Aiguillon,[1] who told him that the surest way of obtaining the favour he sought would be to endeavour to interest Madame du Barry in his *protégé's* case, and promised to take him to the countess's apartments later in the day. We will follow the example of M. Vatel and allow Belleval to relate the sequel in his own words, thereby presenting the reader with probably the best pen-portrait of Madame du Barry which we have:

"At the hour appointed, I presented myself at M. d'Aiguillon's hôtel, in full uniform, and he, faithful to his promise, was waiting for me, and went straight to the favourite's apartments, like one to whom doors are always open.

"I had already often seen the countess, but from a distance; enough to allow me to judge of her renowned beauty in the *ensemble,* but not enough to study its details. She was carelessly sitting, or rather I should say reclining, on a large fauteuil, and wore a dress of white material with garlands of roses, which I see even now as I write, fifteen years later.

"Madame du Barry was one of the prettiest women at the Court, where there were so many, and assuredly the most bewitching, on account of the perfections of her whole person. Her hair, which she often wore without powder, was fair and a most beautiful colour, and she had such a profusion that she was at a loss to know what to do with it. Her blue eyes, widely open, had a kind and frank expression, and she fixed

[1] Armand Vignerod Duplessis Richelieu (1720-1788), son of Armand Louis de Vignerod, Marquis de Richelieu, Duc d'Aiguillon, and Anne Charlotte de Crussol-Florensac. Until his father's death, in 1750, he bore the title of Duc d'Agénois.

them upon those to whom she spoke, and seemed to follow in their faces the effect of her words. She had a tiny nose, a very small mouth, and a skin of dazzling whiteness. In short, she quickly fascinated every one, and I well-nigh forgot my petition in the delight I experienced in gazing at her. I was then about twenty-five years of age. She readily perceived my embarrassment, as did the Duc d'Aiguillon, who very adroitly turned it off with one of those compliments which he knew so well how to make. I then presented my petition, adding some explanation and laying stress on the necessity there was for haste, and on the hope that we all placed in her for saving the life of this unhappy Charpentier.

" 'I give you my promise to speak to the King, Monsieur,' she answered, 'and I trust that his Majesty will not refuse me this favour. Monsieur le Duc knows well that his friends are mine, and I thank him for not forgetting it,' she added, turning towards him with a charming smile. She then questioned me about my family, and as to how long I had served, and dismissed us, telling me that I should soon have news from her. She gave her hand to the Duc d'Aiguillon, who kissed it, observing: 'This is for the Captain-Lieutenant; is there nothing for the company?' which made her laugh; and she bestowed upon me the same favour, of which I hastened to take advantage.

"The following day, while I was on guard, a lackey, in the well-known livery of the countess, who had been to our hôtel to inquire for me, approached and informed me that his mistress expected me at six o'clock. At the hour appointed, I presented myself at the door of her apartment and was admitted. There were several persons there, and the King was standing with his back against the chimney-piece. On perceiving me, Madame du Barry said to his Majesty: 'Sire, here is my *chevau-léger*, who comes to render his thanks to your Majesty.'

" 'Thank, in the first place, Madame la Comtesse,' said Louis XV. to me, 'and tell your *protégé* that, if I pardon him, he must, by his attention to my service, cause the fault of which he has been guilty to be forgotten.'

"I do not very well know what answer I made the King; but the Duc d'Aiguillon, who was present, assured me that I had said all that was necessary, and that the King had been satisfied with me and pleased that I had had the tact to choose Madame du Barry to ask for Charpentier's pardon. The same evening, the news was despatched to Provins, where the poor man was expecting nothing but death. He afterwards made a good soldier, and became an example to his regiment.

"The story which I told my comrades of the goodness of the countess was received with great applause, and the Vicomte du Barry, our cornet, had nothing but praises and compliments to report to her. We always believed that he did so, for on every occasion she showed a marked preference for the *chevau-légers* above all the other troops of the King's Household. For my part, I was always afterwards treated with kindness, and I often met her at the hôtel of the Duchesse d'Aiguillon, to whom she was much attached on account of her husband. I never again visited her apartments, save on two occasions, to seek M. d'Aiguillon on business connected with our company, when I had not found him at his hôtel and the matter was urgent. But the place of a simple *chevau-léger* was not in the midst of all the courtiers who thronged her apartment, to pay their court to her or to meet his Majesty there. She understood that, and had the delicacy—though she treated me very kindly when I

met her—never to ask why I did not visit her, as
many women would have done. It was a different
matter at the Duc d'Aiguillon's, who was our chief,
and where the 'red-coats' often found themselves, or
at the Maréchale de Mirepoix's, where I also went
frequently. 'Ah! there is my *chevau-léger*,' was the
phrase which the countess never failed to employ when
she caught sight of me, and she would inquire if there
was anything she could do for me. As I invariably
replied that there was not, she said, 'He always replies "No," when there are so many who would answer "Yes." My dear duke, are they all like that in
your company?' 'Assuredly not,' answered the Duc
d'Aiguillon, and the laughter and gaiety which followed seemed as if it would never come to an end.'[2]

The Duc d'Aiguillon, who figures in the above incident, was Choiseul's most bitter enemy. The an-
tagonism between them was something more than the
conflict of personalities; it was one of principles and
ideas. "M. de Choiseul belonged to the Jansenists, to
the Parliamentarians, to the party of reform in
Church and State, to the first awakening of Liberty, to
the conspiracy of the future. M. d'Aiguillon belonged
to the traditions of his family, to the school of his
great-uncle, Cardinal de Richelieu, to the wisdom of
the past; to the theory of the right of absolute power,
to the party of social discipline, to the doctrine which
makes of monarchical government a good pleasure
tempered by a theocracy. In these two men everything is antagonistic, the internal administration of
the country as well as the plan of her alliances on the
map of Europe. They are the two champions and the
two extremities of their age."[3]

[2] *Souvenirs d'un Chevau-léger*, p. 128, *et seq.*
[3] E. and J. de Goncourt's *La Du Barry*, p. 48.

After having been in disgrace for a number of years, in consequence of the attachment which had once existed between himself and the King's mistress, Madame de Châteauroux, d'Aiguillon was eventually restored to favour and made Governor of Brittany, in which capacity he gained the victory of Saint-Cast over an English force which had landed there with the intention of ravaging the coast. His internal administration of that somewhat unruly province was less happy, and though M. Vatel, whose predilection for Madame du Barry appears to extend to her friends, has attempted his defence, there can be little doubt that his conduct, which aroused the bitterest hostility among all classes, was tyrannical and high-handed to the last degree, if not worse.

The Parliament of Brittany was almost as independent as that of Paris, and, in 1764, that court forbade the collection of a tax which the Governor had levied without obtaining its consent. The recalcitrant magistrates were summoned to Versailles, in the hope that the frown of Majesty might overcome their resistance, but they declined to yield, whereupon d'Aiguillon arrested several, including the *procureur-général,* La Chalotais,[*] on a charge of sending threat-

[*] D'Aiguillon was particularly bitter against La Chalotais, who had accused him of personal cowardice at the battle of Saint-Cast. It appears that, in the course of the conflict, the duke mounted to the top of a windmill, in order to direct the operations of his troops. La Chalotais remarked that in the battle "the troops were covered with glory, and their general with meal"; in other words, that the duke had gone into the mill to seek shelter. The charge, which was not made until eight years after the event, was, of course, groundless, as all contemporary accounts of the battle agree in eulogising the conduct of d'Aiguillon, and, whatever his faults may have been, he was certainly not lacking in courage, and, when a mere lad, had been twice severely wounded and mentioned in despatches for conspicuous bravery. However, the hatred with which the arbitrary governor was regarded was such that the slander found ready credence, and has been repeated by several historians.

ening anonymous letters to the King, exiled others, and organised a new Parliament. The Bretons, however, resisted the new tribunal with all their native stubbornness, and, after a struggle of four years, the Government gave way, the old judges were restored to their places, and d'Aiguillon recalled.

The duke returned to Versailles, eager for revenge upon Choiseul, to whose machinations he attributed the check which his projects had sustained, and placed himself at the head of the devout party, the sworn enemies of the Minister. The position of this party and of its leader had, however, been much weakened of late years by the expulsion of the Jesuits and the successive deaths of the Dauphin—the intimate friend and protector of the duke—the Dauphiness and the Queen; and d'Aiguillon's prospects of triumphing over his enemy seemed small indeed.

Under these circumstances, it was absolutely necessary for d'Aiguillon to seek new allies, and, accordingly, he turned towards Madame du Barry, who, he judged, would be ready enough to respond to the advances of one who was not only an important personage himself, but able to secure for her the countenance and support of some of the greatest names in France. A consummate courtier, the former lover of Madame de Châteauroux had no difficulty in gaining a complete ascendency over the easy-natured favourite, who soon conceived for him a sincere friendship, which, if any reliance is to be placed in contemporary gossip, was not long in developing into a warmer feeling.

As an earnest of favours to come, on the death of the Duc de Chaulnes, in the autumn of 1769, Madame du Barry succeeded in procuring for d'Aiguillon the post of Captain-Lieutenant of the *Chevau-légers* of the King's Household. This was not only a lucrative, but a very important, position, as it afforded its possessor frequent opportunities for private interviews with the King;[5] and Choiseul, anxious that it should be filled by one of his own party, had endeavoured to obtain it for his nephew, the Vicomte de Choiseul. The news that the relative of the Minister had been passed over in favour of the nominee of the mistress created general surprise, and plainly indicated that the influence of the once all-powerful Choiseul was no longer to be undisputed.

The *rapprochement* between d'Aiguillon and Madame du Barry assuring as it did to the former an advocate with the King, and to the latter the support of the devout party, greatly strengthened the hands of both in the struggle against their common enemy. Nevertheless, it may be doubted whether they would have ventured so quickly to assume the aggressive had not circumstances secured them the adhesion of two allies as ambitious and unscrupulous as d'Aiguillon himself and far more able, the Chancellor Maupeou and the Abbé Terray.

René Nicolas de Maupeou came of an ancient Parliamentary family, who more than a century before had counted fifty kinsfolk by blood and marriage in the Parliament of Paris alone. His father, René Charles de Maupeou, had successively filled the posts of First President, *garde-des-sceaux* and vice-chancellor, and in September 1768, on the resignation of Lamoignon, had been appointed Chancellor, a position which he resigned twenty-four hours later in favour of his son.

The elder Maupeou, who is described as "of noble and majestic figure, dignified countenance, and ami-

[5] The King himself was Captain of the *Chevau-légers*, and both he and Louis XIV. always wore the uniform of the corps when with the army in the field.

able disposition," seems to have been both popular and respected; the younger, in nearly every respect the exact antithesis of his father, was probably the best hated man of his time; indeed, it would be difficult to name any Minister who has been to the same degree the object of public execration. If we are to credit only half of what we read about him, it would appear that such a monster of malevolence, ingratitude, avarice, treachery, hypocrisy, and general depravity had never before been seen, while "he bore on his countenance all the signs of the baseness of his soul, and his person inspired an instinctive repulsion."[6]

However that may be, Maupeou was a man of considerable ability and extraordinary tenacity of purpose, an indefatigable worker—he rose as early as four o'clock in the morning—a shrewd judge of his fellows, and gifted with a perfect genius for subterranean intrigue.

Maupeou had owed his appointment to Choiseul,[7] and had at first affected for his patron an almost repulsive idolatry. He was wont to declare that nothing could induce him to change his residence, because from his windows he could at least perceive the chimneys of the Hôtel de Choiseul; boasted that "he

[6] Here is his portrait drawn by his biographer, M. Flammermont:
"He was 'a little black man.' He had a low forehead, bushy and very black eyebrows, keen, cold, piercing eyes, a prominent nose, a large and disagreeable mouth, a retreating chin, a bilious complexion, generally white, often yellow, and sometimes green; at the Court they called him ' la bigarrade (sour orange).' In a word, he was frankly hideous."—Le Chancelier Maupeou et les Parlements, p. 7.

[7] Choiseul was not blind to the dangerous and intriguing character of Maupeou, but he deemed himself strong enough to be able to ignore it. When some of his friends protested against the appointment, he replied: " I am aware that Maupeou is a scoundrel, but he is the most capable person for the Chancellorship. If he misbehaves himself, I shall get rid of him."

bore on his heart the livery of the Minister," and
never spoke of him but as "our good duke." But
even while thus protesting his unswerving devotion to
his interests, Maupeou was diligently seeking the
means to effect his ruin.

The Chancellor's desire to secure the fall of Choiseul
was not, as was the case with d'Aiguillon, prompted
by any personal feeling, but simply by expediency; the
Minister stood between Maupeou and the realisation
of a project whereby he hoped to assure for ever his
political fortunes.

For more than forty years the relations between the
Crown and the Parliaments had been exceedingly
strained. The magistrates, who derived their authority from the King, were no longer satisfied with exercising their judicial functions; they now sought to
band themselves together and form a new organisa-
tion in the body politic, a tribunal which should be the
organ of the nation, the guardian of its liberties, interests, and rights, the judge between the King and
people, the interpreter of the sovereign's will.

Such pretensions, as may be imagined, were strongly
resented by Louis XV., who entertained as exalted a
conception of the royal prerogative as his predecessor,
and who repeatedly asserted in his solemn declarations,
in his beds of justice, that the will of the sovereign
was paramount and must be obeyed.

The importance of the question at issue can hardly
be overestimated. The Parliaments did not lay claim
to the right of remonstrance—that was not contested;
they claimed to enjoy the right of refusing to register
the royal edicts; in other words, to impose an *absolute veto* on the measures of the King. "If it was
decided in favour of the King," wrote Madame
d'Epinay, voicing, in all probability, the opinion of her
friend Rousseau, the consequence would be to render

him absolutely despotic. If it was decided in favour of the Parliament, the King would possess hardly more authority than the King of England."[8]

Although the difference between the parties was of such long standing, a settlement seemed as far off as ever; and, in the meanwhile, undignified and vexatious disputes were of frequent occurrence, which on several occasions had been carried to such lengths as to throw the whole judicial machinery of the realm into hopeless disorder for months together. The King would submit an edict to the Parliament; the Parliament would remonstrate; the King would hold a Bed of Justice and insist on the registration of the edict; the Parliament would refuse and suspend its functions; the King would order the recalcitrant judges to resume their duties and exile those who disobeyed, with the result that all litigation would come to a standstill and great hardships be inflicted on unfortunate suitors, who were compelled to wait for redress until a truce had been concluded.

Out of this *impasse* the keen eye of Maupeou perceived that there were but two ways of escape: the re-establishment of the States-General, or the overthrow of the existing Parliamentary institutions and the creation of new courts, the members of which should be compelled to confine themselves to their judicial functions. For the first, the time was not yet ripe, in addition to which it would not have in any any way furthered his designs, which were to strengthen the authority of the Crown, *"en la retirant de la poussière du greffe, où elle était menacée de s'ensevelir,"* and by so doing render himself indispensable to the King. But the second might be accomplished if Louis XV. could be inspired with the resolution necessary for a vigorous *coup d'état.*

[8] Cited by M. Vatel in *Histoire de Madame du Barry,* ii. 15.

To carry out any measure of this kind, however, so long as Choiseul retained his credit with the King, was out of the question, for Choiseul had continued the policy of his predecessor, Cardinal de Bernis, or rather that of their common protectress, Madame de Pompadour, and supported the Parliaments, who were devoted to him. The first step, therefore, to the overthrow of the Parliaments must be the overthrow of Choiseul; and it was with this object in view that the Chancellor determined to cast in his lot with d'Aiguillon and Madame du Barry.[9]

The Abbé Terray, who followed the Chancellor into the camp of the favourite, was, like Maupeou, a member of the Parliament; like him, ambitious and absolutely devoid of principle; and, by a singular coincidence, like him again, a man of singularly unprepossessing appearance. "He was a very extraordinary being, this Abbé Terray, and, happily, of a very rare species. His exterior was rugged, sinister, even terrifying: a tall, bent figure, haggard eyes, a furtive glance, which conveyed the impression of falseness and perfidy, uncouth manners, a harsh voice, a dry conversation, no openness of soul, judging every human being unfavourably because he judged them by himself, a laugh rare and caustic.[10] Although he was harsh to the last degree to those unable to resist or injure him, he showed himself immoderately complaisant and disgracefully servile towards those whom he believed to have credit. Never did there exist a more icy heart or one more inaccessible to affections,

[9] M. Flammermont's *Le Chancelier Maupeou et les Parlements,* p. 153. *Biographie générale,* article *Maupeou,* by M. Grégoire.
[10] On one occasion, when dining at the house of a friend, who knew his character intimately, Terray began to laugh, upon which his host remarked to his neighbour at the table, "See! the abbé is laughing. Some one must have met with misfortune."

save that for sensual pleasures, or for money, as a
means of procuring those pleasures."[11]

Such is the description given of him by one of his
contemporaries.

Terray's intellectual qualities, however, as his critic
readily admits, were vastly superior to his moral, and,
employed for worthier ends, might have atoned for
his vices. Heir to a wealthy uncle enriched by specu-
lations in Mississippi stock, he had largely increased
his patrimony through his connection with the scandalous Malisset Association, formed to raise the price
of grain, and in which Louis XV. himself was pop-
ularly believed to be interested, and was now a rich
man.   In the Parliament of Paris, which he had
entered when very young, he had early gained distinction and had taken a leading part in the campaign
against the Jesuits, receiving as the reward of his
services the rich abbey of Molesmes. At this period
he had been a follower of Choiseul, but chagrin at the
duke's refusal to recognise his claims to advancement
and, more particularly, to the post of Comptroller-
General, when vacated by Laverdi in the autumn of
1768, had decided him to join his fortunes to those
of Maupeou and work with him for the downfall of
the haughty Minister.

The cabal gained its first success in the closing days
of 1769.

Maynon d'Invau, who had replaced Laverdi as
Comptroller-General in the autumn of the previous
year, had found his new post very far from a bed of
roses, for the difficulties which his predecessor had
bequeathed him[12] were aggravated by the growing an-

[11] Montyon's *Particularités et Observations sur les Contrôleurs-
Généraux des Finances de* 1660 *à* 1791.

[12] Laverdi had left the debt 115 millions since the Peace; the
sinking-fund was only a bait, for much more was borrowed than
was extinguished. In January 1769, the revenue had been fore-

tagonism between Choiseul and Maupeou, and between the King and the magistracy. His expedients for remedying the lamentable condition of the finances having been rejected by the Parliament of Paris, and a bed of justice having failed to bring the recalcitrant judges to reason, he endeavoured to steer a middle course between the wishes of the Court and the Parliament; and in a council held at Versailles, on December 21, laid upon the table a modified form of his original proposals, containing a scheme for the reduction of expenses and the abolition of a number of financial offices, as a concession to the gentlemen of the robe.

Choiseul supported his *protégé:* Maupeou attacked him vigorously; the King sided with the Chancellor, broke up the council in a passion, and, retiring to his cabinet, slammed the door violently behind him. Then Maupeou was sent for, and remained in conference with the King for half an hour, as the result of which it was decided, in anticipation of Maynon d'Invau's resignation, which was tendered almost immediately, to offer the post of Comptroller-General to Terray, whom the Chancellor declared to be the only man capable of initiating and carrying through the measures that were needed.

The fall of Maynon d'Invau and the appointment of Terray was a severe blow to the prestige of Choiseul, and though the Minister himself affected to make light of the matter, its significance was not lost upon his friends. "I supped on Tuesday with the grand-papa (Choiseul)," writes Madame du Deffand to Walpole; "he is still in the best of spirits; he will be like Charles VII., of whom it was said that no one could lose a kingdom more gaily."[13]

stalled to the amount of thirty-two and a half million livres.— Martin's *Histoire de France jusqu'en* 1789, xvi. 246.
[13] Letter of December 26, 1769.

CHAPTER X

THE year 1770 opened for Madame du Barry with a fresh proof of the royal favour. On the counterscarp of the fortifications of Nantes stood a number of houses, booths, and shops, the property of the Crown. The rent derived from these structures, estimated by contemporary writers at 40,000 livres per annum, had in 1769 been bestowed by Louis XV. on the Duchesse de Lauraguais, who, however, only lived to enjoy it a few months, and, on January 1, the King, by way of a New Year's gift, handed his mistress a brevet conferring a life interest in *Les Loges de Nantes* upon her.

This present was extremely acceptable to Madame du Barry, who had not yet received any considerable pecuniary favours, and had, therefore, been able to indulge in but few of the hundred extravagances for which her soul yearned. Deeming it inadvisable, until her position was assured, to make application to the King, she had been compelled to have recourse to the *"Roué,"* who, in confident expectation of a bountiful return, had cast his bread upon the waters freely enough. However, in the years to come, the countess was destined to receive ample compensation for these few months of self-denial, and her astute brother-in-law to reap a rich reward for having, as he affirmed, well-nigh beggared himself in assisting the lady to maintain her new dignity.[1]

[1] In his letter to Malesherbes, already cited, the *"Roué"* says: "In order to sustain her new position during the first fifteen months, during which she received no pecuniary favour, I engaged the remainder of my fortune."

Early in the following spring, the favourite removed from the apartments on the *rez-de-chaussée* of the Cour Royale, which she had occupied since her installation at Versailles, to those of the late Dauphiness, Marie Josèphe of Saxony. These apartments, which had never before been occupied by a mistress, were situated on the second floor of the château, above the Cabinets of Louis XV., and formed part of what were known as the Petits Cabinets.[2] In the interval between the death of the Dauphiness and the installation of Madame du Barry they had undergone various modifications, and now comprised an ante-chamber, a dining-room, a *cabinet de compagnie,* a private cabinet, a library, an *arrière-bibliothèque,* a wardrobe and a bath-room; while a private staircase communicating with the King's apartments on the floor below enabled the monarch to visit his mistress at any hour he pleased without being observed.[3]

Although preparations for Madame du Barry's occupation of these apartments seem to have been in progress throughout the previous winter, the lady was dissatisfied with their condition; and, accordingly, advantage was taken of the annual visit of the Court to Fontainebleau in the following autumn to have

[2] The " Petits Cabinets," sometimes called the " Petits Appartements," were the portion of the King's apartments situated above his Cabinets, or state rooms, which were on the first floor of the château. Here Louis XV. had his library, kitchens, where he occasionally amused himself by experiments in cooking, of which he was almost as fond as his successor of carpentry, distilleries, a bath-room and, on one of the upper terraces, his aviaries. Here also he gave supper-parties to his intimate friends and received visits from *maîtresses de passage.* Without being entirely cut off from the rest of the château, the Petits Cabinets had only just enough communication as was required by the servants, and no one, not even members of the Royal Family, ever entered the sacred precincts, except by invitation of the King.

[3] See the plan in M. de Nolhac's *Le Chateau de Versailles sous Louis XV.*

them redecorated and regilded, an army of workmen being employed in order to complete the work before the favourite's return. Two years later, the countess came to the conclusion that the bath-room was not quite as commodious as it might be made, and insisted on new baths being constructed; a request, or command, which was duly complied with, although at this time the unfortunate Director of the Board of Works appears to have been in dire straits for lack of funds, and writes to Terray, the Comptroller-General:

" Monsieur,—The Royal Family are impatiently demanding various arrangements which have been submitted by me to his Majesty and commanded by him. Madame la Comtesse du Barry has demanded new baths in her apartment, which his Majesty has likewise commanded, and the work will cost 15,000 livres. I have not a *single sol* wherewith to carry out his Majesty's wishes. I again implore you to place me in a position to do so."

Madame du Barry's installation in these apartments marks a new step in her triumphant career. So striking a mark of the royal favour as the conferment of a lodging in the Petits Cabinets, the very apartments, too, which had formerly been occupied by the second lady in the land, was not likely to be ignored, and many of those who had hitherto held aloof from the mistress now deemed it incumbent upon them to pay their court to her. " I remarked," writes the Duc de Croy, " that little by little people went more and more to visit the countess. She was established in a lodging in the Cabinets, the same in which Madame la Dauphine died. From all this she derived the advantage of being generally acknowledged as a lady of the Court;

she went to all the *fêtes* pell-mell with the others; people gradually became accustomed to it."[4]

In the face of these renewed proofs of the King's infatuation, before the association of d'Aiguillon, Maupeou and Terray, the defection of men whom he had always believed devoted to his interests, and of high-born dames, who, he perceived, were only awaiting a favourable opportunity to follow the example of Maréchale de Mirepoix and the Comtesse de Valentinois, and openly take part with the favourite, Choiseul began to be seriously alarmed and to find, as he confided to Dumouriez, that "the jade was occasioning him considerable embarrassment."[5] However, he consoled himself with the reflection that with the arrival of the Dauphiness-elect, the Archduchess Marie Antoinette, everything would be changed. A young princess, accustomed at her mother's Court to hear the name of the Duc de Choiseul mentioned with esteem and affection as the firm friend of Austria and the negotiator of her own marriage, would not hesitate to accord him all the support in her power. And this support would be no mean factor in the situation. Beautiful and fascinating as she was reported to be, she could hardly fail to obtain influence over a monarch so susceptible to feminine charms as Louis XV., who, for very shame's sake, must hesitate to flaunt before the eyes of a young girl brought up amid virtuous surroundings his low-born mistress. The result would be that decorum would once more reign at Court; Madame du Barry would be relegated to the background; the cabal which had formed around her would be powerless to harm him, and he would be able to crush his enemies at his leisure.

[4] *Mémoires inédits du Duc de Croy,* Bibliothèque de l'Institut, cited by M. de Nolhac.

[5] *La Vie et les Mémoires du Général Dumouriez* (edit. Berville and Barrière), i. 143.

Thus Choiseul reasoned, but, unhappily for himself, he underrated, as he had from the very first, the strength and permanency of Louis's senile passion, and failed to perceive that the friendship and support of a princess who, while able to annoy, might be powerless to injure, the lady whom the King delighted to honour, would be a broken reed indeed.

Marie Antoinette arrived at Strasburg on May 7; on the 14th, she was met by Louis XV., the Dauphin, and *Mesdames,* at the Pont de Berne, in the Forest of Compiègne, and conducted to Versailles, where the marriage was immediately celebrated.

On the evening before the ceremony, a supper, at which the whole of the Royal Family and a few of the most favoured courtiers were present, was given at the Château of La Muette, where the royal party had broken their journey, upon which occasion the King presented the young princess, amongst other jewels, with the famous pearl necklace threaded on a single string, which had been brought to France by Anne of Austria, and bequeathed by her to future queens and dauphinesses.*

Another incident connected with the banquet was of a less pleasing nature, for Louis XV. had the unpardonably bad taste to invite Madame du Barry, although up to the present he had never yet ventured to introduce his mistress to the same table as the Royal Family.

The Austrian Ambassador, Mercy-Argenteau, who had been commissioned by his " Sacred Majesty," as he styles Maria Theresa, to report to her the minutest details concerning her daughter, could scarcely believe

---

* The smallest of the pearls composing this necklace was said to be as large as a filbert. Magnificent though they were, however, they were surpassed, according to Mademoiselle de Montpensier, by the pearls of the Maréchale de l'Hôpital, which *le Grand Monarque* purchased and presented to Madame de Montespan.

the evidence of his eyes. " It appears inconceivable," he writes, " that the King should choose this moment to accord to the favourite an honour which has been refused her up to the present."[7]

" What is the Comtesse du Barry's function at Court?" inquired Marie Antoinette, observing with surprise the attentions which the infatuated monarch lavished upon the favourite.

" To amuse the King," was the diplomatic answer of the courtier addressed.

" Then," rejoined the young girl, with all the candour of her fifteen years, " I intend to be her rival."

" A rivalry indeed ensued," remarks M. de Nolhac, " very different from the one she imagined, between innocence and vice, a contest secret at first, but soon apparent, and affecting the highest political interests."[8]

Beautiful, joyous, and affectionate, eager to please, grateful for every attention, Marie Antoinette speedily won golden opinions from Louis XV., who, we feel bound to observe, appears to have treated her with a kindness which might well have merited more consideration for his domestic tranquillity than the princess afterwards exhibited. With Madame du Barry, too, contrary to the general impression which seems to prevail, nothing occurred during the first few weeks to presage the storm which was ere long to arise and defy all the efforts of Louis XV., Mercy, and Maria Theresa to calm. The Dauphiness, though speedily made aware of the true nature of the mysterious function of " amusing " the King, remained for some time in ignorance of the favourite's humble origin and eventful past; and, acting on the advice of the sage Mercy and her reader, the Abbé de Vermond, made no distinction between Madame du Barry and other ladies

---

[7] Mercy *to* Kaunitz, May 17, 1770.
[8] *Marie Antoinette et Madame du Barry, Revue des Deux Mondes,* May, 1896.

of the Court; that is to say, she treated her with courtesy on the occasions on which they happened to meet at the card-table or elsewhere. The favourite, on her side, " who knew how to put on decorum with *le grand habit,*" showed towards the Dauphiness an extreme deference bordering on servility, and was evidently prepared to go to any lengths to propitiate the new power.

About the middle of June, Madame du Barry summoned up sufficient courage to make advances, and, accordingly, presented herself before the Dauphiness at her *lever,* upon which Mercy reports to Maria Theresa:

" Madame du Barry believed it incumbent upon her to pay her court one morning to her Royal Highness; that princess received her without affectation; the latter conducted herself with dignity and in a manner that could give offence to no one."⁹

To be received " without affectation" was, probably, quite as much as the favourite felt that she had the right to expect, and in the freedom of her apartments she lisped to the delighted King, like his mistress grateful for small mercies, her opinion that *" cette petite rousse était sarmante."*

Matters continued thus till the early part of July, when an unfortunate incident came to mar the harmony of Versailles, if harmony could ever be said to exist in a Court which was without its equal in Europe as a forcing-house for envy, hatred, malice, and all uncharitableness.

It happened that the Dauphin had for governor a certain Duc de la Vauguyon, of whom we have had occasion to speak in an earlier chapter, a despicable old intriguer, who passed for a *dévot,* and was in the habit of listening at keyholes and suchlike places, in the hope

⁹ Letter of June 15, 1770.

of gleaning information which might further his designs.[10]   Through hatred of Choiseul, he had espoused
the cause of Madame du Barry, and, for a similar
reason, had viewed with strong disapprobation the
Austrian marriage, which had been the work of his
enemy.   Being powerless to prevent it, he now sought
to render it as unhappy as possible, in order that he
might retain his hitherto unbounded influence over the
mind of his pupil and complete his task of embittering
him against Choiseul.[11]

In pursuance of this amiable resolution, he, through
his son, the Duc de Saint-Mégrin, persuaded Madame
du Barry to obtain the King's consent to the Dauphin's
inclusion in certain supper-parties which Louis was in
the habit of giving to his intimate friends at Saint-
Hubert, a hunting-lodge situated between the forests
of Rambouillet and Saint-Léger, and at which, says
Mercy, " decorum was not always scrupulously observed."[12] By this means the duke, apparently, hoped to
bring about a *rapprochement* between the Dauphin and
Madame du Barry—he had been at great pains to conceal the lady's past from his pupil—and, at the same
time, cause dissension between the young prince and
Marie Antoinette, who, he was aware, had conceived
a strong aversion to the favourite, though she had
hitherto contrived to keep her feelings under control.

[10] " A singular incident happened the other day. I was alone
with my husband when M. de la Vauguyon stealthily approached
the door, in order to listen. A *valet-de-chambre,* who is either
a fool or a very honest man, opened it, and M. de la Vauguyon,
not having time to withdraw, was found posted there like a
sentinel."—Marie Antoinette *to* Maria Theresa, July 9, 1770.
[11] Some writers allege that La Vauguyon went so far as to endeavour to persuade the young prince that Choiseul had caused
his father and mother, the late Dauphin and Dauphiness, to be
poisoned, but dull-witted as the future Louis XVI. undoubtedly
was, it is difficult to believe that any one could have supposed
him capable of crediting so monstrous a charge.
[12] Mercy *to* Maria Theresa, July 14, 1770.

The Dauphin attended one of the suppers, where he was not a little astonished at the levity which prevailed, and particularly at the freedom with which Madame du Barry treated his august grandfather. However, as he was an exceedingly timid and reserved youth—though he had been married nearly two months, he had not yet ventured to claim his conjugal privileges—it is probable that he would have kept his opinion of such proceedings to himself, had not *Mesdames,* alarmed at the danger which threatened the innocence of their nephew, taken upon themselves to give him a little history of the favourite, not forgetting a few of the most striking episodes in her life; and this information made such an impression upon the mind of the Dauphin that from that moment " he bestowed upon the Comtesse du Barry frequent marks of his aversion."[13]

Nor was this all; for, in a conversation with Marie Antoinette on July 8, in the course of which he solemnly announced to the blushing princess his intention, during the approaching visit of the Court to Compiègne, to live with her *" dans toute l'étendue re l'intimité qui comporte leur union,"*[14] the name of Madame du Barry happened to be mentioned, upon which the Dauphin repeated to his wife all that his aunts had told him concerning that lady.

The day after this conversation we find the Dauphiness writing to Maria Theresa as follows:

" The King has shown me a thousand kindnesses,

[13] Mercy *to* Maria Theresa, July 14, 1770.
[14] But he did not carry out his resolution. On January 3, 1774 —three and a half years later—Maria Theresa wrote to Mercy: " The coldness of the Dauphin, a young husband of twenty years of age, towards a pretty wife, is more than I can conceive. In spite of all the assertions of the faculty, my suspicions increase as to the physical constitution of the prince, and I have little to count upon but the good offices of the Emperor, who, on his arrival at Versailles, will perhaps find means to compel this indolent husband to acquit himself better of his duty."

and I love him tenderly; but it is pitiable to see his infatuation for Madame du Barry, who is the most foolish and impertinent creature imaginable. She played
every evening with us at Marly, and on two or three
occasions found herself at my side; but she did not
address me, neither did I attempt to enter into conversation with her; but, when obliged, I have spoken to
her."

And three days later:

" I have forgotten to tell you that I wrote yesterday
to the King; I was very frightened, being aware that
Madame du Barry reads everything. But you may be
persuaded, my dear mother, that I shall commit no
mistake either for or against her."

But the influences at work around her were too
strong to permit of the little Dauphiness carrying out
this diplomatic resolution. Apart from the Dauphin,
who was still only a boy, and too shy and reserved to
invite her confidence, Marie Antoinette had no one to
whom she could turn for guidance amid the shoals and
quicksands of the Court. Her *dame d'honneur,* the
Comtesse de Noailles, possessed the rare merit of not
being an intriguer, but she carried flattery to lengths
which irritated the Dauphiness, and, besides, was but
little qualified to give advice, save on matters of Court
ceremonial, her devotion to which procured her from
her young mistress the name of *"Madame l'Etiquette";*
while none of the other ladies of her Household possessed any particular attraction for the princess, which
was scarcely surprising, as the majority were indebted
for their positions to La Vauguyon or the favourite.[15]

In her isolation, the young girl turned towards her
aunts, the three *Mesdames*—the fourth, Madame
Louise, had, a few months before, succeeded in wrest-
ing from Louis XV. a reluctant permission to enter

[15] M. de Nolhac's *Marie Antoinette, Dauphine,* p. 142.

the Carmelites of Saint-Denis—whose friendship
Maria Theresa, aware of the reputation of these princesses for piety and virtue, but not, unfortunately, of
their predilection for petty intrigue, had advised her to
cultivate.

Mesdames were enchanted to find their niece so
ready to seek their society and accept their guidance.
They received her with open arms, gave her the key
to a private door leading to Madame Adélaïde's apartments, in which the sisters were in the habit of holding
their little Court, so that she might come thither un-
attended and at any hour she pleased, racked their
brains to devise new means of amusing her, and ca-
ressed and flattered her to the top of her bent. From
thence to obtain influence over her mind, to imbue her
with their own prejudices, to dictate to her the attitude
she should assume towards the different members of
the Court, was but a step. " The insinuations of the
old princesses, falling incessantly on the mind of the
young girl," says M. de la Rocheterie, " ended by
making an impression upon it, however strong the
protest of her good sense, as the continual dropping of
water ends by wearing away even the hardest rock.
This deplorable ascendency extended itself over everything, mingled with everything, touched everything."[16]

Mesdames hated Madame du Barry and all her supporters, though a wholesome dread of their royal
father's anger prevented them from showing their
antipathy in too marked a manner. But the frank,
impetuous little Dauphiness was quite incapable of
dissimulating her dislike, and the princesses meanly "incited her to a resentment which they dared not exhibit
themselves." So long, however, as the Court was at
Compiègne occasions of peril were rare; Marie Antoinette did not see Madame du Barry, except at a dis-

[16]*Histoire de Marie Antoinette*, i. 91.

tance, at Mass, the chase, or the *grand couvert,* and
had, therefore, no opportunity of testifying the aversion and contempt which she now entertained for the
favourite. On the other hand, the Duc de la Vauguyon
and his confederate, Madame de Marsan, the *gouvernante* of the Dauphin's sisters, Clotilde and Elisabeth,
who came every day to pay their court to the Dauphiness, found themselves treated with a coldness which
excited general remark and showed the Du Barry party
that they had now to reckon with a new adversary.

Towards the end of July, the Court paid a short visit
to Choisy, and it was while there that a false move on
the part of Madame du Barry, which directly touched
the Dauphiness, greatly accentuated Marie Antoinette's
dislike of the favourite and ruined any slight chance
that might have remained to the latter of eventually
overcoming the hostility of the princess.

To amuse the Dauphiness, the King gave orders for
some comedies to be performed in the theatre of the
château. This theatre was a very small one, and could
with difficulty accommodate the various members of
the Royal Family and their respective suites, and one
evening it happened that Madame du Barry, arriving
late with her two inseparables, the Maréchale de Mirepoix and the Comtesse de Valentinois, found all the
front seats occupied by the *dames du palais* of the
Dauphiness. They requested them to make way, but
the *dames* declined, and a war of words ensued, wherein one of Marie Antoinette's ladies, the Comtesse de
Gramont, who is described by Madame du Deffand as
" foolish, impudent, and talkative," greatly distinguished herself. Some of the shafts she discharged
would appear to have been very keenly barbed and
to have found their mark; any way, next morning
Madame du Barry, instead of allowing the affair to
rest, as policy should certainly have dictated, having

regard to the official position of the delinquent, complained to the King, who promptly exiled the Comtesse de Gramont fifteen leagues from the Court.

This incident created an immense sensation. The Comtesse de Gramont was the sister-in-law of the duchess of that name, and a leading light of the Choiseul party, which was highly incensed at the exile of one of its members, and besought the Dauphiness to intercede for her with the King. This Marie Antoinette, who was herself very indignant, promised to do; but Mercy intervened, and, on his advice, she confined herself to expressing her regret that punishment should have been inflicted on one of her ladies without any official notification having been made to her, as etiquette demanded. Louis XV., though perfectly well aware that it was the punishment, and not the breach of etiquette, that was being made the subject of protest, was much relieved at escaping so easily from an awkward position, laid the blame on the negligence of his *Commander des Ordres,* promised that it should not occur again, and made many affectionate speeches to the Dauphiness.

Three months later, while the Court was at Fontainebleau, the exiled *dame du palais* wrote to her mistress, informing her that she was ill and urgently in need of the best medical advice, and begging her to obtain the King's permission for her to come to Paris. There was in all probability nothing more serious the matter with the countess than the malady from which all ladies excluded for a season from the delights of Versailles and the capital suffered, to wit, *ennui.* But the kind heart of Marie Antoinette was touched, and after a dinner *au grand couvert,* at which all the Royal Family were present, she took the opportunity of soliciting the return of the exile " in a manner full of grace and sweetness."

The King demurred, and hinted that it would be as well if Madame du Barry's pardon were obtained. The Dauphiness exclaimed: " Think what a grief it would be to me, papa, if a lady attached to my service were to die in your disgrace!"   But she did not act upon the hint, in consequence of which, according to Mercy, Madame du Barry " showed at first some inclination to oppose the desire of Madame la Dauphine."   Finally, a courier having been despatched to obtain a certificate of ill-health from the complaisant medical adviser of the Comtesse de Gramont, that lady was permitted to reside in Paris, but no further concession was made, and the Court remained forbidden ground.

Whether the King's refusal to pardon the countess was due to the influence of Madame du Barry is very doubtful.   Vindictiveness was so entirely alien to the favourite's character, and it was so obviously to her interests to endeavour to conciliate the Dauphiness, that we are inclined to think that she offered no opposition to the lady's return to Court, and may even, contrary to Mercy's assertion, have seconded the solicitations of the princess; but that Louis XV., having determined to make an example, was not to be turned from his purpose.   However that may be, it is certain that Marie Antoinette, whose pride was deeply wounded by what she chose to regard as a personal affront, never forgave Madame du Barry her share in the affair, and henceforth treated her with the utmost disdain, and tacitly encouraged her *entourage* to do likewise, to the intense chagrin of the favourite and the annoyance of the King.

On the other hand, the Dauphiness lost no opportunity of bestowing marks of her favour upon Choiseul, his wife and sister.   In so doing, of course, she was only acting in accordance with the instructions of

Maria Theresa, who had charged her daughter never to forget that Choiseul had been the negotiator of her marriage, and that she owed her proud position entirely to him. But, as matters stood, the result was most unfortunate for the duke; for Madame du Barry and her friends had little difficulty in persuading the King that the attitude adopted by Marie Antoinette towards the favourite was directly attributable to the influence of the Choiseuls; and as the Dauphiness's favour declined, that of the Minister declined also.

CHAPTER XI

BUT, in the meanwhile, events of far more importance than the relations between a Dauphiness and a favourite, at least in the eyes of all save the most contemptible of palace intriguers, had arisen to occupy public attention.

The indignation of the Bretons against d'Aiguillon had been very far from appeased by the restoration of their Parliament and the recall of the duke. They had not ceased to demand justice upon their late governor, whom, besides the grievances relative to his administration, they accused of suborning witnesses to assist in the conviction of La Chalotais and others; and at length d'Aiguillon found himself compelled to request the King to allow him to be brought to trial, in order that he might have an opportunity of refuting the charges against him. Formal proceedings were accordingly commenced before the Parliament of Paris (April 14, 1770), Louis himself presiding at the opening sitting and " comporting himself like a kind father in the midst of beloved children."[1] Before, however, the trial had been in progress very long, it became evident that the judges were animated by no friendly feelings towards the duke, and determined to submit his conduct in Brittany to the most searching investigation. D'Aiguillon began to be seriously alarmed (" The best reasons," he wrote to his friend, the Chevalier de Balleroy, " have difficulty in overcoming prejudice, partiality and intrigue"), and to see before him a

[1] Hardy's *Journal des événements qu'ils parviennent à ma connaissance.*

humiliating sentence and possibly severe punishment, for there can be very little doubt that the charges against him were in the main but too well justified, though, according to his apologist, M. Marcel Marion,[2] many of the witnesses for the prosecution perjured themselves in the most shameful manner.

It was now that d'Aiguillon reaped the reward of his foresight in securing the friendship of one who had the ear of the King. Whether, as contemporary gossip alleges, Madame du Barry had become the mistress of the duke is, to say the least, doubtful—it would seem indeed to rest on no better evidence than the charge that Madame de Pompadour was the mistress of Choiseul—but, at the same time, there can be no question that the favourite was sincerely attached to d'Aiguillon, and, as soon as she understood the danger which threatened him, exerted all her influence to induce the King to put a stop to the trial.

Her task was not a difficult one. The feeling of absolute authority was, as we have already observed, as strong in Louis XV. as his predecessor, and he had from the first regarded with disfavour an investigation into the conduct of a person who had been the representative of royalty in Brittany and might well plead the orders of the King for many of the acts which had aroused so much indignation in that province. Moreover, it is highly probable that Maupeou, who perceived in an interference with the course of the trial an excellent opportunity for a great quarrel with the Parliament, supported by his counsels the solicitations of Madame du Barry, and thus removed any lingering scruples which the King might still have entertained about perpetrating so scandalous an abuse of his power.

Accordingly, on July 27, 1770, a Bed of Justice was

[2] *La Bretagne et le Duc d'Aiguillon,* 1753-1770, par M. Marcel Marion (Paris, 1898).

held at Versailles, and the Parliament informed that a prosecution which tended to submit to its inspection the secrecy of the King's administration, the execution of his orders, and the personal use of his authority, could not be allowed to continue, declared the conduct both of d'Aiguillon and of the Breton magistrates whom he had persecuted " irreproachable," annulled the proceedings, and imposed the most absolute silence on all concerned.[3]

It would have been difficult to show more utter disregard for all judicial forms. " It seemed," says an indignant contemporary writer, " that the King had been induced to give the greatest *éclat* to this assembly, merely that it might more absolutely become the object of the derision of France and of all Europe. He was perhaps the only person in his kingdom who was not ashamed of it. That very evening he invited the Duc d'Aiguillon to be of the party to Marly,[4] and admitted him to the honour of supping with him.[5]

The Parliament returned from the Bed of Justice " transported with rage," and, on July 2, threw down the gauntlet to royal absolutism and fulminated a decree setting forth that the proceedings on which the King had seen fit to impose his veto contained " the basis of grave proofs compromising the honour of the Duc d'Aiguillon," whom they, in consequence, declared incapable of exercising any functions belonging to the

[3] Martin's *Histoire de France jusqu'en* 1789, xvi. 279.

[4] Only a small portion of the Court accompanied the King on his visits to Marly, and Louis XV. always nominated those whom he desired should be of the party.

[5] *Vie privée de Louis XV.*, vol. iv. p. 141. As we recently saw this book referred to in an English weekly review as if it were a mere *chronique scandaleuse*, we may here remark that such is very far from being the case. The title is, indeed, somewhat of a misnomer, as the work is far more concerned with the *public* than the private actions of Louis XV., and is of no small value to the serious historian, if only for the admirable account it contains of the struggle between the King and the Parliaments.

peerage until he had purged himself therefrom by due process of law.

The Council quashed the decree of the Parliament. The Parliament, after fruitless remonstrances, decreed anew that the prosecution could not be considered terminated by an arbitrary act of absolute authority, and were, as usual, supported by the provincial courts. The Parliaments of Rennes and Bordeaux were particularly violent. The former ordered two memorials in favour of d'Aiguillon to be burned by the public executioner, refused to register the royal edict of June 27, and sent energetic remonstrances to the Chancellor. The latter forbade the inhabitants of the duchy of Aiguillon to bring their appeals before it, thus confirming the decree of the Parliament of Paris depriving the duke of his privileges. The King replied by compelling the Parliament of Rennes to register the obnoxious edict by force, caused two of its members, both noblemen, to be arrested and imprisoned at Compiègne, and threw Dupaty, the attorney-general of the Parliament of Bordeaux, into a gloomy dungeon in the Château of Pierre-Encise, at the gates of Lyons, from which, however, he was presently released, through the mediation of Madame du Barry.[6]

Urged on by Maupeou, who had persuaded him to regard the union between the Parliaments as a criminal confederation directed against his royal authority, and by the favourite, " who felt herself personally affected" by the decree which pronounced the honour of her *protégé* compromised, Louis XV. now determined on a *coup d'Etat* to bring the insolent judges to reason. At a meeting of the Council on the evening of September 2, he announced his intention of holding a Bed of

[6] Martin's *Histoire de France jusqu'en* 1789, xvi. 280. Vatel's *Histoire de Madame du Barry,* i. 424. Flammermont's *Le Chancelier Maupeou et les Parlements,* p. 87, *et seq.*

Justice on the following day, not at Versailles, but in
Paris, at the Palais de Justice; and early next morning the Parisians were astonished to hear the sound of
cannon and to see the King, who seldom visited his
capital, drive into the Place Louis XV., escorted by
four companies of musketeers, and enter the Palais,
accompanied by the Chancellor in his robes of office.[7]

The monarch entered the Salle des Séances, where
the members of the Parliament were assembled, took his
seat, and having, through the mouth of Maupeou, up-
braided them with their insubordinate conduct in the
most unmeasured terms, caused all the documents connected with the prosecution of d'Aiguillon to be handed
over to him, ordered the decrees and resolutions
against the duke to be effaced from the registers, and
forbade the Parliament ever to reopen the affair on
any pretext whatsoever.

The magistrates appear to have been too thunder-
struck by this unwonted display of energy, on the part
of a sovereign whose feebleness had become a byword,
to have taken any steps for three days, when they met
and passed a resolution accusng the King of " a pre-
meditated plan to change the form of government, and
to substitute for the equable force of laws the irregular
concussions of arbitrary power"; after which they
adjourned for the autumn vacation, and for three
months there was peace.

When, on September 2, Louis XV. had announced
to the Council his intention to hold a bed of justice on
the following day, Choiseul, shrewdly suspecting what
was in the air, had begged the King to excuse him
from attending, on the plea that he had arranged to
start that evening for La Ferté-Vidame, to pay a

7 Letter of Madame du Deffand *to* Horace Walpole, September
3, 1770.

long-promised visit to La Borde, the Court banker; indeed, from the very commencement of the prosecution of d'Aiguillon the Minister had maintained an attitude of the strictest neutrality. There can be no question that his sympathies were entirely with the Parliaments, and almost equally certain that he had encouraged the Breton magistrates at first to resist and afterwards to attack the duke. But he was too keen-sighted to imagine that there was much hope of the Parliaments compelling the King to yield, spurred on as Louis was by the favourite, incited, in her turn, by her reputed lover, d'Aiguillon.

Madame du Barry and her allies, however, were determined to prevent their adversary from deriving any advantage from this policy of self-effacement, and did not scruple to charge him with concealing his hand and secretly sustaining the magistrates in their resistance; and, unfortunately for the Minster, an act of extraordinary indiscretion on the part of his evil genius, Madame de Gramont, lent but too much colour to these accusations.

On August 20, Mercy reports to Maria Theresa that " the Duc de Choiseul had had a violent altercation with the Duc de Richelieu, owing to the latter having declared that the Duchesse de Gramont, while passing through Provence and Languedoc, on her way to the waters of Barèges, had sought to stir up the Parliaments of those provinces against the decisions of the Court in the affair of the Duc d'Aiguillon."

It is probable, as M. Flammermont observes, that this was a calumny, and that Madame de Gramont had confined herself to stating her own opinions on the matter which the whole kingdom was discussing. The duchess was not the woman to mince her words where her successful rival and her brother's most bitter enemy were concerned, but that did not prove that she was the mouthpiece of a conspiracy organised by Choiseul.[8] Nevertheless, the incident was not without its effect upon the King, who from that moment treated the Minister with marked coldness, and, though he continued to transact business with him and invite him to his supper-parties, did not honour him with a single word of kindness or confidence.[9]

In point of fact, Choiseul at this period had far too much on his hands to spend his time in encouraging the Parliaments to resist the King by decrees and remonstrances. He was meditating a stroke whereby he intended to rid himself of his enemies and render his services indispensable to his royal master.

In 1766, a small English settlement, which received the name of Port Egmont, after the Earl of Egmont, First Lord of the Admiralty, had been established on one of the Falkland Islands, a group the importance of which was then greatly overestimated. It was far from a valuable possession, but Spain, which still asserted a nominal supremacy over a large portion of the South Seas, took umbrage, and, without making any formal complaint to the English Government, in June 1770 the Governor of Buenos Ayres, Don Francesco Buccarelli, despatched an armament, which compelled the little garrison to surrender and carried them away prisoners.

When the news of this high-handed proceeding reached London, the English Government sent orders to its representative at Madrid to demand in peremptory terms the restitution of the Falkland Islands and the disavowal of Buccarelli's action, and, in view of a possible refusal, active preparations were made for war.[10]

[8] M. Flammermont's *Le Chancelier Maupeou et les Parlements*, p. 101.   [9] *Vie privée de Louis XV.*, iv. 146.
[10] Stanhope's " History of England from the Peace of Utrecht," v. 416, *et seq.*

Spain was in no condition to go to war, and, unsup-
ported, would probably have shrunk from so unequal a
struggle. But, by the terms of the Family Compact of
1761, France was bound to come to her aid, with men
and ships, against any Power with which she might become involved in hostilities; and, relying on the support of his ally, Carlos III. declined to grant the full
measure of reparation that England claimed, and intimated very plainly that he was prepared to abide by
the consequences.

Everything now depended upon France, for Grimaldi, the Spanish Prime Minister, who governed his
master, was devoted to French interests, and might be
relied upon to act in accordance with the wishes of the
Cabinet of Versailles.[11] If France were unwilling to
go to war and advised conciliation, Spain would undoubtedly comply with England's demands; if, on the
other hand, she counselled resistance, hostilities must
as certainly follow.

The conduct of Choiseul at this juncture has been
the subject of much discussion, and with good reason,
since it varied with the changes in the political situation
in France. M. Gaston Maugras, his latest biographer,
asserts that the Minister's despatches prove beyond
a doubt that he was sincerely desirous of preserving
the peace.[12] This may be true in regard to the later
despatches, though even in some of these there is a
ring of insincerity; but the earlier ones, and particularly those written in the summer of 1770, are distinctly
belligerent in tone and, in our judgment, there can be

[11] "His (Grimaldi's) doctrine is absolutely French; guided in
everything by the French closet, he ever has the French interest
in view, and considers Spain in a secondary light. I do not
accuse him of being a false servant, as I really think he considers such a system most salutary for the master he serves; at
least he has caused him to adopt it."—"Diaries and Correspondence of James Harris, first Earl of Malmesbury," i. 56.

[12] *Le Duc et la Duchesse de Choiseul.*

no question that Choiseul both desired war and did his utmost to bring it about.

That such should have been the case is scarcely a matter for surprise, when we consider that however disastrous such a conflict might have been to France, it would undoubtedly have been to the personal advantage of the Minister. D'Aiguillon, Maupeou, and Terray, aided by Madame du Barry, were working assiduously to effect his downfall and, he had grave reason to believe, were already within measurable distance of attaining their object. But, in the event of war, their machinations would be completely checkmated; nay more, they would recoil upon their own heads, for then Choiseul, who was familiar with the condition and needs of both army and navy, who possessed the confidence of the Courts of Madrid and Vienna, and could count upon the support of the magistracy, would become an indispensable man; while his rivals, whose intrigues had exasperated the Parliament and enhanced the difficulty of obtaining its consent to the fresh taxation which hostilities would render necessary, would be sent about their business.[13] " I have no reason to doubt," wrote Mercy, " that the Duc de Choiseul believed that war would strengthen his position and render his services necessary."[14]

But if Choiseul desired war, it was far otherwise with his master. Whatever his faults have been, Louis XV. was not lacking in intelligence, and to enter upon another conflict while France was still suffering from the exhaustion produced by the last, over a mere question of etiquette in which she had not the smallest interest, appeared to him, as indeed it was, the height of insanity. Moreover, war would mean the triumph of the Parliament and the sacrifice of the Chancellor and

[13] Mr. J. B. Perkins' "France under Louis XV.," ii. 247.
[14] Mercy *to* Maria Theresa, September 19, 1770.

the Comptroller-General, and probably d'Aiguillon as
well, to its resentment, for the Parliament would then
be in a position to dictate terms to the King, and there
could be little doubt what those terms would be.
Nothing, Louis determined, should induce him to submit to so great a humiliation, and he intimated his
wishes to Choiseul in unmistakable terms.

Choiseul had, of course, no option but to obey, and,
accordingly, made some attempts to quench the flame
which he had been so industriously fanning. But the
belligerent tone of his earlier despatches had done their
work but too well; Spain, in the belief that France
would support her, had been actively engaged in pre-
paring for hostilities, the people were clamouring for
war, and Grimaldi replied that, if he advised Carlos III.
to accede to the English demands, he would be stoned
by the populace. Little hope of a settlement now remained, and in October Choiseul asked the Council for
8,000,000 livres wherewith to prepare for the coming
struggle.[15]

Some further weeks were wasted in fruitless negotiations, and, on December 3, Francès, the French
Ambassador at St. James's, informed Choiseul that the
English Government were at the end of their patience
and that war was inevitable. The Minister thereupon
adopted a course which, we venture to think, must entirely destroy any claim which he might otherwise have
upon our sympathy. He took upon himself to send
Prince Masserano, the Spanish Ambassador in London, contrary instructions to those given him by the
King of Spain, and to beg him to present to the English Government *sub spe rati* a plan of accommodation.[16] At the same time, however, he wrote to Gri-

[15] Mr. J. B. Perkins' "France under Louis XV.," ii. 249.
[16] Masserano did not dare to present this plan himself to the
English Government, but requested the French Ambassador to

maldi at Madrid informing him of what he had done, and explaining that his object was " to silence the lying tongues that represent to the King that I am stirring up war through personal ambition."

" It is obvious," observes that well-informed and impartial historian, M. Flammermont, " that Choiseul had presented this plan because he was almost certain that it would not be ratified by Spain, and that war was inevitable. He desired to prove his good-will and to show that he was devoted to the cause of peace in order to silence his enemies, but at the bottom of his heart he desired war and was secretly prepared for it."[17]

Choiseul's enemies, indeed, were fully alive to the gravity of the situation as regarded themselves, and were putting forth every effort to crush the Minister ere he could contrive to involve the country in war in order to crush them. Their designs were facilitated by the fact that the quarrel between the King and the Parliament of Paris had now reached an acute stage. At the opening of the winter session on December 3, an edict had been issued interdicting all joint action between the Parliament of Paris and the provin-

lay it before Lord North. Francès complied and writes to Choiseul :

" MONSEIGNEUR,—The Prime Minister (Lord North) granted me a rendezvous on Thursday, to give me an answer in regard to the new plan. He had given a dinner to the lord Sandwich (sic) ; the repast lasted a long time, and the guests were intoxicated with wine. At length, at nine o'clock in the evening, I found my lord North, who was as drunk as a hackney-coachman, while all the members of the British Council were as mellow (bien conditionnés) as their chief. The circumstance, in a little affair affecting the fate of three crowns, is not without interest."

The Ambassador adds that Lord North, although so drunk, seemed to grasp every point that was put before him as easily as if he had been perfectly sober, "car ces messieurs conservent machinalement de la logique et du raissonement dans l'ivrognerie par l'habitude qu'ils en ont contractée."

[17] M. Flammermont's Le Chancelier Maupeou et les Parlements, p. 175, et seq.

cial Parliaments, and all opposition to the enforcement of royal edicts, under pain of deprivation of office. This edict the judges indignantly refused to register; indeed, to have done so would have been to admit themselves wholly in the wrong, and there can be no doubt that it had been framed by Maupeou with the deliberate intention of bringing matters to a crisis. After a bed of justice had been held at Versailles, where the angry magistrates were further exasperated by the sight of their enemy, d'Aiguillon, whom they had decreed suspended from the privileges of his rank, seated among the peers, and various futile remonstrances had been addressed to the King, the Parliament declared that " their profound affliction did not leave their minds sufficiently free to decide upon the fortunes, lives, and honour of the King's subjects," and closed the Law Courts.[18]

The cabal was not slow to profit by the turn which events had taken. Maupeou entreated the King to dismiss Choiseul, declaring that the disgrace of the duke would have the immediate effect of assuring peace abroad, by compelling Spain to accede to England's demands, and at home, by demonstrating to the Parliament that it could no longer reckon on the support of a powerful Minister, and on the embarrassments that a great war would occasion the Government. His arguments were supported by Terray, who felt that he would certainly be disgraced if Choiseul were not, by d'Aiguillon, who feared that the Parliament would resume its proceedings against him if Maupeou and Terray were exiled, and, finally by Madame du Barry, "who loved the Duc d'Aiguillon too tenderly to abandon him on this occasion." Choiseul, on his side, defended himself vigorously, and

[18] *Vie privée de Louis XV.,* iv. 146. Martin's *Histoire de France jusqu'en* 1789, xv. 282.

did not hesitate to carry the war into the enemy's camp, assuring the King that the wisest course to adopt in regard to the Parliament would be to conciliate it by the dismissal of the Chancellor and the Comptroller-General, in which event the judges would doubtless accept the recent edict, with certain indispensable modifications, and lend themselves to any fresh taxation which circumstances might render necessary.

Louis XV. was at a loss what to do. On the one hand, he felt that Choiseul was the best of his Ministers, and that he would cover himself with odium by sacrificing to a low-born favourite and an unworthy cabal the man who had consolidated the Austrian alliance, negotiated the Family Compact, annexed Corsica to France, and reestablished his armies and his fleet; added to which he was ashamed to abandon his cousin, the King of Spain, at the moment when his concurrence was absolutely necessary. But he feared and hated the Parliament, from which he hoped Maupeou and Terray were about to deliver him, and, above all, he desired to have peace and quiet in his private life, and to put an end to the incessant complaints and solicitations of his mistress.[19]

While the King hesitated, events abroad were hastening to a crisis. Wearying of the obstinacy of Spain, the English Government sent orders to Harris[20] to leave Madrid, and if Choiseul had remained in office there can be little doubt that hostilities would have been commenced by England, and that France

[19] M. Flammermont's *Le Chancelier Maupeou et les Parlements*, p. 179.

[20] James Harris, afterwards first Earl of Malmesbury. He was at this time only twenty-four, but had already given promise of those great abilities which were to cause Talleyrand to observe: *"Je crois que Lord Malmesbury était le plus habile Ministre que vous aviez de son temps; c'était inutile de le devancer; il falloit de suivre de près."*

would have come to the assistance of her ally, under the terms of the Family Compact.

The intervention of the Prince de Condé determined Louis to follow the counsels of the favourite and her supporters and dismiss Choiseul. During the visit to Compiègne, in the preceding summer, the cabal, apprehensive that its attacks upon the chief Minister might be attributed by the King to motives of personal enmity and private ambition, had deemed it prudent to seek some ally whose high position placed him above such suspicions and who enjoyed the confidence of the monarch. They found these qualifications in Condé, who was badly disposed towards Choiseul, to whose influence he ascribed the fact that the hand of the wealthy Mademoiselle de Penthièvre had been bestowed upon the Duc de Chartres, instead of upon his own son, the Duc de Bourbon, and, moreover, aspired to the command of the army, an aspiration which the Minister had not seen fit to encourage.

Proposals of alliance were accordingly made to the prince, some writers say by Terray, who was chief of his council, others through the Princesse de Monaco, his mistress, who had been gained over to the interests of the cabal by Cromot, chief clerk of the Exchequer, a bitter enemy of Choiseul; and Condé accepted the rôle that was offered him on three conditions: first, that the appointment of Choiseul's successor at the Ministry of War should rest with him; secondly, that he should have the command of the army in the event of war; and thirdly, that the post of Grand Master of the Artillery should be revived in his favour.

The prince conducted his manœuvres with so much skill that up to the last moment Choiseul was unaware who was the principal agent of his ruin. On December 19, Condé came over from Chantilly and had an audience of the King, and as soon as he had suc-

ceeded in triumphing over the irresolution of the
monarch and had obtained his promise that Choiseul
should be dismissed, returned home.

However, Louis still hesitated. To a person of his
vacillating temperament, to make a resolution is one
thing, to give effect to it is quite another, and though
that same evening he wrote the *lettre-de-cachet* announcing his disgrace to Choiseul, he could not make
up his mind to send it, and for three days carried it
about in his pocket.[21]

The cabal was in the utmost alarm, for any day now
might bring the news that England had declared war,
in which event all its fine schemes would collapse like
a house of cards. Then Maupeou burned his boats.
Requesting an audience of the King, he reiterated his
conviction that Choiseul was deceiving him and
secretly doing his utmost to plunge the country into
war, which would necessitate the abandonment of the
campaign against the Parliament and the sacrifice of
himself and Terray to the resentment of the judges;
and begged his Majesty's leave to retire from office,
instead of waiting to be dismissed.[22] At the same time,
Madame du Barry, prompted by d'Aiguillon, suggested to the King that he should send for and question the Abbé de la Ville, chief clerk of the Foreign
Office, from whom he would be able to acertain what
were the real intentions of the Minister regarding the
Anglo-Spanish quarrel.

This Abbé de la Ville had begun life as a Jesuit,
and, though he had long since abandoned that Order,

[21] According to the *Vie privée de Louis XV.*, the king had one
evening, some little time before this, "when inflamed with love
and heated with wine," written a *lettre-de-cachet* at the instance
of the favourite; but, on coming to his senses the following
morning, had promptly destroyed it.

[22] M. Flammermont's *Le Chancelier Maupeou et les Parlements,*
p. 182.

had not failed to profit by the lessons he had learned in his youth. He had a grudge against Choiseul, "who despised his advice, his experience, and his person," and was only too ready to betray him to any one who was in a position to remunerate his treachery.

According to Besenval, when questioned by Louis XV. the abbé replied that, as it was his chief's invariable practice to write even the most unimportant despatches with his own hand, he was unable to enlighten him as to the Minister's real intentions. But it would be very easy for his Majesty to ascertain. Let him send for M. de Choiseul and order him to draft a letter to the King of Spain which should declare to that prince that his Majesty was absolutely determined to maintain peace, and that no consideration would induce him to involve his kingdom in war. If, said he, the Minister obeyed without hesitation, it would be a proof that he was sincerely desirous for peace; if, on the contrary, he raised objections, no one could doubt that he was working for war.

"The plot," remarks the chronicler, "was adroitly woven, and could not fail to attain its object; for it was easy to calculate that M. de Choiseul, who had just despatched a courier to Spain with proposals of accommodation, would reply to the King that, before writing to that Court, it was necessary to await the answer to the last plan that he had sent to it; that if it were accepted, the letter would be unnecessary; if it were rejected, there would be still time to write."[23]

This incident, as related by Besenval, which is to be found in the works of the Goncourts, Carlyle, and other writers of authority, has been generally accepted, but it is doubtful whether the baron's version is the

[23] *Mémoires du Baron de Besenval* (edit. Berville and Barrière), i. 267 *et seq.*

correct one. Recent research has revealed that many
of the despatches of Choiseul preserved in the Spanish Archives are not in the handwriting of the Minister himself, but are only signed by him,[24] and we
are, therefore, of opinion that the Abbé de la Ville
was cognisant of Choiseul's negotiations, and that
what he really did was to communicate to Louis XV.
the contents of his chief's last despatch to Grimaldi,
written on December 19, in which, while mildly ad-
vising peace, Choiseul added these words:

"If you do not adopt this course (*i.e.*, come to
terms with England), it will be necessary to begin war
at the same time, that is to say, towards the end of
January; and, in that event, you must advise me of
the day on which you propose to seize the English
vessels in your ports."[25]

However that may be, Louis XV. determined to
have a final explanation with Choiseul; and at a meeting of the Council held on December 23, the King,
"with a certain quivering of the chin, which was always the indication of a troubled mind," insisted on
the latter informing him at once what was the exact
situation of affairs, and obtained the Minister's confession that war was inevitable, and that it was
necessary to prepare for it. Then the monarch cried
furiously, *"Monsieur, je vous avais dit que je ne
voulais point la guerre,"* and he ordered Choiseul to
enjoin immediately upon the Marquis d'Ossun, the
French Ambassador at Madrid, to make the greatest
efforts to induce Carlos III. to subscribe to the English conditions.

[24] M. Vatel, to whom the credit of this discovery belongs, takes
advantage of it to endeavour to discredit the whole story about
the Abbé de la Ville, in the interests of Madame du Barry, but
there can be no doubt that Besenval was well informed in regard
to the main facts.
[25] Cited by Mr. J. B. Perkins in "France under Louis XV.," ii.
249.

The same day a courier carried to Spain the last despatch of Choiseul, and another, sent by a different route, a letter from Louis XV. to his cousin, imploring him to make some sacrifice for the sake of peace, and a note announcing to d'Ossun the disgrace of his chief Minister.

In the same Council, Choiseul, though unaware of the despatch of the second courier, comprehended that his dismissal had been decided upon. As he offered the pen to the King to sign the marriage contract of the Duc de la Rochefoucauld, Louis, with frowning brow, snatched it out of his hand, and, after using it, flung it angrily on the table, instead of returning it to the duke.[26]

The following morning, the 24th, Choiseul's ante-chamber was, as usual, crowded with suitors. The Duc de la Vrillière,[27] *Commandeur des Ordres* to the King (*"le grand congédieur ordinaire"*), entered, requested an immediate audience of the Minister, and, with some hypocritical words of condolence—he was one of Madame du Barry's henchmen, and, like Richelieu, an uncle of d'Aiguillon—handed him the *lettre-de-cachet* which Louis had written three days before.

"I order my cousin to deliver his resignation of his offices of Secretary of State and *Surintendant des*

[26]*Mémoires du Baron de Besenval* (edit. Berville and Barrière), i. 270. *Le Chancelier Maupeou et les Parlements*, 182 *et seq.*

[27] Louis Phelypeaux, better known under his former title of Comte de Saint-Florentin. He had been created a duke the previous year. The three names by which he was known at different periods of his life, Phelypeaux, Saint-Florentin, and La Vrillière, procured him the following mordant epitaph:

  " *Ci-git, malgré son rang, un homme fort commun,
    Ayant porté trois noms et n'en laissant aucun.*"—

M. Maugras's *La Disgrâce du Duc et de la Duchesse de Choiseul*, p. i.

Postes into the hands of the Duc de la Vrillière and
to retire to Chanteloup until further orders from me.
"LOUIS."[28]

Such were the terms in which Louis XV. dismissed
the Minister to whom had been confided for twelve
years the destinies of France.

Choiseul was required to leave Versailles within two
hours, while only twenty-four were allowed him in
which to make his preparations for quitting the capital.
He started at once for Paris, where he found the
duchess about to sit down to dinner.

"You have the appearance of an exiled man," said
she, laughing. "But sit down, your dinner will not
taste the worse for that." And they dined with excellent appetites.[29]

That Choiseul deserved his fate there can, we think,
be little doubt. No condemnation indeed can well be
too strong for a Minister who, for the sake of out-
witting his private enemies and preserving his own
ascendency, is prepared to plunge his country into all
the horrors of war. Nevertheless, the Parisians, who

[28] *Revue de Paris,* 1829, vol. iv. 62; communicated by Gabriel,
Duc de Choiseul, who possessed the original letter.

The instructions to La Vrillière, also in the King's handwriting,
show to what a point he had carried his irritation against the
disgraced Minister: "The Duc de La Vrillière will deliver the
accompanying orders to MM. de Choiseul (Choiseul and his
cousin, the Duc de Choiseul-Praslin, Minister of the Marine),
and will bring me their resignations. Were it not on account
of Madame de Choiseul, I would have exiled her husband elsewhere, as his estate is situated in his government (Touraine);
but he will conduct himself as if he were not residing there, and
will see no one, except his family and those to whom I may
give permission to visit him."

The *lettre-de-cachet* exiling the Duc de Praslin contained only
two lines: "I have no further need of your services, and I exile
you to Praslin, whither you will betake yourself within twenty-
four hours."

[29] M. Maugras's *La Disgrâce du Duc et la Duchesse de Choiseul,* p. 3.

did not know what we know to-day, and who saw in
him only an able and patriotic statesman sacrificed to
the machinations of an unpopular cabal, chose to make
of him a kind of hero. As soon as the news of his
disgrace reached the capital, the whole city was in a
ferment of excitement. Expressions of regret and
indignation were heard on every side, and all classes
united in manifestations of sympathy. Although he
had been forbidden to receive visits from any but members of his own family during the short time he was
permitted to remain in Paris, and two exempts had
been stationed by the Lieutenant of Police at his door
to ensure that this order was observed, his numerous
friends, headed by the Duc de Chartres, famous in
after years under the name of Philippe Egalité, forced
their way into the house to offer him their condolences
and bid him farewell. All the streets leading to the
Rue de Richelieu, in which the Hôtel de Choiseul was
situated, were so blocked with the carriages of people
who came to inscribe their names in his visitors' book,
as a last token of esteem and affection "for the great
Minister whom France had lost," that for some hours
ordinary traffic was entirely suspended. As, in spite
of the large emoluments of his different offices and his
wife's wealth, he was known to have contracted immense debts and to be embarrassed for money, his
friends hastened to place their credit at his disposal,
and within a few hours these offers amounted to no
less a sum than four million livres.[30]

The exiled Minister's departure on the morrow par-
took of the nature of a veritable triumph. An enormous crowd lined the streets from his hôtel to the
Barrière d'Enfer, while the windows and even the
roofs of the houses were thronged with spectators;

[30] M. Flammermont's *Le Chancelier Maupeou et les Parlements,*
p. 186. Belleval's *Souvenirs d'un Chevau-léger,* p. 143.

and when the coach containing the duke and duchess appeared, followed by a long cortège of their friends' carriages, the multitude broke forth into loud and continued acclamations. "Never has disgrace been accompanied by so much glory," wrote Madame du Deffand. "There is no such example in histories ancient or modern."

The popular excitement continued long after the departure of Choiseul and showed itself in a hundred different ways. Portraits and busts of the duke were seen everywhere; medals were struck to perpetuate the memory of the event; snuff-boxes bearing on one side the head of Choiseul and on the other that of Sully, the great Minister of Henri IV., were sold in the streets;[31] and Moreau painted a charming picture representing Choiseul supporting France, Glory in the act of depositing a crown of laurel on the duke's head, while people prostrated themselves at his feet, and Envy, in a corner, turned away her head in anger. Verses in praise of the fallen Minister and satirising his enemies and the King circulated everywhere, and the following song obtained a great vogue:

> " Le Bien-Aimé de l'Almanach
> N'est pas le Bien-Aimé de France.
> Il fait tout *ab hoc et ab hac*
> Le Bien-Aimé de l'Almanach.

> " Il met tout dans le même sac
> Et la Justice et la Finance;
> Le Bien-Aimé de l'Almanach
> N'est pas le Bien-Aimé de France." [32]

Until now Ministers in exile had received few marks of sympathy or attachment, even from their

[31] " *Tiens!* " cried the witty actress, Sophie Arnould, on being shown one of these. " They have put the receipts and the expenses together."

[32] Cited in *Anecdotes sur Madame la Comtesse du Barry*, p. 193.

relatives and dearest friends. Maurepas at Bourges, Machault at Arnouville, d'Argenson at Ormes, and Bernis at Soissons had lived in the most complete isolation; people dared not mention their names at Court, much less openly brave the royal displeasure by visiting them. But times had changed. The age and feebleness of the King and the disunion in the Royal Family had permeated the whole Court with a spirit of independence and insubordination hitherto unknown, and which, in the ensuing reign, was to assume alarming proportions. The Dauphiness and the Duc de Chartres did not attempt to conceal the regret with which the exile of Choiseul inspired them, and the frequency of the requests made to him for permission to visit the disgraced Minister compelled Louis to give a sort of qualified consent, and he, accordingly, replied to all applicants, " I neither permit nor forbid you."[33]

Thenceforth a continuous stream of prominent persons repaired to Chanteloup, where Choiseul, notwithstanding his enormous debts, lived in almost regal state and dispensed the most magnificent hospitality. " During the four years that the exile of the Minister lasted," says Dutens, " there was scarcely a day on which some person from the Court did not arrive at or leave Chanteloup, and the King was surprised to learn that its salons were frequently more brilliant than those of Versailles. The secrets of the Cabinet were as well known there as at Versailles, and the er-

[33] M. Maugras's *La Disgrâce du Duc et de la Duchesse de Choiseul,* p. 78.

The ex-Comptroller-General, Maynon d'Invau, having requested permission, La Vrillière wrote: " I have submitted to the King the letter wherein you ask permission to go to Chanteloup, and his Majesty has done me the honour to reply that he has never accorded any one permission to go there, but that he has not refused, and that he has left those who have asked the liberty of themselves deciding what they will do."—E. and J. de Goncourt's *La Du Barry,* p. 118.

rors of the new Ministry were so strictly examined that the company of Chanteloup was dreaded as a tribunal. Even the King became curious to learn its decisions, and he frequently asked those who returned thence, 'What do they say at Chanteloup?' "[34]

[34]*Mémoires d'un voyageur qui se repose,* ii. 86. The memoirs of the time contain some interesting particulars about this magnificent château and the splendour which Choiseul maintained there. Cheverny says that those who drove up at night fancied they were entering Versailles, owing to the immense extent of the buildings and the lavish manner in which they were lighted up, both within and without; and that he occupied twenty minutes in passing along the corridors of the château from the apartments allotted to him to those of a fellow-guest. Dutens describes it as "a delightful place, where the most complete and the most magnificent establishment was kept up that I have seen at the house of any great nobleman in Europe"; and tells us that, on the occasion when he visited it, there were four hundred persons living in the house, including those in the service of the duke, fifty-four of whom were in livery, and that the account for bread alone amounted to three hundred livres a day. Small wonder that Choiseul's friends had to come to his assistance!

CHAPTER XII

CHOISEUL disgraced, Spain, as had been foreseen, hastened to comply with the English demands, and Louis XV. and Maupeou found their hands free to deal with the Parliament, which, it will be remembered, had closed the courts as a protest against the edict of December 3.

This was a step to which the Parliament had had recourse before on several occasions, and generally with some degree of success. Closing the courts often brought temporary exile and other annoyances to the judges, but the vexation to the Government and inconvenience to the community at large caused by the suspension of justice had ended in the magistracy obtaining concessions.

The present rupture, however, was destined to have a very different termination. In *lettres de jussion,* five times repeated, the King ordered the Parliament to resume its functions, and the members as often refused to obey. On the night of January 19-20, each judge was roused from his slumbers by two Musketeers, who presented him with an order from the King to resume his duties, to which he was to answer a simple yes or no in writing, and that immediately and without taking counsel with any one. A few, alarmed by this nocturnal summons, were afraid to signify a formal disobedience to the royal commands, but the majority stood firm; and when, on the following morning, the Parliament was hurriedly convened to discuss the situation, the weaker members repudiated the promise which fear had extorted from them,

164

and the whole body reiterated its defiance of the King.

Maupeou had long since determined to be content with no half-measures; if the members of the Parliament declined to exercise the duties of judges, they should cease to be judges, and give place to those who would know better than to oppose the King's edicts. Moreover, quite apart from all considerations of the royal authority, a reform in the judicial system was urgently needed, and Despotism masquerading in the garb of Progress was a spectacle which appealed irresistibly to his cynical mind. He, accordingly, resolved to strike a final and decisive blow without delay.

That night, the unfortunate judges were again awakened, on this occasion by an officer of the Council, who notified to them a decree of that body declaring their offices confiscated, and forbidding them for the future to exercise any of their functions or even to assume the title of members of the Parliament. To this officer succeeded Musketeers, bearing *lettres-de-cachet,* which exiled them to distant provinces.[1]

These measures created the most unbounded amazement and indignation, even among those who had hitherto had but little sympathy with the Parliament, for not only had an institution which had been powerful in the days of Saint-Louis and Philippe le Bel been swept away at a single stroke, but an outrageous attack had been made on the sanctity of vested interests. Judicial dignities could only be acquired by inheritance or purchase; some had been handed down from father to son through many generations; others had repeatedly changed hands for very large sums of money, and all had until that moment been regarded as sound a form of investment as land or houses. It

[1] *Vie privée de Louis XV.,* iv. 153, *et seq.*

is true that the dispossessed magistrates were subsequently permitted to demand compensation; but the price fixed was very far below the value of their offices, and the knowledge that the Government did not hesitate to invade the rights of property aroused a feeling of uneasiness throughout the entire community.[2]

In Paris, the popular indignation assumed its usual form, and a storm of *chansons,* pamphlets, and epigrams, some of them couched in the most threatening language, rained upon Maupeou.[3] But, undeterred by the public clamour and the violent remonstrances of the provincial Parliaments,[4] the Chancellor steadily pursued the course he had marked out for himself. On January 23, the members of the Council of State were provisionally commissioned to render justice at the Palais, and were installed with great pomp, amid the hooting of the populace. A month later, an edict established six superior councils at Arras, Blois, Châlons, Clermont-Ferrand, Lyons, and Poitiers, all of which towns had hitherto been included within the

---

[2] Mr. J. B. Perkins's "France under Louis XV.," ii. 271.

[3] Here is an extract from a pamphlet cited in *Les Fastes de Louis XV.:*

"Maupeou is the most abominable monster that hell has ever vomited forth to distress the kingdom, the most damnable hypocrite, the most determined villain that has ever been seen on earth. The Jacques Cléments, Ravaillacs and Damiens may yield him the first place in their parricidal gang. The Sicilian Vespers, the Saint-Bartholomew, the defeats of Poitiers, Azincourt, and Malplaquet were lucky days for the nation in comparison with that on which this traitor was born, for they only destroyed some Frenchmen, whereas this impious wretch would wipe out the very name. What good citizen, if any such are still left us, would not solicit the honour to load, charge, and fire the weapon which should revenge the nation and deliver it for ever from the villain who has ruined it?"

[4] The provincial Parliaments met with substantially the same fate as the Parliament of Paris; the unruly members being deprived of their offices and their places filled by men more amenable to the royal will.

jurisdiction of the Parliament of Paris, to the great loss and inconvenience of litigants residing therein, who had been compelled to carry their appeals to the capital. The members of these new courts were strictly forbidden to receive any term-fees, judges' fees, or other perquisites over and above their salaries. On April 9, the Cour des Aides was swept away, and its members and its jurisdiction divided between the new Parliament and the superior councils. Finally, on the 13th of the same month, a Bed of Justice was held in which were read three edicts: the first, abolishing the old Parliament; the second, abolishing the Cour des Aides; the third, transforming the old Grand Council into the new Parliament.

After the edicts had been read, Louis XV. rose and terminated the sitting with these words: " You have heard my will; I desire that you will conform to it. I order you to commence your functions on Monday; my Chancellor will install you. I forbid any deliberations contrary to my edicts and all representations in favour of my former Parliament, for I will never change."

Madame du Barry assisted at this ceremony, " hidden behind a gauze curtain." As she was leaving the Palais, she encountered the Duc de Nivernais, who, with ten other peers, had given his opinion against the registration of the edicts.[5]

" I hope, Monsieur le Duc," said she, " that you will cease to oppose the King's wishes, for, as you have heard his Majesty say, he will never change."

[5] The Princes of the Blood (with the single exception of the Comte de la Marche), headed by the Duc d'Orléans and the Prince de Condé, had refused to attend the bed of justice, and sent a vigorous protest to the King, " couched in harsh and barbaric language." Louis seized the protest and threw it into the fire, and forbade the princes to appear in his presence or in that of the Dauphin and Dauphiness.

"True, Madame," replied the gallant duke; "but when he said that he was looking at you."

It has frequently been asserted that, but for the assistance he derived from the *caquetage* of Madame du Barry, Maupeou would never have succeeded in inducing Louis XV. to sanction the destruction of the Parliaments. Historians like Michelet and Henri Martin have given the weight of their authority to this charge, which, however, appears to rest on no better foundation than an anecdote related by the *Nouvelles à la main*.[6] Writing under date March 25, 1771, Bachaumont says:

"The Empress of Russia has carried off the picture-gallery of the Comte de Thiers, a distinguished amateur, who had a very fine collection. M. Marigny (Director-General of the Board of Works, an office which included the supervision of the art-collections of France) has had the mortification of seeing these treasures go to a foreign country, for lack of funds to purchase them for the King. Among the pictures was a full-length portrait of Charles I., King of England, by Van Dyck. This is the only one which has remained in France. The Comtesse du Barry, who displays more and more taste for the arts, gave orders for it to be bought. She paid 24,000 livres for it, and when she was reproved for having selected this picture among so many which would have been more suitable,

[6] *Nouvelles à la main* was the name given in the seventeenth century to clandestinely printed gazettes, which contained news of the Court and the town, generally in a highly piquant form. They were prohibited by the Parliament of Paris in 1620, and in 1666 and 1670 the penalty of whipping and the galleys was decreed against the vendors. They still continued to be circulated however, and it was not until some years later that La Reynie, the Lieutenant of Police, contrived to suppress them. They reappeared under the Regency, when Madame Doublet published a weekly journal, entitled *Nouvelles à la main,* which was continued by Bachaumont, and, after his death, by Pidansat de Mairobert.

pretended that she was recovering a family portrait. In fact, the Du Barrys claim to be related to the House of Stuart."

On October 22, the *Nouvelles,* which was now edited by the ingenious Pidansat de Mairobert, Bachaumont having died in the preceding April, returns to the subject of Charles I.'s portrait:

" People are talking much of the full-length portrait of Charles I., purchased for 20,000 livres by Madame du Barry. This lady has placed it in her apartments, together with that of the King, and, it appears, not without design. It is asserted that she shows it to the King, whenever his Majesty, relapsing into his normal kindness of disposition, seems to weary of violence and inclines towards clemency. She tells him that perhaps his Parliament would have made some attempt similar to that of England, if the Chancellor had not foreseen their insane and criminal designs and checked them before they had reached the degree of baseness and wickedness required to put them into execution.[7] However absurd and atrocious such an imputation may be, it reinflames the prince for the moment, and it is from the foot of this picture that proceed the destroying thunderbolts that smite the magistrates and pulverise them in the remotest corners of the realm.

" One is well assured that a calumny so atrocious and so deliberate cannot proceed from the tender and ingenuous heart of Madame la Comtesse du Barry, and that the alarms with which she inspires the King are instigated by advisers whose policy is as clever as it is infernal."

[7] " Behold that unfortunate monarch," said she to him. " Your Parliament would perhaps have ended by treating you as he was treated by the Parliament of England, if you had not had a Minister to oppose their designs and set their menaces at defiance."—*Vie privée de Louis XV.,* iv. 160.

" This anecdote, justified by events, is attested by courtiers whose testimony carries great weight."

The portrait referred to by the *Nouvelles* is the beautiful painting, now in the Louvre, representing the King followed by a squire leading his horse, which the famous engraving of Le Strange has helped to popularise. Considerable doubt exists as to whether this portrait ever belonged to Baron de Thiers, but, contrary to the opinion expressed by Mr. R. B. Douglas, in his " Life and Times of Madame du Barry," there is none whatever that it was at one time the property of the favourite. Here, however, is what M. Jules Guiffrey, the great French authority on Van Dyck and his works, has to say on the subject:

" The Louvre Catalogue states that the portrait comes from the collection of Louis XV. and that it had belonged to Baron de Thiers, who, as is known, sold his fine collection bodily to the Empress of Russia. Here there is a twofold error. It is, to say the least, very doubtful if the portrait of Charles I. ever formed part of Baron de Thiers's collection. It is also related that the picture figured at the beginning of the eighteenth century in the collection of the Comtesse de Verrue, who gave it to the Marquis de Lassay. Nevertheless, it is not mentioned in the catalogue of the countess's pictures, published for the first time by M. Charles Blanc in the *Trésor de la Curiosité*. The collection of the Marquis de Lassay fell partly, as is known to the Comte de la Guiche; in the latter's lot was *Charles I.* The collection of the Comte de la Guiche was sold by auction in 1770; but the famous picture found no purchasers, and the heirs withdrew it at 17,000 livres. It was, no doubt, in consequence of this fruitless effort to sell the picture that the Comtesse du Barry, in quest of distinguished ancestors, to atone for the lowliness of her extraction, made direct offers to the owners. A bargain was struck, and the favourite became the possessor of the picture. She bought it for herself, and not for the King, as has often been asserted. Only at the commencement of the succeeding reign did she consent to surrender it and sell it to King Louis XVI., as will be gathered from the correspondence which we shall now cite.

"After the death of Louis XV., the Comtesse du Barry, pressed by her numerous creditors, was reduced to parting with a portion of the riches of every kind which royal liberality had showered upon her. The *Charles I.* included in this enforced liquidation was offered to M. d'Angiviller, Director-General of the Board of Works. The architect Le Doux, who had done much work for Madame du Barry, undertook the negotiations. We have not been able to find his letter, but the three following notes render that document unnecessary and all comment superfluous:

"*'Letter of* M. D'ANGIVILLER *to* M. LE DOUX.

"'I have received, Monsieur, the letter wherein you acquaint me with Madame du Barry's fixed intention to sell the portrait of Charles I. and of the offer which has been made to her. I will not let the opportunity of acquiring this valuable work escape. I therefore secure it on behalf of the King for the price of 24,000 livres (1000 louis) which has been offered for it, and this sum will be paid down on delivery of the picture.
"'I am, Monsieur, &c.'"[8]

The remaining two letters mentioned by M. Guiffrey merely refer to arrangements for the removal of the picture from Louveciennes and the payment of the purchase-money.

[8] M. Guiffrey's *Antoine Van Dyck, sa vie et son œuvre* (Paris, 1882), p. 180 *et seq.*

Thus it will be seen that the portrait of Charles I. did belong to Madame du Barry, and that she sold it to Louis XVI. for the exact sum which the *Nouvelles* state that she had paid for it. What amount of truth there was in the story of the use the lady made of her purchase it is very difficult to say. As Sheridan remarked of Dundas, the writers of the *Nouvelles* were no doubt largely indebted to their imagination for their facts; but, on the other hand, they were frequently well-informed, and hardly deserve the scorn which Madame du Barry's two champions, M. Vatel and Mr. Douglas, so unsparingly mete out to them. These writers ridicule the story on the ground that the sale of the Thiers collection took place at a later date than that stated by the *Nouvelles,* in fact some months after the old Parliament of Paris had been sent about its business, so that the portrait of Charles I.[9] could not have been in Madame du Barry's possession early enough to be used as a bogey to frighten the King. But, from the passage from M. Guiffrey's work which we have just cited, it would appear that the portrait was acquired, not at the sale of Baron de Thiers's pictures in the autumn of 1771, but from the heirs of the Comte de la Guiche some time in 1770, that is to say, *before* the suppression of the Parliament, which entirely refutes their arguments and strengthens the case against the favourite.

However, if for lack of trustworthy evidence, Madame du Barry must be acquitted of the Machiavelian conduct attributed to her, for we should hesitate to condemn any one on the testimony of Bachaumont and his *confrères,* though, as we have observed, they were not nearly so black as M. Vatel and Mr. Douglas appear to imagine, she was unquestionably, in some

[9] Van Dyck valued this picture at £200, but was persuaded to reduce his charge to half that amount.

degree, responsible for the quashing of the proceedings against d'Aiguillon, and cannot, therefore, be held altogether blameless for the later developments of the quarrel between the King and the magistracy.

While Maupeou was waging war on the Parliaments, d'Aiguillon was engaged in the congenial task of inciting Madame du Barry to persecute the friends of Choiseul. Jarente, Bishop of Orléans, who had persuaded Madame Adélaïde to intercede with the King for the recall of Choiseul, was deprived of the distribution of benefices; d'Usson was recalled from Stockholm; the appointment of the Baron de Breteuil as Ambassador at the Austrian Court was revoked, just as he was on the point of starting for Vienna; Rulhière was deprived of his pension and his place in the Foreign Office; the unfortunate Prince de Beauvau, whose imperious wife had taken so prominent a part in the attacks upon the favourite, lost his post of Governor of Languedoc, though he was over a million livres in debt; and *lettres-de-cachet* were suspended over the heads of the Archbishop of Toulouse, Malesherbes, the Duc de Duras, and even Sartine, the Lieutenant of Police. D'Aiguillon and the favourite dealt blows on every side, and as they could not strike their feminine adversaries directly, they struck at them through their husbands, their lovers, or their brothers.

Desolation and alarm reigned in the salons whence had proceeded the quips and gibes and epigrams against Madame du Barry and her reputed lover, for no one knew upon whom the next blow might fall.

" The lady is more supreme than her predecessor or even Cardinal de Fleury," wrote Madame du Deffand to Horace Walpole; " she is exasperated to the last degree. We are passing through a terrible time here; it is impossible to foresee where it will end."[10]

But great as was the influence of Madame du Barry over her royal adorer, she was for some months unable to overcome the reluctance of the King to promote d'Aiguillon to the Foreign Office, which was the goal of that intriguing nobleman's ambition. Louis had always disliked d'Aiguillon—he had never been able to pardon him for having been, for a time, his successful rival in the affections of Madame de Châteauroux —and to make a Foreign Minister of a man who was but yesterday an accused person was to defy public opinion to an extent from which a far bolder monarch than himself might well recoil. Moreover, the duke's pretensions encountered serious obstacles in the opposition of the Prince de Condé, who, until he fell into disgrace on account of his sympathy with the Parliament, exercised considerable influence, and at the beginning of January succeeded in thrusting one of his *protégés,* the Marquis de Monteynard, into the Ministry of War; and from a rival candidate, whose qualifications for the post were far superior to his own.

This was the Comte de Broglie, surnamed " the little intriguer," who had formerly been French Ambassador at Warsaw, and, in 1767, had succeeded Tercier as conductor of the secret diplomatic correspondence of Louis XV. Broglie had nothing to aid him on the side of Condé, who had a long-standing grievance against the count's elder brother, the Maréchal de Broglie, dating back to the time of the Seven Years' War:[11] but he had public opinion on his side, especially

---

[10] Letter of March 26, 1771.

[11] This resentment was so bitter that it survived the fall of the Monarchy, and twenty years later, during the emigration, the prince and the old marshal, commanding the same troops and involved in the same disasters, could hardly bring themselves

among the representatives of foreign Courts, and had the support of the Maréchale de Mirepoix and Mademoiselle " Chon " du Barry, the sister-in-law of the favourite.

For five months the post of Minister for Foreign Affairs remained vacant; while clouds were gathering upon the horizon, the French agents abroad and the Ambassadors in Paris were complaining every day of the absolute ignorance in which they were left, and foreign princes waited about at Versailles until a successor to Choiseul should be appointed.[12] D'Aiguillon intrigued against Broglie, Broglie intrigued against d'Aiguillon,[13] and Condé intrigued against both. Madame du Barry supported her *protégé;* Monteynard, the new Minister for War, Maupeou, and Terray

to speak to one another.—The Duc de Broglie's *Le Secret du Roi,* ii. 339.

[12] *Ibid.* 352.

[13] Broglie bombarded Louis XV. with letters, in which he carried flattery and servility to their utmost limits. In one written on January 14, 1771, he says: " The knowledge that, under the sole direction of your Majesty, the King of Spain has been compelled to accept the conditions imposed by England has occasioned the greatest joy. The value of this most fortunate peace is infinitely augmented in the eyes of your subjects by the knowledge that they owe it to your paternal care, and everybody exclaims with enthusiasm and regret, ' Why does not the King do everything and decide upon everything, himself? nothing would then be wanting to our happiness and his glory.' " And this at a time when the most distinguished persons in France were flocking to Chanteloup, and *"Le Bien Aimé de l'Almanach"* was being sung at every street corner!

In another letter, the count informs the King that " he should indeed be flattered if Madame du Barry entertained a sufficiently good opinion of him to lead her to desire that the Ministry of Foreign Affairs should be conferred upon him."—*Le Secret du Roi,* ii. 343, 352.

The servility of Broglie, however, must not blind us to the fact that he was by far the most suitable candidate for the post to which he aspired. He was the first French statesman to foresee the designs of the Eastern Powers upon Poland, and had he been appointed to the Foreign Office, would have undoubtedly striven his utmost to checkmate them.

sided with Condé; while the Maréchale de Mirepoix
and Mademoiselle " Chon " espoused the cause of the
diplomatist, who also had the assistance of a certain
fascinating Chevalier de Jaucourt, called by his friends
" *Clair-de-lune*," owing to his talent for relating ghost-
stories, who endeavoured to frustrate d'Aiguillon's
ambitions by supplanting him in the affections of the
favourite.

" It is almost impossible that your Majesty should
form a correct idea of the horrible confusion which
reigns here," wrote Mercy to Maria Theresa. " The
throne is disgraced by the extensive and indecent influence of the favourite and her partisans. The nation
shows its feeling by seditious remarks and disloyal
pamphlets, in which the person of the sovereign is
not spared.[14] Versailles is the abode of treachery,
spite, and hatred; everything is done through motives
of personal interest, and all honourable feeling dis-
carded."[15]

At length, in June, Condé having in the meantime
fallen into disgrace, Louis XV. grew weary of the importunities of his mistress, and allowed a reluctant
consent to be wrung from him that the Foreign Office
should be given to d'Aiguillon, to the indignation of
Broglie, the disgust of the whole nation, and the
amazement of Europe.[16]

The nomination of her *protégé* was celebrated by

[14] One morning, a placard bearing the following words was
found affixed to the King's statue by Bouchardon, in the Place
Louis XV.: " By order of the Mint. A Louis badly struck must
be struck again." This, of course, referred to the attempted
assassination of the King by Damiens, on January 5, 1757, and
was nothing less than a thinly veiled incitement to regicide.

[15] Letter of April 16, 1771.

[16] The Marine, which had likewise been a bone of contention,
had been filled in the previous April by the appointment of
Boynes, a creature of d'Aiguillon. Until then its duties had been
discharged by Terray.

Madame du Barry, in the following September, by a grand dinner at Louveciennes, at which were present the wife of the new Minister, the dowager Duchesse d'Aiguillon—" *la grosse duchesse,*" as Madame du Deffand styles her—the Maréchale de Mirepoix, the Princesse de Montmorency, the Comtesse de Valentinois, the Chancellor and all the Ministers of State, and the whole of the Corps Diplomatique, with the exception of the Ambassadors of Spain and Naples.[17] These Ministers, acting presumably on instructions from their Courts, had declined to visit the favourite, and Fuentes, the Spanish Ambassador, went so far as to refuse invitations to functions at which the lady was to be present. The representative of Great Britain, on the other hand, showed most gratifying complacence, and, in February 1772, gave a dinner-party exclusively to the d'Aiguillon and Du Barry faction.

At the Salon of 1771 Madame du Barry was again in evidence. Two important works were consecrated to the favourite—one, a bust in terra-cotta, by Pajou; the other, a full-length portrait, by Drouais, in which the lady was represented as one of the Muses.[18] The bust in terra-cotta by Pajou, the marble reproduction of which, exhibited at the Salon of 1773, and now in the Louvre, is by many considered that sculptor's *chef-d'œuvre,* was generally admired and

[17] Madame du Deffand *to* Horace Walpole, September 25, 1771.
[18] Here is a contemporary description of the portrait: "The Comtesse du Barry is painted as a Muse. She is seated, and is partly veiled by light and transparent draperies, which are gathered up below the left breast, leaving the legs uncovered to the knees, and revealing the outline of the rest of her figure. In her right hand she holds a harp and a crown of flowers; in the left she carries other flowers. The foreground of the picture is filled by books, paint-brushes, and various attributes of the arts."—Cited by M. Vatel in *Histoire de Madame du Barry,* ii. 83.

warmly praised by the *Mercure*. But the picture was
not so fortunate, as the devout, " who only care to
see women veiled from head to foot," were shocked
at the mythological nudity of the figure; and Madame
du Barry, hearing of this, ordered it to be at once removed from the walls of the Salon.

In February 1771, the Prince Royal of Sweden, the
future Gustavus III., arrived in Paris, accompanied
by his younger brother, Frederick. The ostensible
object of his visit was to improve his mind by a course
of foreign travel, and he took up his quarters at the
Swedish Legation, Rue de Grenelle Saint-Germain,
under the name of the Graf von Gothland. But, in
point of fact, he had been sent by his mother, Queen
Ulrica, sister of Frederick the Great, on the invitation
of Choiseul, to solicit French assistance in the difficult
enterprise which was to end in his *coup d'Etat* of
August 19, 1772.

When Choiseul's invitation was sent the duke was,
of course, still in office; but the young prince reached
Paris to find his hoped-for ally exiled and his enemies
wrangling over his departments; and was, in consequence, placed in a somewhat embarrassing position.
Acting, however, on the advice of Creutz,[19] the saga-
cious and popular Swedish Ambassador, he resolved to
pay court to all parties, and won golden opinions from
all. One day, he sent his compliments to Chanteloup
through Madame du Deffand, and the next he supped
at Rueil with the d'Aiguillons, Richelieu, and Maupeou. On another, he showed himself in the salon of
the Comtesse d'Egmont[20] in the Rue Louis-le-Grand,

[19] Gustaf Philip Creutz (1729-1785), the most celebrated
Swedish poet of the eighteenth century, author of the beautiful
idyll *Atis och Camilla*, and the exquisite pastoral *Daphné*.
[20] Sophie Jeanne Armande Elisabeth Septimainie de Vignerod
du Plessis de Richelieu, daughter of the notorious Duc de Riche-

and on a fourth went to the Palais-Bourbon to visit
the Prince de Condé. Nor did he neglect to render
homage to the reigning sultana, whose heart he quite
won by presenting a rich collar, some writers say of
gold, others of diamonds, to her favourite lapdog.
" *On raconte ici* (Vienna) *des bassesses du Roi de
Suède*[21] *vis-à-vis cette femme*," writes Maria Theresa.
" *Quelle honte!* "[22]

On November 13, Madame du Deffand informs her
friend at Strawberry Hill: " The Idol (Madame du
Barry) is at the height of her glory; she has written to
the King of Sweden; her letter did not reach the
King; but, as it was announced to him, he has fore-
stalled her and written to her *des choses charmantes
et admirables*."

At this time a rumour was afloat that " the Idol "
had sent, or was about to send, her portrait to Gustavus, and poor Madame d'Egmont, who had promised
hers to the monarch, was in despair and addressed the
most pathetic letters to Stockholm.

" Place me then in a position to send you my portrait," she writes.   " I cannot do so without a positive

lieu, by his second marriage with Elisabeth Sophie de Lorraine,
and wife of Casimir, Marquis de Pignatelli, Duc de Bisaccia,
Comte d'Egmont. At her husband's hôtel, and also at that of
her father, she kept a brilliant salon, which was frequented by
diplomatists, like Mercy, Lord Stormont, Creutz, Gleichen, and
Fuentes; painters and sculptors, like Roslin, Le Moyne, Chardin,
and Hall; and men of letters, like Jean Jacques Rousseau and
Ruhlière. Her salon was at this time a centre of resistance to
Maupeou, whose reforms Madame d'Egmont and her friend, the
Comtesse de Brionne, opposed with great energy. Brought into
connection with Gustavus III. by Creutz, the countess encouraged and aided him in his efforts to obtain the support of
France for the projects he meditated in Sweden. An affection
"très vive et qui parait avoir été pure," sprung up between the
two, and they corresponded regularly until the lady's untimely
death in October 1773.

[21] Gustavus had received the news of the death of his father
and his succession to the throne of Sweden on March 1.

[22] Letter to Mercy-Argenteau, April 1, 1771.

assurance that you have not nor will have that of Madame du Barry." She returns to the charge in another letter: " Sire, it is said that you have asked for the portrait of Madame du Barry; they go even so far as to assert that you have written to her. I have denied it at all costs, but it has been persisted in in so positive a manner that I implore you to authorise me to contradict it. No, it cannot be." Finally, in a third letter, she says: " I ask again for an answer concerning the portrait of Madame du Barry. Deign then to give me your word of honour that you neither have nor ever intend to have it."[28]

At the beginning of January 1772, a difficulty arose about the payment of the subsidies which had been promised by France to Gustavus to assist him in the execution of the projects he was meditating in Sweden, d'Aiguillon declaring that it was absolutely impossible to obtain the money. The poet-ambassador in the Rue Grenelle Saint-Germain, however, knew his Versailles as intimately as did Mercy himself, and forthwith wrote to his master:

" In this terrible situation, here are the expedients that I propose to your Majesty: (1) To write a very touching letter to the King, *a very flattering one to Madame du Barry,* and one full of confidence and friendship to the Duc d'Aiguillon. This is of the most vital importance . . . ."

Gustavus lost not a moment in despatching the touching, flattering, and friendly epistles to their respective destinations, and on the 16th of the same month the delighted Creutz sends a courier to announce that his Majesty's letters have produced the desired effect: " The lady who enjoys the confidence of the King takes the most lively interest in all that concerns the King of Sweden. She speaks to me continually,

[28] Geffroy's *Gustave III. et la Cour de France,* i. 242.

and charges me to convey her good wishes to your Majesty."[24]

And so it came about that, through the intercession of the flattered favourite, the empty French Treasury was compelled to disgorge the needed subsidies, and the King of Sweden enabled to pave the way for the revolution which was to bring his haughty nobility into subjection to the Crown.

The rumour of the previous autumn that Madame du Barry intended to bestow her portrait on Gustavus would appear to have been well grounded, for shortly after the Baron de Lieven had brought to Versailles the official announcement of the *coup d'Etat* of August 19, 1772, on which occasion the favourite had joined her felicitations to those of Louis XV., we find Creutz writing to his sovereign as follows:

" Madame du Barry was wishful to send to your Majesty her bust (by Pajou) and the portrait of herself by Greuze;[25] but this would oblige your Majesty to send her your portrait and to write to her; and I, accordingly, allowed the matter to drop. It is, however, very essential to spare the feelings of Madame du Barry, and I implore your Majesty to place me in a position to say some flattering things to her. I am high in her favour, but I am embarrassed what answer to make to her should she come again to propose to me to send her portrait. The King is extremely sensitive in regard to everything which concerns her, and he neither pardons nor forgets the slightest thing that may wound her."[26]

[24] Geffroy's *Gustave III. et la Cour de France,* i. 148.
[25] This portrait figures among the objects chosen by the commission of arts at Louvèciennes, after the execution of the countess in 1793. It is described in the catalogue as " an unfinished picture representing the Dubarry as a Bacchante."—E. and J. de Goncourt's *La Du Barry,* p. 75, note.
[26] Geffroy's *Gustave III. et la Cour de France,* i. 212.

Gustavus replied very graciously to Madame du Barry's felicitations,[27] but he did not mention the portrait, and nothing more was heard about it. Almost at the same time, he gave to Madame d'Egmont the solemn promise that she had demanded that he would never accept any portrait of the favourite; and, in August 1773, two months before her untimely death, that lady sent him a charming miniature of herself by the Swedish painter Hall, which is now in the National Museum in Stockholm.[28]

Never had favourite worked for the fall of a Minister with less personal animosity than Madame du Barry for that of Choiseul. But for the continual promptings of the ignoble triumvirate whose tool she had had the misfortune to become, and particularly of d'Aiguillon, who had striven to inspire her with something of his own hatred of Choiseul, it is doubtful whether she would ever have embarked upon the struggle with the Minister, much less have carried it through to the bitter end. What resentment she had entertained for her adversary disappeared with his departure from the Court, and gave place to a feeling of sympathy and regret, of which an incident which occurred twelve months later affords us a striking proof.

When he had received the King's orders to retire to Chanteloup, Choiseul had been deprived of all his

[27] Here is the King's letter:
"The interest that you take in my success renders it the more agreeable to me. Baron de Lieven has given me a faithful account of the good will that you have shown for me, and I thank you for it sincerely. I reckon with confidence on the sentiments that you have always manifested for me, and I do not doubt that I shall often have occasion to speak to you of the gratitude with which I am very truly, Madame la comtesse du Barry. . . ."
[28] The Comtesse d'Armaillé's *La Comtesse d'Egmont d'après les lettres inédites à Gustave III.*, p. 275.

offices, with one exception, which, from a pecuniary point of view, was the most important. This was the post of Colonel-General of the Swiss troops in the French service, carrying with it a salary of 100,000 livres.

An impression appears to have prevailed that the office in question once conferred could not be taken away, and Louis XV., in bestowing it upon the duke in 1762, had assured him that he should hold it for life.

Moreover, the King, at the instance of Carlos III., had given his word that no further steps should be taken against the fallen Minister; and as the months went by and the salary continued to be paid to him, Choiseul became convinced that he would be allowed to retain his command. His astonishment and indignation, therefore, may be imagined when, on the night of December 6, 1771, a courier from the Court arrived at Chanteloup, bearing a letter from d'Aiguillon to Choiseul's friend, the Duc de Châtelet,[29] who was on a visit there, in which the duke was requested to inform his host that the King, having discovered that the post of Colonel-General of the Swiss was one which could only be held during his good pleasure, had decided that the welfare of his service would not permit him to leave it any longer in the hands of M. de Choiseul, who must, accordingly, send in his resignation forthwith. His Majesty would then be willing to consider the question of compensation, although he did not recognise that M. de Choiseul had any claim to be indemnified. The letter concluded with an intimation that the King's decision was irrevocable, and

---

[29] Louis Marie François du Châtelet d'Harancourt, son of Voltaire's " divine Emilie," and believed to be " one of the works of the philosopher." He had been French Ambassador at St. James's and Vienna, and was Colonel of the Régiment du Roi.

the words, *"Ce que dessus est ma façon de vouloir,"* in Louis' own hand.[30]

Du Châtelet duly communicated the contents of this very unwelcome epistle to Choiseul, who thereupon addressed to the King, not the resignation demanded, but a long letter, wherein, after protesting against the manner in which he was being treated, he demanded as compensation for the loss of his post (1) liberty to visit any part of France, Paris and the Court excepted; (2) settlement of all the debts he had contracted while in office, including three or four million livres which he had borrowed from his wife, and two million due to creditors;[31] (3) a revenue of 40,000 livres on the forest of Haguenau, of which he had been *grand bailli*, and forest rights worth about 800,000 livres; (4) a pension of 50,000 livres, with reversion to the duchess.

These modest demands were carried to Versailles by Du Châtelet, who was charged to deliver the letter into his Majesty's own hand, and not to intercede in his favour with either Ministers or mistress, "whose marks of interest would humiliate him."

However, Du Châtelet took upon himself to ignore these instructions and went to d'Aiguillon, whom he had known since boyhood. His reception in this quarter was far from encouraging. The Minister appeared surprised and "shocked" at the demands of M. de Choiseul, as well he might be, and though he

[30] M. Maugras's *La Disgrâce du Duc et de la Duchesse de Choiseul*, p. 149. Madame du Deffand *to* Horace Walpole, January 6, 1772.

[31] A few days after his dismissal from office, Choiseul had asked the King for three million livres to pay his debts. Louis assented and signed an order on the Treasury for that amount, but omitted to add the words, *"Bon pour trois millions,"* an omission which the Minister did not discover until some hours later. He had intended to ask the King to rectify the error at the next meeting of the Council, but, unfortunately for him, that meeting happened to be the one in which the King decided on his disgrace.

promised to procure an audience of the King for Du
Châtelet, did so with such very bad grace that his
visitor had a shrewd suspicion that it was to his machinations that Choiseul owed the loss of his post, which,
indeed, was the case,[32] and that he would use his influence to hinder Louis from granting the compensation asked for.

Much perturbed by the turn that events were taking,
Du Châtelet decided to have recourse to Madame du
Barry, and, having obtained an interview with the
lady, " exposed to her with warmth the enormity of
the injustice done to M. de Choiseul and the harshness
and bad faith of his enemies."

The favourite received him very kindly, informed
him that as " there was not a crown in the Treasury "[33]
there might be some difficulty in complying with M.
de Choiseul's demands, and that the question of liberty
to leave Chanteloup had better not be raised for the
present, but readily promised to do all in her power
to further his efforts on his friend's behalf. " I was
satisfied with her replies," writes Du Châtelet to
Choiseul. " She told me that she entertained no ill-
feeling towards you; that she would be charmed to
avail herself of the present occasion to prove it; that
what had happened in the past was entirely your fault;
that, at the beginning, she had done everything she
could to prevent it; but that you must feel that matters
could not be again on the same footing as they once
were, not as regarded herself, for she was a mere no-

[32] D'Aiguillon appears to have instigated the Dauphin's brother,
the Comte de Provence, to ask for Choiseul's post. The count,
however, did not obtain it, as the Dauphin was so angry when
he heard what Provence had done that he protested against his
appointment; and the command of the Swiss was, in consequence, given to the youngest of the three brothers, the Comte
d'Artois, a boy of sixteen.
[33] Belleval tells us that such was the penury of the Treasury
at this period that the pay of the troops was in arrears.

body, but in regard to the King, whom you continually offended in the object of his affections."

Du Châtelet obtained the desired audience of the King, but it availed him little.

"Is that the resignation that you have there?" asked Louis, perceiving the letter in the duke's hand.

"No, Sire, but the proposals that M. de Choiseul has the honour to make to your Majesty."

"I do not wish to hear his proposals—I want his resignation," rejoined the King. And he declined to receive the letter, and referred Du Châtelet back to d'Aiguillon.[84]

Here, as may be supposed, he received scant consolation, so he despatched a courier to Chanteloup with a letter conjuring Choiseul "in the name of God to yield to force," lest worse evils should befall him, after which he rushed off to Madame du Barry, whom he informed that he was in despair, that his friend's interests were his own, that his honour was compromised, and so forth.

Madame du Barry appeared "touched" and "even terrified" by his agitation, declared that she was sincere in her desire to help him, and said that, although she knew nothing about finance, she would endeavour to obtain for Choiseul a pension of 100,000 livres. "She concluded," writes Du Châtelet to Choiseul, "by assuring me that d'Aiguillon had no power over her; that she gave audience to all who came to her, and did as she wished. She promised to let me know on the morrow how she had succeeded."

Next day, the favourite sought out the King, and remained closeted with him for two hours and a half, pleading the cause of the man who had persecuted her so cruelly. "So long an interview augured well for

[84] Madame du Deffand *to* Horace Walpole, January 6, 1772.

me," writes Du Châtelet, " and I flattered myself somewhat on my success."[35]

The King was very angry with Madame du Barry
for interfering, as was d'Aiguillon also; but at the
next meeting of the Council the matter was discussed,
and Du Châtelet informed that his Majesty was willing to accord Choiseul a pension of 50,000 livres, with
reversion to the duchess, and 200,000 livres in cash.

In the meantime, Choiseul had sent in an uncon-
ditional resignation of his post, a judicious step, which
so delighted poor Du Châtelet, who was becoming
quite ill with anxiety, that, " in a transport of joy, he
twice kissed the courier who brought the letter."
However, if we are to believe Besenval, who was then
staying at Chanteloup, the good effect produced by
the resignation must have been largely discounted by a
letter which Choiseul sent through the post, " intended to be brought to the notice of the King and
calculated to exasperate him."

In great alarm, Du Châtelet followed the Court to
Choisy to entreat Madame du Barry to continue her
exertions on his friend's behalf, and found her with
the King and d'Aiguillon in the salon. After listening
to what he had to say, she turned to d'Aiguillon and
said, " It must be so." Then she engaged the King
and Minister in conversation, with the result that, as
the former took his place at the card-table, he exclaimed, " A pension of 60,000 livres and 100,000
écus (300,000 livres) in cash."[36]

And so, thanks to the efforts of the faithful Du
Châtelet and the good offices of the kind-hearted
favourite—who certainly on this occasion gave an example of Christian charity which *Mesdames* and some

[35] *Mémoires de M. le Duc de Choiseul, écrits par lui-même,* ii. 1,
et seq.
[36] *Mémoires du Baron de Besenval,* i. 290.

of their devout friends would have done well to imitate—Choiseul received very handsome compensation for the loss of his command, and was enabled to pay his bread bill, though apparently not much besides, as when he died, on May 8, 1785, he was several million livres in debt.

It would be pleasing could we record that Madame du Barry's services met with some recognition from her former adversary. Such, unfortunately, was very far from being the case. Not only did she never receive a single word of thanks, but in the duke's unpublished Memoirs we find her described more than once by an exceedingly unpleasant term; and we cannot, therefore, subscribe to the opinion of Choiseul's enthusiastic biographer, M. Maugras, that it would have been impossible for any one to have shown in misfortune " *une âme plus forte et plus elevée.*"[37]

[37] *La disgrâce du Duc et de la Duchesse de Choiseul,* p. 168.

CHAPTER XIII

THE position of Madame du Barry after the disgrace of Choiseul recalls that of Madame de Pompadour after the dismissal of her implacable enemy, the Comte d'Argenson, in February 1757. So long as the two Ministers in question retained their credit, neither lady could feel absolutely secure; the moment they had contrived their ruin, all restraints were removed, all fears banished, and they began to reign in real earnest.

But there the comparison ends. " The life, the whole life, of Madame de Pompadour belongs to history. It is a life of affairs, of intrigues, of negotiations, the maintenance of a political rôle, a public exercise of power, a commerce at all hours with Ministers, with Secretaries of State, with men of the sword, with men of money, with men of the robe, a control of the interests of the nation, and of the will of the King, an influence on the destinies of France and of Europe."[1]

Madame du Barry, as we have observed elsewhere, cared for none of these things.[2] Her adversary, Choiseul, overthrown, her *protégé*, d'Aiguillon, promoted, she hastened to resign the uncongenial part which circumstances had, for a few months, forced her to play, and became again merely " *la mieux entretenue du royaume.*"

[1] E. and J. de Goncourt's *La Du Barry*, p. 122.
[2] She did, however, out of curiosity, attend one meeting of the Council, at which she sat upon the arm of the King's chair and played many " *petites singeries enfantines.*"

Nevertheless, she did not fail to appreciate the victory she had won, the sense of increased security, the knowledge that no longer need she be on her guard lest some trifling indiscretion should be seized upon and converted by a powerful and unscrupulous foe into a formidable weapon against her; and, after her own fashion, she enjoyed its fruits as fully as ever had Madame de Pompadour. For the first two years of her reign there had been some bounds to her extravagance; now there were none, even as there seemed no limits to the infatuation of the old King and the shameful complaisance of the Comptroller-General, who not only persuaded Louis XV. to double her monthly pension of 30,000 livres, but instructed Beaujon, the banker of the Court, that the drafts of Madame du Barry were to be accepted as " orders of the King," with the result that in four years the lady drew upon the Treasury for no less a sum than 6,427,803 livres![3]

And so the coffers of the State became the cash-box of the favourite, and the money wrung from the pockets of the luckless taxpayers by the adventurous Terray was poured out in a ceaseless flood on a host of modistes and milliners, goldsmiths and jewellers, furniture dealers and bric-à-brac merchants; on silks and laces, on pendants, and earrings, and bracelets, on superb toilette-sets[4] and costly porcelain, and, what is perhaps less reprehensible, on pictures and statuary,

[3] In addition to all this, on the death of the Comte de Clermont, in 1772, she was accorded one-third of his pension of 300,000 livres, and she is also believed to have received immense sums from the sale of monopolies, offices, commissions in the army and so forth.

[4] Jacques Roettiers, the famous goldsmith, received orders from the King for a " toilette tout en or " for Madame du Barry, but the cost prevented its completion. The accounts sent in by Roettiers père et fils to the favourite were as follows: January 1770, 34,795 livres; August 1771, 156,028 livres; May 1772, 56,657 livres; November 1773, 93,606 livres.

and even books—books gorgeously bound in red
morocco and stamped with the Du Barry arms and
device. Her toilettes and jewels and equipages were
the admiration and despair of all the ladies of the
Court. Pagelle, the renowned modiste of the *Trois
Gallants* in the Rue Saint-Honoré, provided her with
" *un grand habit de satin blanc chiné en argent, brodé
en paillons verts et roses,*" &c., &c.—the full description
of the garment would occupy the better part of a page
—at a cost of 10,500 livres; Vanot, of the Rue Saint-
Denis, with " *une tres-belle toilette de point d'Argentan
et son surtout,*" and " *une parure de déshabillé,*" which
cost respectively 9000, and 7000 livres; while gowns
at 2000, 3000 and 4000 livres figure in her accounts
with almost monotonous regularity. She had a *parure*
of diamonds valued at 450,000 livres, a dinner-service
of Sèvres porcelain for which she paid 21,438 livres,
and a magnificent *vis-à-vis,* the panels of which were
decorated with her arms and "the famous battle-cry,
' *Boutez-en-avant,*' " encircled by doves, pierced hearts,
quivers, torches—" in short, all the attributes of the
god of Paphos." This resplendent equipage, which
was the gift of the grateful d'Aiguillon, was reported
to have cost 52,000 livres.

The apartments of the favourite at Versailles formed
a series of boudoirs, each of which seemed to those
who entered for the first time more elegant than another. The chimney-piece in the salon was adorned
with a magnificent clock, " around which a world of
porcelain figures disported themselves." In the same
room were two commodes of priceless lacquer, one relieved by figures in gold, the other decorated with fine
porcelain *plaques,* which, we are told, had not their
equals in Europe. From the ceiling hung a lustre of
rock-crystal, which had cost 16,000 livres, and in a
corner stood a beautiful piano, the work of the famous

Clicot, the case of which was of rosewood, exquisitely
inlaid and lavishly gilded. The cabinet contained a
writing-table plated with porcelain, and an inkstand
which was a masterpiece of the goldsmith's art; while
in the bedroom was a wonderful clock, which represented " the Three Graces supporting the vase of
Time," and Love indicating the hour with his arrow.
" The most exquisite objects of art, marvels of up-
holstery, bronzes, marbles, statuettes, abounded in this
asylum of voluptuous pleasure. It was the last word
of luxury."[5]

A whole regiment of servants was employed to do
the bidding of the mistress of all these treasures:
eight *valets-de-chambre* and a like number of footmen, two coachmen, three postilions, three running-
footmen, two sedan-chairmen, five grooms, a *maître
d'hôtel,* a clerk to keep the household accounts, two
valets de garde-robe, a Swiss and two gardeners.

Never had such gorgeous menials been seen before.
On ordinary occasions, the *valets-de-chambre* and
footmen contented themselves with " coats of chamois
cloth gallooned with silver, waistcoats and breeches
of chamois silk, with buttons, garters, and buckles of
silver." But on occasions of ceremony, as, for instance,
when the King dined or supped with their mistress, they
appeared arrayed in " coats of scarlet cloth gallooned
with gold and with *basques* of white Naples silk, scarlet silk waistcoats and breeches, with gold buttons,
garters, and buckles." The coachmen were attired in
sky-blue cloth, and chamois waistcoats with silver buttons; the running-footmen, postilions—the lady was
never drawn by less than four horses—and grooms, in
blue and silver; the sedan-chairmen in scarlet and

---

[5] E. and J. de Goncourt's *La Du Barry,* p. 34 *et seq.* Imbert de
Saint Armand's *Les Femmes de Versailles: Les Dernières Années
de Louis XV* 142 *et seq.*

silver; while the rest of the household wore a blue livery gallooned with silver.

Until the close of the year 1772 Madame du Barry had no residence at Versailles, save her apartments in the château; the majority of her servants being lodged at the Hôtel de Luynes, as it was impossible for their mistress to accommodate more than a few of them. This arrangement was not without its inconveniences, so, in December 1772, the favourite purchased from Binet, first *valet-de-chambre* to the Dauphin, for 80,-000 livres, an hôtel, or rather pavilion, situated at the corner of the Avenue de Paris and the Rue de Montboron. Her new acquisition, however, proved to be far too small for the lady's requirements, and she, accordingly, bought some four acres of land between the pavilion and the Rue de Montboron, and instructed the architect Ledoux to build her an hôtel here. For some reason, which, curiously enough, is not stated, the erection of this hôtel, the chief feature of which was a splendid porch, appears to have given umbrage to the Dauphin, but, according to M. Le Roi, the more he objected, the more ostentatiously was the work pressed on.

About the middle of December 1770, Madame du Barry, finding that, notwithstanding the alterations and additions designed by Gabriel, her château of Louveciennes was still too small to permit of her entertaining on the scale she desired, had commissioned the architect Ledoux to construct a pavilion beside it; and at the beginning of January 1772 the building was completed.[6]

This beautiful pavilion, about which so much has been written, consisted of a simple *rez-de-chaussée*

[6] Some writers have stated that the pavilion was completed in three months, and that Ledoux owed his place in the Academy of Architecture to the amazing celerity with which he carried out the work; but this was not the case.

built of Saint-Leu stone, surmounted by a belvedere.
It was about twenty to twenty-five feet in height and
the same in breadth, with five windows on each side.

A flight of seven or eight steps led up to a peristyle
of four Ionic columns, the pediment of which was
adorned by a Bacchanalian dance of children in low-
relief, the work of Lecomte.

The vestibule, which served on great occasions as
a dining-room, was built of grey marble with four
Corinthian pilasters. Between the pilasters, the capi-
tals of which were lavishly gilded, were placed four
groups of women holding horns of plenty, beautifully
executed by Lecomte and Pajou. At either end of
the vestibule were tribunes for the accommodation of
musicians, and over the door leading into the main
salon was the portrait of a person decorated with the
cordon bleu, probably the King. Around the room ran
a frieze of Cupids, amidst which were placed the
united arms of Madame du Barry and her husband.[7]

Behind the vestibule was the main salon, on either
side of which were two smaller salons. The main
salon contained *dessus-de-portes* by Fragonard,[8] some

---

[7] And not, says M. Vatel, those of Madame du Barry and
Louis XV., as the Goncourts state, which may be seen by exam-
ining the beautiful water-colour by Moreau *le jeune,* now in the
Louvre, of which we shall presently speak. The arms which
Madame du Barry had invented for the mythical Vaubernier
were a chevron, a hand, and two roses.

[8] Fragonard was also commissioned to paint four panels for
this room, but they did not take their place upon the walls for
which they were destined, the reason being, according to the
writer of an interesting article in the " New York Critic " (November 1901), that the artist had been a shade too explicit in
the matter of portraiture. " Louis XV. resented being painted
even as a young and fanciful shepherd in company with the
favourite. The royal sybarite refused to sanction any record of
his profligacy, and Fragonard's idyl, which traced in such persuasive accents the love of King and courtesan, was supplanted
by decorations in no way comparable to this dream of youthful
tenderness." These panels are now in the possession of Mr.
Pierpont Morgan.

The sculptor Pajou modelling the bust of Madame du Barry, by many considered his masterpiece, now in the Museum of the Louvre.

—p. 177

From the painting by Henri Cain.

beautiful arabesques, delicately carved by Métivier and Feuillet, and a console in which the celebrated Gouthière had surpassed himself. But, according to Madame Vigée Lebrun, the finest ornament of the room was the superb view which its windows commanded, embracing as it did Saint-Germain, Le Vésinet, Saint-Denis, the Seine in all its windings, and, in the misty distance, Paris.

Of the two smaller salons, that on the right, the ceiling, of which had been painted by Restout and the *dessus-de-portes* by Drouais, contained four magnificent pictures by Vien, symbolical of "the progress of love in the heart of young girls," and two little marble figures from the chisel of Vassé, one an *Amour,* the other representing Folly with a mask in his hand; that on the left was adorned with mirrors, which reflected a superb mantelpiece of lapis lazuli. On the ceiling Briard had painted an allegory of love in the country.[9]

"Nothing could be more rich, nothing more gorgeous, than the furniture and decorations of the interior," says a contemporary writer; "the tables, the chimney-pieces, the locks, the window-fastenings, &c., all are of exquisite finish and excessive delicacy." The chronicler, however, blames this excess of richness and elegance as being in bad taste. "It is neither richness nor delicate workmanship which constitute beauty; it is the art of giving to each object the character which belongs to it."[10]

Outside the pavilion were two marble figures, the work of the sculptor Allegrain; one representing Diana pursued by Actæon, the other a bather—a woman—emerging from the water. The head of

[9] Dulaure's *Nouvelle Description des environs de Paris* (Paris, 1786), ii. 17, *et seq.* E. and J. de Concourt's *La Du Barry,* p. 130. *Vatel's Histoire de Madame du Barry,* ii. 116, *et seq.*

[10] Dulaure's *Nouvelle Description des environs de Paris* (Paris, 1786), ii. 19.

Diana reproduced very plainly the features of Madame du Barry.

The Louvre possesses a beautiful water-colour by Moreau *le jeune*, representing a *fête* given by Madame du Barry to Louis XV. at Louveciennes, on December 27, 1771, probably for the inauguration of the new pavilion. The drawing is thus admirably described by M. Vatel:

"We are in the grand dining-room of the pavilion, recognisable by its tribunes and the four groups of women by Lecomte and Pajou, only one sees that the horns of plenty that they hold are utilised to serve as torches. Above is an Olympian ceiling, which recalls to mind the Salon d'Hercule at Versailles; below a square porch in black and white marble. A dazzling clearness, rendered by the painter with consummate art, pervades the whole room. The lustres of Gouthière blaze like the lights in a picture of Schalken; everything breathes a festal air.

"The King sits by Madame du Barry's side, a score of persons are at the supper-table; great ladies and beribboned noblemen.

"About the table move a crowd of lackeys, carrying dishes or waiting upon the guests; some of them with their three-cornered hats on their heads, their swords by their sides, their red coats and blue facings, would appear to be Gardes Suisses.

"The King seems to have his own private servants, attentive behind his chair. He is speaking to no one, and is isolated and grave in the midst of this joyous atmosphere; his hand rests nonchalantly on the table near his plate; his glance is mournful; his expressionless face is that of a bored man.

"On his right is Madame du Barry, perfectly recognisable. One would say that Moreau had copied or recalled the bust of Pajou. She wears a white or rose-coloured gown. We can distinguish her diamond earrings and the necklace which descends to her bare and opulent bosom.

"Next her, some little distance away, is a great nobleman wearing the *cordon bleu*. We seem to recognise in him the Maréchal de Richelieu, to judge by his statuette in the Louvre and the portrait in the Bibliothèque de l'Arsenal. His neighbour might be, according to a pure supposition on our part, the Maréchale de Mirepoix; she is turning round and placing something, probably sweetmeats, in the hand of Zamor.[11] The latter is recognisable by his tawny complexion, his size, and his costume. On his head is a white cap adorned with a plume, and he wears a rose-coloured coat and high black boots. Another personage, who is dressed in Madame du Barry's livery, attracts attention by the air of importance with which he carries in his arms a little greyhound, probably that of the mistress of the house.

" We observe one of her servants approach the favourite with an appearance of eagerness, a dish in

[11] Zamor was Madame du Barry's Indian page. Many writers call him a negro; but this is incorrect, as he was a native of Bengal, who had been brought to France by the captain of an English ship. He was about seven years old when the countess took him into her service—a step which, as we shall see hereafter, she had bitter reason to regret. His mistress had him taught to read and write, and, on July 4, 1772, he was baptized at the Church of Notre Dame at Versailles, the sponsors being " the High and Puissant Prince Louis François Joseph de Bourbon, Comte de la Marche, represented by his concierge, and the High and Puissant Dame Benedicte de Vaubergny (*sic*) Comtesse du Barry, represented by her *femme-de-chambre*." Zamor was a great favourite with Madame du Barry and also with the old King, to whom his impish pranks caused great amusement. According to the *Anecdotes,* Louis rewarded his antics by appointing him Governor of the Château and Pavilion of Louveciennes, with a salary of 600 livres, and ordered Maupeou to draw up the brevet of the appointment and affix thereto the great seal; but this, like the story of Zamor collecting cockchafers and putting them into the Chancellor's wig, is probably a myth.

one hand, his serviette in the other; he seems to be
whispering in her ear, and to be informing her of
some important incident connected with his duties.
Madame du Barry listens attentively, and her eyes
appear to be in search of something.

"The elaborate supper is not an orgy; it is a Court
banquet, ceremoniously served, in accordance with all
the rules of etiquette. The morganatic couple permit
themselves in public a familiarity which gives us an
excellent idea of the position of a *maîtresse déclarée*."[12]

[12] Vatel's *Histoire de Madame du Barry,* ii. 123, *et seq.*

CHAPTER XIV

ALTHOUGH Madame du Barry's influence over Louis XV. was, in all probability, greater than that of her predecessor in the King's affections, her hopes of obtaining the almost general recognition of her position which had been accorded to Madame de Pompadour, during the latter part of her reign, were fated never to be realised. For this there were several reasons. One lay, of course, in the difference between the personalities of the two favourites. The life of Madame de Pompadour previous to her " elevation" had been irreproachable, while she was one of the most accomplished women of her time —a woman, indeed, who, had she but been born to the purple, any nation might have been proud to welcome as its queen. The early career of Madame du Barry, as we have seen, was not one which would bear investigation, and, beyond her gaiety and good nature, she had no qualities which might serve to reconcile the Court to her sway. Another reason was the resentment aroused by the dismissal of Choiseul. Madame de Pompadour, it is true, had been directly responsible for the dismissal of half a dozen Ministers; but neither Orry, Maurepas, the two d'Argensons, Machault, nor Bernis had had any very considerable following, and their misfortunes had been, in consequence, received with comparative indifference, whereas Choiseul's partisans comprised the most intellectual portion of the nation, and his fall was regarded as a public calamity. A third cause was to

be found in the fact that, even in the few years that
had elapsed since the death of Madame de Pompadour, the doctrines which were steadily undermining
the whole social fabric had made material progress;
new ideas, new conceptions of monarchy and its duties,
were spreading fast among all classes; people were
no longer inclined to regard with complacence the
spectacle of a royal mistress squandering the public
money upon a hundred whims and caprices.

But it would appear to have been to a different
cause to which Madame du Barry attributed her failure to overcome the hostility of an influential section
of the Court, and to remove which all her efforts were
now directed. This was the attitude persisted in by
the young Dauphiness, who, in spite of the representations of Mercy, could not be prevailed upon to accord "the most foolish and impertinent creature imaginable" the slightest mark of recognition, and treated
her and her partisans with the utmost disdain.

Towards the end of June 1771, d'Aiguillon, who
had met with a very icy reception from Marie Antoinette on the occasion of his presentation to her as
Minister of Foreign Affairs, had an interview with
Mercy, in which, after eulogising the beauty, grace,
intelligence, and so forth of the Dauphiness, he informed the Ambassador that he had been commanded
by the King to intimate to him that his Majesty had
observed with annoyance "signs of an aversion too
strongly marked towards the persons who composed
the intimate society of the King"; that not only did
the princess refuse them the recognition due to members of the Court, but added "words of satire and
hatred"; that this was creating much ill-feeling, and
destroying the tenderness of the King towards her,
and that it was very essential that it should cease.

Mercy hastened to express his regret and his conviction that the blame for the unfortunate state of affairs of which d'Aiguillon had spoken rested not with the princess herself, but with those who had dared to speak to her " of things she ought never to know or to see"; hinted at the " pernicious counsels " of *Mesdames,* and assured the Minister that " the least tender and affectionate insinuations coming from the King" could not fail to produce their effect, and that he would do everything in his power to further his Majesty's wishes. " It is clear," he writes to Maria Theresa, " that the proceeding of the Duc d'Aiguillon had been planned on the advice of Madame du Barry, with the intention of gradually inducing Madame la Dauphine to treat the favourite better."

The Empress, who had been much alarmed by the evidence of Madame du Barry's influence afforded by the fall of Choiseul, and was very dubious as to the attitude of d'Aiguillon towards the Franco-Austrian alliance, and still more so with regard to the reception her designs upon Poland were likely to meet with at Versailles, lost no time in despatching a letter of re-monstrance to her daughter. She informs her that she has been told that her reception of d'Aiguillon had left much to be desired; that she held herself aloof from all his party; that they were of the King's Court as well as herself; and that she should submit to his Majesty's will " with the respect and obedience of a child." " It ought to suffice for your favour that the King distinguishes such or such an one, without ex-amining their merits."

She concludes by warning her against *Mesdames,* who, " filled with virtue and possessing real merit, have never learned how to make themselves loved or respected either by their father or the public. Everything which is said or done in their circle is common knowledge, and, in the end, all will be laid at your door, and you alone will bear the blame."[1]

Her words, joined to the representations of Mercy, were not without effect. On July 24, the Ambassador writes from Compiègne that, on receipt of the Empress's letter, the princess had become very grave and thoughtful; that the same evening, while playing lansquenet with the King and the Royal Family, she had found herself seated next to Madame du Barry, and had shown how highly she valued the Imperial advice by displaying "neither disgust nor temper," but, on the contrary, speaking to the favourite, whenever the incidents of the game required that she should do so, "gracefully and without affectation, saying neither too much nor too little." Nor was this all, for next day the Duc d'Aiguillon, happening to present himself while the princess was at play, met with an extremely gracious reception, "the Dauphiness speaking to him frequently with a charming air of gaiety"; which condescension appears to have so astonished the new Minister that, consummate courtier though he was, he could only reply in monosyllables.

Maria Theresa expresses her satisfaction at the good news in her next letter to Mercy:

"I am very pleased that my daughter has begun to treat the Duc d'Aiguillon better. Without entering into their personalities, she ought to be the same to all the members of the dominant party, even to the Comtesse du Barry, and speak to her on any unimportant matter as she would to every other lady whom the King admits to his Court; she should even distinguish her. She ought to ignore what this woman is and treat her well, without condescending to anything unworthy."[2]

And to Marie Antoinette she writes:

[1] Letter of July 9, 1771.   [2] Letter of August 10, 1771.

" Mercy informs me that you have, on his advice, begun to treat the ruling party with courtesy, and have even addressed a few vague remarks in that direction, which have had a marvellous effect. I do not enlarge upon this matter; Mercy is charged to speak to you freely; I am only delighted that you lend yourself so promptly to his counsel."[3]

Madame du Barry, however, was not satisfied with "a few vague remarks"; she desired a more formal recognition of her position from the first lady in the land, and had made up her mind to obtain it; and, accordingly, gave the King no rest until he had promised that he would himself interview Mercy, with a view to putting an end to the cruel humiliations which, she declared, were rendering her life miserable.

" I was invited to sup with the Comtesse de Valentinois," writes the Ambassador, " and repaired thither with the Nuncio and the Sardinian Ambassador. We found there the Duc and Duchesse d'Aguillon, the Duc de la Vrillière, a *dame du palais,* some other ladies in the service of the Comtesse de Provence,[4] and the Comtesse du Barry. It was the first time that I had found myself in the company of this woman. The Sardinian Ambassador spoke to her first as to a person with whom he was well acquainted; the Nuncio showed himself very anxious to join in the conversation. I thought it incumbent upon me to show more reserve, and it was not until the favourite had addressed me that I allowed myself to converse freely with her. I received, on her side, a more gracious reception than the others were accorded. I did not sit down to table, and the Comtesse du Barry, giving as her reason that she was compelled to return to her apartments before

[3] Letter of August 17, 1771.
[4] Louis Marie Joséphine of Savoy, daughter of Victor Amadeus III., King of Sardinia. She had been married to the Comte de Provence, June 14, 1771.

eleven o'clock, did not sup either. The conversation
was interrupted by the Duc d'Aiguillon, who, taking
me aside, informed me that the King desired to speak
to me in private, and that he had charged him to propose that, the following day, on his return from the
chase, I should repair to the Comtesse du Barry's
apartments, where his Majesty would see me. I replied
without hesitation that I would go wherever the King
required me."

The following morning, the Dauphiness received the
Ambassadors, and, approaching Mercy, said in a low
voice: " I felicitate you on the good company in which
you supped on Sunday."

" Madame," replied Mercy, " an event much more
remarkable is going to happen to-day, and to-morrow I
shall have the honour of rendering an account of it to
your Royal Highness."

That evening, at seven o'clock, the Ambassador presented himself at the favourite's apartments in the
château. D'Aiguillon came to meet him, and informed
him that the King had just returned from hunting
and was dressing, after which he carried off two or
three persons who were present into an adjoining
room, under the pretence of looking at a picture, leaving Mercy alone with Madame du Barry.

The favourite seized the opportunity to tell the Ambassador how delighted she was that the King's idea
of giving him audience in her apartments had afforded
her an opportunity of making his acquaintance, and
that she wished to take advantage of it to speak to him
of a painful subject which affected her deeply. She
was not ignorant, she said, that, for a long time past,
people had been engaged in endeavours to ruin her
with the Dauphiness, and that, to effect their object,
" they had had recourse to the most atrocious calum-
nies" in daring to attribute to her disrespectful words

concerning her Royal Highness. So far from having to reproach herself with a crime so terrible, she had always been numbered among those who "justly extolled the charms of the archduchess." Although the princess had constantly treated her with severity and a kind of contempt, she had never indulged in any complaints against her Royal Highness, but only against those who inspired her to these marks of dislike, and that whenever a question had arisen of granting some request made by the Dauphiness, she had used her influence with the King in the princess's favour.

Mercy assured the favourite that she was under a complete misapprehension in supposing the Dauphiness capable of sentiments so contrary to her character, and, we may suppose, paid the lady many pretty compliments, which pleased her so much that she became quite familiar, confided to her guest some interesting details about her life, her plans for amusing the King, her opinion of certain personages of the Court, and so forth.

The confidences were interrupted by the arrival of Louis XV., who entered by the private staircase between his apartments and those of his mistress.

" Must I retire, *Monsieur?*" inquired Madame du Barry.

Mercy's astonishment at hearing the most Christian King addressed by such an appellation was so profound that he would appear to have had some difficulty in persuading himself that he was not dreaming.[5] But his Majesty seemed to take it quite as a matter of

[5] " Although I pass my life here in witnessing extraordinary things, I am not often able to regard them as dreams. I have seen the King in company with Madame du Barry; she calls him ' Monsieur,' and treats him as an equal. He takes it in very good part, and even in my presence, did not appear annoyed at his favourite behaving thus."—Letter of Mercy *to* Kaunitz, September 2, 1771.

course, and smilingly intimated to the favourite that
he wished to be alone with the Ambassador, upon
which the lady withdrew, and the King, turning to
Mercy, said: "Up to the present you have been the
Ambassador of the Empress; now I beg you to be
my Ambassador, at least for a time." Then, with
much embarrassment, he began to speak of Marie
Antoinette, declaring that he loved the princess with all
his heart, that he found her charming, but that she was
young and impressionable, and, since her husband was
not in a position to advise her, it was impossible that
she should escape the snares that intrigue laid for her;
that he had remarked with displeasure that she had
conceived certain prejudices and dislikes, obviously
the result of the evil counsels of those by whom she
was surrounded, and that she was treating very badly
certain persons whom he had admitted to his private
circle of friends. "See Madame la Dauphine frequently," he concluded. "I authorise you to say to her,
on my behalf, whatever you think necessary; she is
being given bad advice, and must not be allowed to
follow it. You see what confidence I have in you,
since I tell you what is in my mind in regard to the
private life of my family."

Mercy endeavoured to make the King comprehend
that it would be far better, as the matter under discussion was of so very delicate a nature, if his Majesty
would take upon himself the task of remonstrating
with the Dauphiness. But Louis, as is well known, had
an invincible repugnance to personal explanations with
members of the Royal Family, and on the rare occasions on which he contrived to summon up sufficient
courage to reprimand them, invariably had recourse
to writing; and the Ambassador, finding his representations useless, consented to accept the commission
offered him, and left the château, not altogether dis-

pleased at finding that he had become, in the short space of two days, the friend of the favourite and the confidant of the King.

In accordance with his promise to Louis XV., Mercy lost no time in seeking an interview with Marie Antoinette, and pointing out to her the inconsistency of her attitude towards the mistress. If, said he, you wish to show by your behaviour that you are aware of the rôle that Madame du Barry plays at Court, your dignity requires that you should request the King to forbid this woman to appear henceforth in your presence; if, on the contrary, you wish to appear ignorant of the true position of the favourite, you ought to treat her as you would any other lady of the Court, and, when occasion offers, speak to her, were it only once, "which would put an end to all specious pretext for recriminations." Then he advised her to have a few minutes' conversation with the King on the matter, and persuaded the Abbé de Vermond to urge the same course upon the princess. But whatever effect their representations had was quickly undone by *Mesdames;* Marie Antoinette declared that "her courage failed her," and all that she could be prevailed upon to promise was to speak once to the favourite.

The Ambassador at once communicated this welcome intelligence to Madame du Barry, upon which that lady announced her intention of joining the circle of the Dauphiness on the following Sunday, and giving the princess an opportunity of redeeming her promise. Mercy hurried off to warn Marie Antoinette, who answered that she was prepared to keep her word, but insisted that he should be present. It was then arranged that on Sunday, at the close of the evening's card-playing, Mercy was to approach the favourite and engage her in conversation, and that the Dauphiness, in passing round the room, should stop and speak to him,

and then, as if taking an opportunity, address a few
words to Madame du Barry. Marie Antoinette declared that this was the only way in which she could
bring herself to do what he wished, as she felt so
afraid, and Mercy implored her to be firm, and strictly
enjoined upon her to say nothing about their plan to
her aunts. This the Dauphiness promised readily
enough, but broke her word, with what result we shall
now see.

" In the evening," says Mercy, " I went to the
assembly; the Comtesse du Barry was present with her
friends. Madame la Dauphine called me aside, and
told me that she was frightened, but that her intentions
remained unchanged. The game being at an end, her
Royal Highness sent me to place myself beside the
favourite, whom I engaged in conversation. In a moment all eyes were turned upon us. Madame la Dauphine began to speak to the ladies present; she reached
my side, and was not two paces away, when Madame
Adélaïde, who had not lost sight of her for a moment,
raised her voice and exclaimed: 'Let us go; it is
time to await the King at my sister Victoire's.' At
these words Madame la Dauphine turned away, and
the whole scheme came to nothing."

That same evening, presumably in anticipation of
victory, all the Ambassadors, including the Papal
Nuncio—who seems to have been one of the most as-
siduous of the favourite's courtiers, though the story
of his having put on the lady's slippers one morning
at her toilette is probably a myth—had been invited to
supper by Madame du Barry. Mercy was one of those
present, and was agreeably surprised to find that, " in
spite of the little humiliation which she had just experienced at the hands of Madame la Dauphine," his
fair hostess treated him with the utmost graciousness.
He explained to d'Aiguillon, who was among the

guests, what had passed that evening, and flattered himself that he had succeeded in throwing all the blame on the shoulders of *Mesdames*.

Presently, the King, on his way from the Council to sup, with the Royal Family, came in for a moment, impatient to learn the result of the Ambassador's little scheme, and, later in the evening returned, and, " having as it were pushed me into a corner," said, in a very confused manner: " Ah well! M. de Mercy, you have seen the Dauphiness? Your advice bears but little fruit; I shall have to come to your help"; and then turned away without giving the Ambassador time to reply.

To any one unacquainted with Louis XV.'s character those words might have been understood to imply that he meditated a personal remonstrance with the Dauphiness or *Mesdames*. But Mercy knew that it was perfectly hopeless to expect anything of the kind, and that the monarch would probably confine the marks of his displeasure to " sulks and silence" whenever the offending parties happened to approach him, and he, accordingly, sent an exhaustive account of the whole affair to Vienna and made strong representations to Marie Antoinette, warning her that comparisons were being made between her conduct and that of the Comtesse de Provence—who had lately made Madame du Barry supremely happy by speaking to her " without affectation,"—and very much to the disadvantage of the Dauphiness. The princess expressed due contrition, and pleaded in extenuation her fear of her aunts!

Mercy's "humble report" to Vienna brought a strong letter of remonstrance from Maria Theresa to her daughter, so strong indeed that the Empress judged it advisable to ask the Ambassador to read it before handing it to the Dauphiness, and to return it, if he considered that the strictures it contained were too severe.

MARIA THERESA *to* MARIE ANTOINETTE.

"Schönbrunn, September 30, 1771.

. . . " Marsy[6] has confirmed what all my letters tell me, namely, that you only act as your aunts direct. I esteem them, I love them, although they have never known how to make themselves either esteemed or loved by their own family or the public; and you wish to follow the same road. This fear and embarrassment of speaking to the King, the best of fathers! That of speaking to people to whom you are advised to speak! Confess this embarrassment, this fear of saying a simple 'Good-morning'; a word about a dress or some other trifle costs you so many grimaces! Actually grimaces, or worse! You have allowed yourself to be dragged into such bondage that your reason and even your duty are no longer able to guide you. I can no longer keep silent. After the conversation with Mercy and all that he impressed upon you that the King desired, that your duty demanded, that you should have dared to fail him! What good reason can you allege? None. You ought neither to know nor see the Barry in any other light than as a lady admitted to the Court and the society of the King. You are his first subject, you owe him obedience and submission; you owe an example to the courtiers, who execute the will of your master. If anything degrading, any familiarities were required of you, neither I nor any one else would counsel them, but an indifferent word, certain attitudes, not for the sake of the lady, but for your grandfather, your master, your benefactor! And you fail him so conspicuously on the first

---

[6] The Abbé de Marsy, a Lorrainer in the Austrian service, who had lately been on a visit to France.

occasion on which you could oblige him, and show him your attachment! Let us see now for what reason? A shameful complaisance for people who have reduced you to dependence, by treating you as a child, procuring you rides on horseback, on donkeys, amusements with children, with dogs. See the great reasons for your preference for them over your master, and which will render you ultimately ridiculous, unloved and unesteemed. You began so well; your judgment when not directed by others is always true and just. Let yourself be guided by Mercy; what happiness could either he or I have except your own happiness and the good of the State? Free yourself from these false ideas; it is for you, after the King, to lead, and not to be led away like a child when you wish to speak. You are afraid to speak to the King, but you are not afraid to disobey and disoblige him. I fear that, for a short time, I must permit you to avoid verbal explanations with him; but I insist that you convince him by all your actions of your respect and affection. . . . I have detained the courier until the first day of the month, and I cannot conceal from you that I was so overwhelmed by the news that he brought me that I needed time to recover. I do not demand that you should break with the company that you frequent; God forbid! But I wish you to take counsel of Mercy in preference to them, to see him more frequently, to speak to him of everything, and to communicate nothing that he says to you to others. Too much complaisance savours of degradation and weakness; you must know how to play your own part if you wish to be esteemed. If you suffer yourself to be discouraged, I foresee great troubles for you, nothing but mischief-making and petty intrigues, which will render your life miserable. I desire to warn you of this; I conjure you to believe the advice of a mother who knows the world and idolises her children, and desires only to pass her last sad days in being of use to them. I embrace you tenderly; do not think me offended, but touched and occupied with your welfare."

The vigorous language in which Maria Theresa addresses her daughter in the aforegoing letter was dictated by more weighty consideration than the young princess's personal welfare. The seizure of Zips by Austrian troops the previous year had been followed by further aggressions in Poland, and Kaunitz was now actively negotiating with Frederick the Great and the Czarina Catherine for a share of that unhappy country. Sorely against her will had the Empress-Queen been brought to acquiesce in the participation of Austria in this iniquitous deed,[7] but having once consented, her scruples were laid aside, and all her energies henceforth devoted to making the best possible bargain with her fellow robbers and overcoming the opposition of the French Court.

That exhausted and ill-governed France would attempt armed intervention between the Eastern Powers and their prey was, of course, out of the question; but, on the other hand, there was every likelihood that she might take serious umbrage at the policy pursued by Austria, with the result that the alliance to which

[7] "When all my lands were invaded, and I knew not where in the world I should find a place to be brought to bed in, I relied on my good right and the help of God. But in this thing, where not only public law cries to Heaven against us, but also natural justice and sound reason, I must confess never in my life to have been in such trouble, and am ashamed to show my face. Let the Prince (Kaunitz) consider what an example we are giving to all the world, if, for a miserable piece of Poland, or Moldavia, or Wallachia, we throw our honour and reputation to the winds. I see well that I am alone, and no more in vigour; therefore I must, though to my very great sorrow, let things take their course."—Letter of Maria Theresa *to* Kaunitz (undated), cited in Carlyle's "Frederick the Great," x. 34.

Maria Theresa looked for support against the steadily increasing power of Prussia might be strained to breaking point. Hence it was, above all things, necessary to maintain the best possible personal relations with Louis XV.; hence her indignation and alarm at the impolitic conduct of her daughter.

Marie Antoinette's repugnance to make even the smallest concession to the feelings of Madame du Barry was not lessened by the persistent attempts of the favourite's partisans to control the appointments in the princess's Household. In the autumn of that year the Dauphiness's *dame d'atours,* the Duchesse de Villars, fell dangerously ill, the doctors who attended her pronounced her recovery hopeless, and the question of her successor at once began to agitate the minds of the intriguers of the Court. Such an opportunity of establishing a spy of his own about the person of the princess seemed too good to be lost, and the Duc de la Vauguyon forthwith determined to secure the post for his daughter-in-law, Madame de Saint-Mégrin. Prompted by him, the poor Duchesse de Villars thereupon wrote a letter to the Dauphin reminding him that the survivorship to the office in question had been promised to Madame de Saint-Mégrin by the late Dauphiness, and begging him to use his influence with the King to secure the nomination of that lady. The Dauphin had by this time contrived to overcome the awe with which he had once regarded the Duc de la Vauguyon, and was no longer submissive to his will. But he had an intense veneration for his mother's memory, and accordingly, without saying a word to Marie Antoinette, wrote to the King, soliciting the coveted appointment for Madame de Saint-Mégrin. Almost at the same moment, Louis received a letter from the Dauphiness protesting against the proposed nomination, a rumor of which had just reached her, and asking that the place might be given to one of her own ladies. The King, anxious to keep the peace, refused both requests, representing that Madame de Saint-Mégrin was too young for so important a charge, and that the Dauphiness was herself too young to be permitted to choose her *dame d'atours*.

Madame de Villars died, and the Dauphiness, in terror lest the Comtesse de Valentinois, Madame de Montmorency, or some other intimate of the favourite should be appointed, renewed her request that the duchess's successor should be chosen from her own Household. The King curtly refused, and expressed a hope that " his dear daughter" would receive whomever he might select for her with respect and submission.

Finally, it was announced that the Duchesse de Cossé had been appointed.

The Duchesse de Cossé was not one of the Du Barry clique, and she was a young woman of irreproachable virtue; but her husband, of whom we shall have a good deal to say hereafter, was one of the favourite's most intimate friends, and it was he who had solicited the appointment and obliged his wife, who cared little for Court life and passed most of her time in Paris, to accept it. When Marie Antoinette received the King's letter informing her of his choice, she "wept with rage," and her aversion to Madame du Barry became, if it were possible, greater than ever.

But the exigencies of the political situation were too strong to permit the Dauphiness to indulge her prejudices much longer; Maria Theresa wrote to Mercy imploring him to induce her daughter " to place herself on a footing more in conformity with the situation of affairs and my interests," and at length Marie Antoinette consented to speak to the favourite.

On New Year's Day it was the custom for all ladies who had been presented to pay their respects to the Royal Family. "I was informed that Madame du Barry had decided to perform that duty," writes Mercy, "and on New Year's Eve had an interview with Madame la Dauphine, and persuaded her Royal Highness, by every means in my power, not to treat the favourite badly. It was with great difficulty that I obtained a promise to this effect. The essential point was that *Mesdames* should not be informed, and this, happily, was attained." On the following morning, Madame du Barry presented herself before the Dauphiness, accompanied by the Duchesse d'Aiguillon and the Maréchale de Mirepoix. Marie Antoinette spoke first to the duchess, then, passing before Madame du Barry, "and regarding her without constraint or affectation," she said to her: "There are a great number of people at Versailles to-day."

At these simple words the Court was in a ferment of excitement. In the evening, the King embraced the Dauphiness tenderly and overwhelmed her with demonstrations of affection; the partisans of the favourite vied with one another in extolling the charms and virtues of the princess, while, on the other hand, *Mesdames* could not contain their indignation, and went so far as to accuse their hitherto docile pupil of treason.

Under the frowns and spiteful remarks of her aunts, poor Marie Antoinette began to repent of the step she had taken. "I went to the dinner of Madame l'Archiduchesse," writes Mercy. "When she rose from table, she said: 'I have followed your advice; here is the Dauphin, who will bear witness to my conduct.' The prince smiled, but said nothing. Then Madame l'Archiduchesse related to me what had passed, and concluded by saying, 'I have spoken this once, but I am quite decided to stop there; that woman shall never hear my voice again.' "[8]

However, a great point had been gained; Marie Antoinette had succeeded, temporarily at least, in shaking off the yoke of *Mesdames,* and, for some time, she continued to follow the counsels of her mother and Mercy, and threw no more obstacles in the path of their diplomacy. And so, for the sake of a few indifferent words from the Dauphiness to the mistress of the King, the old clients of France were abandoned to their fate, and Austria permitted to grab her share of poor distracted Poland without the smallest remonstrance from Versailles. " We must not speak of Polish affairs before you," said Louis XV., smiling, to his grand-daughter one day, " because your relatives are not of the same opinion as ourselves." That was the only hint of disapproval that was ever known to escape him.

That Maria Theresa was well aware that her large share of the " *gâteau des Rois* " depended upon the attitude of her daughter towards " the lady who enjoys the confidence of the King "—as the Swedish Ambassador styles the favourite—is clearly shown by her letters to Mercy. " To ward off these evils " (the possible rupture of the Franco-Austrian alliance) " from the monarchy and the family," she writes, " we must employ every means possible; and there is only my daughter, the Dauphiness, aided by your counsels and acquaintance with your surroundings, who can render this service to her family and her country. Above all, it is necessary that she should cultivate, by constant attentions and affection, the good will of the King, that she should strive to divine his wishes, that she should do nothing to offend him, that *she should treat the favourite well.* I do not require of her anything

[8] Mercy *to* Maria Theresa, January 23, 1772.

degrading, still less intimacy, but *attentions* due in consideration of her grandfather and her master, in consideration of the advantage which will redound to us and to the two Courts. *It may be that the alliance depends upon it!"*

The Court was at Compiègne when the Ambassador received this letter, and he immediately laid it before the Dauphiness, at the same time expatiating upon the influence which the all-powerful favourite might be able to exercise upon the policy of France, and the imperative necessity of conciliating both her and d'Aiguillon, not forgetting to impress upon the princess a due sense of the honour which the Empress was doing her in selecting one so young and inexperienced to co-operate in the union between the two kingdoms.

This lesson, which lasted three-quarters of an hour, was not lost upon Marie Antoinette, who writes to her mother :

" Mercy has shown me your letter, which has much affected me and given me cause for thought. I will do my utmost to contribute to the preservation of the alliance. Where should I be if a rupture occurred between my two families? I trust that *le bon Dieu* will preserve me from this misfortune, and inspire me with what I ought to do; I have prayed to Him earnestly."

That visit to Compiègne was in marked contrast to the one of the preceding year. The Dauphiness was graciousness itself to d'Aiguillon, actually going out of her way to address him, and, on more than one occasion, holding him in conversation for some minutes; and the duke, who was just then feeling very uneasy, owing to the coldness of the King, who had not yet succeeded in overcoming his old dislike of his one-time rival, and his suspicions that Maupeou was engaged in intriguing against him, began to flatter himself that he had found a new means of consolidating his position.

What was of a good deal more importance was that Madame du Barry also had no cause to complain of the princess's treatment of her. She was made happy by some remarks about the state of the weather, which the Dauphiness let fall one day when the favourite joined her circle. It is true that these precious words might very well have been addressed to the Duchesse d'Aiguillon, who accompanied her friend; but Madame du Barry chose to believe that they were intended for her, and retired enchanted to sing the praises of Madame la Dauphine in the ears of the gratified King. Her joy was augmented by finding that Marie Antoinette, importuned by Mercy, had begged the Dauphin to reappear at the supper-parties at the pavilion of the Petit Château, where the favourite did the honours; in consequence of which the prince had for some time refused to attend them, much to the annoyance of the King. And what great results followed from these trifles, which seem to the historian unworthy even of passing mention: these conversations with d'Aiguillon, these few remarks about the weather, the presence of the greedy Dauphin at a supper, from which he very probably returned with a bad attack of indigestion! The Du Barry party, which cared nothing for international politics, except so far as they might subserve its own interests, had no longer anything to gain by combating the Dauphiness, and, on the other hand, much to lose by disobliging the Empress-Queen. The concessions wrung from Marie Antoinette removed the last obstacles in the way of the partition of Poland; Austria signed the Treaties of St. Petersburg, and Versailles remained silent.[9]

But as the difficulties in Eastern Europe disappear-

[9] But Paris did not; pamphlets and satirical prints were to be seen everywhere, and public opinion severely blamed the apathy of the Government.

ed, Marie Antoinette, doubtless being of opinion that
the obligation to do violence to her feelings in the interests of the Court of Vienna was no longer so imperative, began to exhibit signs of restiveness which
filled Mercy with alarm. Towards the end of October,
the Court being now at Fontainebleau, the Ambassador went to visit Madame du Barry, who informed
him that she proposed to pay her respects to the Dauphiness on the following day, and that she looked to
him to ensure her a favourable reception. Mercy intimated that it would be hardly correct for him to open
such negotiations, and that, as the countess had been
satisfied with the manner in which she had been received at Compiègne, they were clearly superfluous.
Nevertheless, the moment he quitted the apartments
of the favourite he did not fail to hasten to Marie
Antoinette, to prepare the princess for the ordeal before her.

Now, it happened that, a few days earlier, the Dauphiness had complained bitterly to Mercy of what she
considered a piece of intolerable impertinence on the
part of Madame du Barry. The favourite, it appeared, had seized upon a piece of the château garden run-
ning level with the apartments of *Mesdames,* and
caused a new pavilion to be built there, the windows of
which commanded a part of the grounds reserved as
a private promenade for the Royal Family. The consequence was that the flame of the princess's dislike to
the mistress was at this particular moment burning
with exceptional vigour, and the Ambassador observed with trepidation "a sort of indecision" in the tone
in which she assured him that all would be well.

He, accordingly, determined to be present at the
reception of the favourite, and to put in an early
appearance in order to speak a word in season before
the crucial moment arrived; and when the Dauphin-

ess returned from Mass the following morning, she
found her mentor awaiting her. " I have been praying
earnestly," said she. " I prayed, ' Oh, God! if thou
wishest me to speak, make me speak. I will act as
Thou deignest to inspire me.' "

" I replied to Madame l'Archiduchesse," writes
Mercy, " that the voice of her august mother was the
only one capable of interpreting the will of God as
regarded her conduct, and that, therefore, she was
already inspired about what to do for the best."

Madame du Barry duly arrived, supported by the
Duchesse d'Aiguillon. Marie Antoinette spoke first to
the duchess, as etiquette prescribed; then looked in the
direction of the countess and observed that " the
weather had been so bad that she had been unable to
go out that day."

" This remark," says Mercy, " was not addressed
very directly to any one, and either owing to the tone
of voice, or the manner which accompanied it, the reception was not one of the best. Happily, M. le Dauphin
was present, and I attributed to this circumstance
Madame l'Archiduchesse's air of coldness and embarrassment. I repeated to the favourite what I had told
her the previous evening, that chance and various incidents determined, to a greater or less extent, her reception; and, finally, I succeeded in persuading her
that in reality she had been well received. She con-
fessed to me that she believed that she had remarked a
kindly intention on the part of Madame la Dauphine,
and that, in fact, she imagined that the presence of M.
le Dauphine had been the obstacle to a more favourable
demonstration. In short, up to the present, this occasion has passed off without comments or discontent,
and that is a great deal more than the actual facts permitted me to hope for."[10]

[10] Mercy *to* Maria Theresa, November 14, 1772.

For the following New Year's Day, Mercy summoned to his aid all the resources of his diplomacy to ensure a favourable reception for Madame du Barry. Not only did he extract a solemn promise from Marie Antoinette to speak directly to the lady, but he persuaded her to exhort the Dauphin, " who never spoke to any one," to do likewise.

The first part of the programme exceeded the Ambassador's fondest expectations. The Dauphin received the favourite most graciously, bowed, smiled, and mumbled something which was understood to be a compliment, to the amazement of the courtiers and the unconcealed delight of the recipient. But alas! her joy and the satisfaction of Mercy were but short-lived for the Dauphiness, evidently thinking that she had done her duty by persuading her husband to civility, declined to even open her lips, and included in this frigid reception the favourite's friends, the Duchesse d'Aiguillon and the Maréchale de Mirepoix.

All Mercy's work seemed again undone; but he rose to the occasion like a man, and argued that Marie Antoinette, in inducing the Dauphin, who feared women as he feared the small-pox, not only to smile upon, but even to speak to Madame du Barry, she had in reality done far more than if she had reserved her efforts for her own reception. His task was rendered the more difficult inasmuch as the favourite's chief adviser, Mademoiselle "Chon" du Barry, had already persuaded her sister-in-law that she had grave cause for complaint against the Dauphiness. However, eventually his diplomacy prevailed, and he left the lady under the impression that she had been rather well treated than otherwise.[11]

The visit of the Court to Compiègne in the following

[11] Mercy to Maria Theresa, January 16, 1773.

July was made the occasion of a very pretty little intrigue. Madame Adélaïde, although she governed her sisters, was, in her turn, governed by her *dame d'atours,* the Comtesse de Narbonne, between whom and d'Aiguillon the bitterest enmity had hitherto existed. D'Aiguillon, however, in the hope of strengthening his own position by reconciling Madame du Barry with the Royal Family, succeeded in persuading the countess that it might be to their common advantage to make peace and enter into an alliance. The countess consented, and a treaty was concluded, the terms of which were as follows: Madame de Narbonne's son was to receive the mayoralty of Bordeaux, and she herself was to be given an interest in the approaching renewal of certain monopolies. In return for these advantages, Madame de Narbonne was to secure better treatment of the favourite by Madame Adélaïde, and induce that princess to use her influence with the Dauphin, the Dauphiness, and the rest of the Royal Family to persuade them to follow her example.

The first part of the scheme succeeded admirably; Madame Adélaïde was easily won over by her *dame d'atours,* in whose counsels she reposed the most implicit confidence, promised that her own treatment of the favourite should henceforth leave nothing to be desired, and wrote a letter to the King, expressing her desire to oblige him in everything. His Majesty, highly gratified, replied with a very affectionate letter, in which he intimated that the best way in which his daughter could oblige him would be by bringing the Dauphin, "who displayed a marked aversion for the fair sex," to show more courtesy towards certain ladies whom the King honoured with his friendship.

Unfortunately, Madame Adélaïde had overrated the prestige which she enjoyed with her relatives; moreover, it was quickly discovered who was responsible for the amazing *volte-face* committed by the princess. The whole Royal Family were furious at the idea of one of its members lending herself to the sordid intrigues of her attendants, and its indignation so frightened poor Madame Adélaïde that she retracted everything, and forbade Madame de Narbonne ever to mention the subject to her again.

CHAPTER XV

THE hostility of Marie Antoinette was not the only annoyance which Madame du Barry had to endure. The *"Roué,"* as we have said elsewhere, had assisted his former mistress during the early days of her favour, when she had prudently kept her extravagance within limits, in confident anticipation of reaping a rich harvest at a later date. In this he was not disappointed. What was the actual amount which he succeeded in extorting from Madame du Barry at various times it is impossible to say, but, to judge from his manner of living, it must have been something enormous.[1] He kept a Parc-aux-Cerfs of his own; he married the sultana of his seraglio to a chevalier of Saint-Louis and settled 2000 écus a year upon her; he gambled as if he had the coffers of the State behind him, losing on one occasion 7000 louis at a single sitting and, on another, when condoled with on his ill-luck, remarking nonchalantly: "Do not distress yourselves, my friends; it is you " (meaning the public treasury) "who will pay for all this."

Nor did he confine his importunities to appeals for financial assistance. He harassed his hapless sister-in-law incessantly with advice, warnings, and plans of

[1] In December 1769 Madame du Barry asked Louis XV. for 600,000 livres for her brother-in-law, without, however, disclosing for whom the money was intended. The infatuated monarch promised that she should have it and applied to the Comptroller-General for the amount. Choiseul, however, got to hear of the matter, and sent the King proofs that the money was to go to the creditors of the Comte Jean, who, of course, remained unpaid.

campaign, and intrigued to get confederates of his
own appointed to important posts in the public service,
once actually endeavouring to secure that of Comptroller-General for a certain Guenée de Brochau;
which, of course, would have meant the hand of M.
du Barry in the Treasury.

At length his conduct became so intolerable that he
was recommended to pass a few months on an estate
at l'Isle-Jourdain, which was among the gifts he had
received from his grateful country, and departed
thither in a very bad humour, after two or three angry
scenes with his sister-in-law, which gave rise to the
belief that he had composed or inspired the following
chanson against the favourite, which had at this time
a considerable vogue:

> " Drôlesse!
> Où prends-tu donc ta fierté?
> Princesse!
> D'où te vient ta dignité?
> Si jamais ton teint se fane ou se pele,
> Au train
> De catin
> Le cri du public te rappelle.
> Drôlesse, &c.
> Lorsque tu vivais de la Messe
> Du moine, ton père Gomard,
> Que la Rançon vendoit sa graisse
> Pour joindre à ton morceau de lard;
> Tu n'étois pas si fière
> Et n'en valois que mieux,
> Baisse ta tête altière,
> Du moins devant mes yeux:
> Ecoute-moi rentre en toi-même,
> Pour éviter de plus grands maux:
> Permets à qui t'aime, qui t'aime,
> De t'offrir encore des sabots.
> Drôlesse!
> Mon esprit est-il baissé?
> Princesse!
> Te souvient-il du passé? "[1]

[1] Madame du Deffand sent a copy of these verses to the
Duchesse de Choiseul, who wrote back that she found them
charming and " *de très bon goût.*"

The titular husband of the favourite, the Comte Guillaume, followed his brother's example, and addressed to his wife threatening letters demanding money. In July 1770, Madame du Barry settled upon him an annuity of 5000 livres; but this seemed to Guillaume a beggarly pittance indeed for the consort of an uncrowned queen, and he renewed his importunities and threats, and became, in fact, so great a nuisance that the lady decided to apply for a separation *de corps et d'habitation.* The case was tried before the Châtelet on February 24, 1772, the countess's plea being the abusive and threatening character of the epistles with which her lord was in the habit of favouring her, three of which were laid before the sympathetic judges. Guillaume did not oppose the application, his silence having apparently been secured by the promise of a further annuity of 16,600 livres, and the separation was duly granted. Madame du Barry seems, however, to have been apprehensive that the insatiable Guillaume might be tempted to appeal against the sentence of the Châtelet, and, accordingly, she applied to the Parliament of Paris to confirm the decision pronounced in her favour, which was done by a decree of April 31, 1772.[3]

Like her predecessor in the post of *maîtresse en titre,* Madame du Barry was one of the kindest of relatives, and seems to have lost no opportunity of pushing the fortunes of her family. She gave her mother, the old sempstress, who had blossomed into the dame de Monvabé, an apartment in the Couvent de Sainte-Elisabeth, a carriage, a *maison de plaisance,* and a little farm at Villiers-sur-Orge and was in the habit of spending a day with her every fortnight. On Anne Bécu's death in October 1788, she bestowed a pension of 2000 livres on her husband, Rançon, "to recom-

[3] Vatel's *Histoire de Madame du Barry,* ii. 139.

pense his good conduct towards his spouse." She also pensioned her aunt Hélène, who called herself Madame de Quantigny, and provided for her four children.[4] Nor did the exactions of the *"Roué"* and her titular husband prevent her from endeavouring to promote the interests of the former's son Adolphe, and her brother-in-law Elie, the youngest of the Du Barry brothers.

Adolphe du Barry, who had assumed the title of viscount, although, of course, he had no more right to the appellation than his father and uncle Guillaume had to that of count, or the still more aspiring Elie to that of marquis,[5] had begun life as page to the King, and later had received a commission in the Régiment du Roi, from which, through his aunt's good offices, he was transferred to the *Chevau-légers* of the Guard, with the rank of *mestre de camp* of cavalry. There was also some talk of appointing him first equerry to the King, but this was prevented by the opposition of the Dauphin, who, on hearing of what was intended, exclaimed, in the midst of a throng of courtiers, "If he receives that post, I will give him my boot in the face at the first *débotté.*"

Several attempts were made by Madame du Barry to arrange a grand marriage for the "viscount." First, she proposed Mademoiselle de Béthune, a descendant of Sully, the celebrated Minister of Henri IV., but the King pointed out to her the absurdity of such pretensions. Then she cast her eyes upon Made-

---

[4] Madame du Barry also placed with Madame de Quantigny a little girl, whom she brought up with her own children. This little girl, who afterwards married the Marquis de Boissaison, was, according to d'Allonville, a daughter of the favourite "by a father, unknown," but the statement lacks confirmation.

[5] The number of pseudo-noblemen at this period was enormous. The genealogist Maugard declared in 1788 that there were in France at least 8000 marquises, counts, and barons, of whom only some 2000 had any legal right to the titles which they bore.

moiselle de Saint-André, a natural daughter of Louis by
Mademoiselle Murphy, of the Parc-aux-Cerfs, who was
being educated at the Couvent de la Présentation, in
the Rue des Postes.   Mademoiselle de Saint-André's
guardian, however, opposed the alliance, on the ground
that the fruit of his Majesty's amours had the right
to look much higher than a "Vicomte" du Barry; and
this appeal to Louis's vanity was successful, greatly to
the vexation of the *"Roué,"* who had suggested the
match to his sister-in-law for reasons of high policy,
his idea being that, in the event of the old King's
death, the fact that the Du Barrys had allied themselves with the Royal Family would hinder his successor from "yielding to the impulses of hatred."[6]

At length, however, a wife was found for Adolphe
in the person of a very lovely young girl, named Mademoiselle de Tournon, a member of a very ancient
family of Auvergne and a connection of the Rohans,
and on July 19, 1773, the marriage was celebrated at
Saint-Roch.

The contract, in which the favourite promised the
happy pair a donation of 200,000 livres,[7] is of great
interest, owing to the signatures; indeed it is probably
one of the most valuable collections of autographs
ever got together on a single document.   They included those of Louis XV., the Dauphin and Marie
Antoinette, the Comte and Comtesse de Provence, and
the three *Mesdames;* beneath which appear the signatures of Madame du Barry, the *"Roué,"*[8] Mademoiselle
"Chon" du Barry, and the bride and bridegroom.

[6] Letter of Jean du Barry published in the *Revue de Paris,*
1836, vol. xxxv.
[7] The principal was never paid, probably owing to the death
of Louis XV. in the following year and the consequent change
in the favourite's fortunes, but Madame du Barry continued to
pay the interest until November 1791.
[8] Jean du Barry figures in the document under the most high-
sounding titles; not only is he Comte du Barry-Cérès and Gov-

It is somewhat surprising to find the signatures of Marie Antoinette and the Dauphin appended to the marriage contract of one of the hated Du Barrys, and all the more so in veiw of the chilling reception which the new "viscountess" received on the occasion of her presentation to them at Compiègne, a few days later.

The favourite, accompanied by the Duchess de Laval and the Comtesse de Montmorency, presented her niece to the King, after which, followed by an immense crowd, the ladies proceeded to the apartments of the Dauphin. At the moment of their entry, the prince was standing in the embrasure of a window, talking to one of his suite and drumming with his fingers on the glass. When the usher announced the approach of the ladies, the Dauphin turned his head, pretended not to see the unfortunate *présentée* or her sponsor, and resumed his conversation and his drumming on the window-pane. As for Marie Antoinette, she coldly returned the ladies' reverences, but did not speak to either of them.

It was the same in the evening at the Dauphiness's card-table, and at her toilette the next morning, at which etiquette required that newly-presented ladies should make their appearance; on neither occasion did the princess address a single word to the viscountess. Not content with these tokens of her displeasure, she refused to allow her to accompany her to the chase in the Royal carriages, and gave strict injunctions to her *dame d'honneur*, the Comtesse de Noailles, that she was not to be invited to her balls.

Marie Antoinette's cruel treatment of this innocent girl, whose only fault was her connection with the favourite, seems to have been the outcome of a ma-

ernor of Lévignac as in 1769, but in the interval he has become Vidame de Chaalons, Comte de l'Isle-Jourdain, Seigneur de Belle-garde, Bretz and half a dozen other manors, and so forth.

licious slander. It was reported to the princess that
Madame du Barry, fearing that the King's affection
for her was on the wane, intended to exploit the beauty
of her niece, in order to retain the royal favour in the
family.   There does not appear to have been the
slightest ground for this accusation beyond the fact
that the young lady bore some resemblance to Madame
de Châteauroux; but it served its purpose, and the
poor Vicomtesse Adolphe had to submit all day to the
covert sneers and ironical smiles of the women of the
Court, few of whom could compare with her in grace
or beauty, and on that account were the more pitiless.

Having secured a wife for her nephew, Madame du
Barry turned her attention to her brother-in-law, the
"Marquis" Elie, for whom, in the following October,
she arranged a marriage with a Mademoiselle de
Fumel, daughter of the Marquis de Fumel, obtaining
for the bridegroom the colonelcy of the Régiment de
la Reine, and for the bride the post of *dame de
compagnie* to the Comtesse d'Artois.[9]

There were now three ladies of the name of Du
Barry at Court—the marchioness, the countess, and the
viscountess—which resulted in considerable confusion,
and contemporary chroniclers not infrequently mistake one Madame du Barry for another.

The new member of the favourite's family met with
much the same reception from the Dauphiness as the
wife of Adolphe had been accorded, in consequence of
which half the Court affected to ignore her existence,
and she was plunged in the depths of despair. After
a while, however, Marie Antoinette, touched with compassion for the unhappy lady, yielded to the entreaties
of Mercy, and, notwithstanding the fierce opposition of
Mesdames, "showed one day that she perceived the

[9] Marie Thérèse of Savoy, younger sister of the Comtesse
de Provence, married to the Comte d'Artois, November 1773.

marchioness's presence"; but towards the poor Vicomtesse Adolphe she remained implacable.

In the autumn of 1773, Madame du Barry received
a compliment which must have gone far to console her
for the mordant verses which so delighted Madame de
Choiseul. The financier La Borde, first Groom of the
Chamber to the King, having occasion to visit Geneva,
was commissioned by the favourite to call upon Voltaire at Ferney, and bestow upon the philosopher, on
her behalf, a kiss on either cheek. The commission
was duly executed, and appears to have greatly delighted the recipient of the kisses, ever susceptible to
flattery, no matter from what source it came, who
hastened to express his gratification in the following
letter:

"MADAME,—M. de la Borde informs me that you
have instructed him to kiss me on both cheeks, on your
behalf.

"Quoi! deux baisers sur la fin de ma vie!
    Quelle passeport vous daignez m'envoyer!
Dieux! c'en est trop, adorable Egérie:
    Je serais mort de plaisir au premier.

"He has shown me your portrait. Do not be
offended, Madame, if I take the liberty of bestowing
upon it the two kisses:

"Vous ne pouvez empêcher cet hommage,
    Faible tribut de quiconque à des yeux:
C'est aux mortels d'adorer votre image;
    L'original était fait pour les Dieux.

"I have heard several selections from *Pandore,* from
M. de la Borde;[10] they appear to me worthy of your
protection. The favour shown to real talent is the
only thing that can augment the *éclat* with which you

[10] La Borde had composed the music to Voltaire's opera of
Pandore.

shine. Deign, Madame, to accept the homage of an old hermit, whose heart knows hardly any other sentiment than that of gratitude."

Voltaire's charming verses soon became public property, as it is highly probable that the poet intended they should be, and are to be found in the *Almanach des Muses* for 1774, the "Correspondence" of Grimm, and the works of several contemporary chroniclers. Madame de Choiseul duly received a version of them from Madame du Deffand, but, needless to observe, did not find them *"de très bon goût,"* and replied that "Voltaire had sullied his pen in his old age."

CHAPTER XVI

THE heart of Louis XV., though not difficult to subjugate, was for the same reason, far from easy to retain; and Madame du Barry, like her predecessors in her exalted office, was called upon to exercise unceasing vigilance in order to safeguard her conquest.

In 1771, Hardy speaks of an intrigue designed to supplant the countess by the Princesse de Monaco, the mistress of the Prince de Condé, or, in default of her, by an English lady, a Miss Smith, and also of a third candidate whose name had not been disclosed. A little later, it appears that a Madame Bèche, the wife of one of the royal musicians, aroused momentary alarm in the camp of the favourite, and to her succeeded Madame d'Amerval, a natural daughter of the Abbé Terray. The King is also said to have cast a favourable eye upon several queens of comedy, among them Mademoiselle Raucourt and the mother of Mademoiselle Mars; but this charge rests upon very untrustworthy evidence.

The only one of the aspirants to the royal heart, however, about whom we possess any details is a Madame Pater, a Dutch lady of good family,[1] who had married a wealthy East Indian merchant.

Madame Pater first visited Paris in 1763, where, we are told, her beauty, joined to a lively wit,[2] excited so much admiration that, on the days on which she re-

[1] She was the eldest of the six daughters of Baron de Newkerke of Nyvenheim.
[2] One evening, Madame Pater was playing whist, when two ladies, both of whom were bitterly jealous of her charms, estab-

ceived, a veritable procession of adorers, "ranging from the Prince de Condé to the most insignificant gentleman of the Court," might be seen wending its way towards her house, in the Faubourg Saint-Honoré. The lady, however, had the misfortune to be afflicted with an exceedingly jealous husband, who had the bad taste to take umbrage at the universal tribute accorded to Madame's charms. For a while he nursed his wrath in silence, but at length he could contain his feelings no longer. Accordingly, one day when the Prince de Condé and several other distinguished admirers were taking their leave, he accompanied them to the door and observed: "I am very sensible, Messieurs, of the honour that you do me in visiting my house; though I do not believe that you can find much diversion here; *je suis toute la journée avec Madame Pater, et la nuit je couche avec elle.*"

After this very plain hint the Prince de Condé, who preferred easier conquests, retired from the field, and the stream of callers sensibly diminished; but by this time the fame of the lady's beauty had reached the ears of the King, who sent the Prince de Soubise to invite Madame Pater to sup with his Majesty at Versailles. The invitation would, no doubt, have been accepted, had the decision rested with the lady, in which case it it not improbable that Jeanne Bécu would never have attained the "sunlit heights." But Monsieur Pater, learning what was in the wind, took alarm, and straightway carried off his wife to Holland, much to the chagrin of the King.[2]

lished themselves behind her chair, and proceeded to dissect her character in stage whispers. Madame Pater pretended not to hear, until presently her partner inquired if she had any "honours," upon which she glanced round at her rivals and replied: "I do not know whether these ladies have left me any."

[2] Comte Fleury's *Louis XV. intime: Les petites maîtresses,* p. 297, *et seq.* Manuel's *La Police de Paris dévoilée,* ii. *passim.*

Ten years elapsed ere Madame Pater returned to the scene of her triumphs. In the interval, she had contrived to secure a separation from the jealous husband, and had taken the name of Baronne de Newkerke. On this occasion she aspired to an important *rôle*. Encouraged by the Duc de Duras, who is said to have been acting under instructions from the exile of Chanteloup, she laid determined siege to the heart of the King; but her ambition soared much higher than the post of *maîtresse en titre:* she had determined to follow in the footsteps of Madame de Maintenon.

Madame Pater's dream of greatness was fated never to be realised, but the conduct of the King must certainly have afforded her good reason to hope for success. He paid her the most marked attention, gave her a handsome pension, and installed her in a suite of apartments on the *rez-de-chaussée* of the Château of Meudon, where she appears to have divided her time between ghostly conferences with a fashionable abbé —she had abjured the Protestant faith and been received into the Catholic Church, by the curé of Saint-Eustache, in order to further her designs—and taking lessons in dancing and deportment from Despréaux, of the Opera.

The latter, who declares that she was the most beautiful woman that he had ever seen, has left us some interesting details about Madame Pater's life at Meudon. He says that every Sunday she dined in the grand vestibule, and afterwards held a sort of Court, which was attended by the governor and all the officials of the château, who treated her with the most profound respect; that occasionally, wearing a mask and leaning on the actor's arm, she condescended to take a promenade in Meudon, "in the midst of a great crowd"; and that the Prince de Lambesc, son of the Comte de Brionne, *grand écuyer de France,* "loved her to madness and offered her his hand and heart"; but that all she would accept from him was a carriage and six horses from the royal stables.[*]

When Louis XV. was seized with his last illness, Madame Pater hastened to Versailles and remained there until the death of the King, apparently in anticipation that, in the event of his recovery, he would fall an easy victim to her persuasions.

After the fatal termination of the King's illness had destroyed her hopes, she consoled herself by marrying the Marquis de Champcenetz, Governor of the Tuileries, and became one of the leaders of the fashionable world. At the beginning of the Revolution she emigrated, but returned during the Directory, and, for some time, appears to have taken an active share in Royalist intrigues. In one of these she was eventually detected, and exiled by Bonaparte. She died in Holland in 1806.

At the time that Madame Pater was indulging in her fond dreams at Meudon, a general impression appears to have prevailed in well-informed circles that Louis XV. would sooner or later seek repose of conscience— to borrow Mercy's phrase—by a second marriage. This belief was due, in a great measure, to the surprising influence which Madame Louise, the Carmelite, had lately acquired over her royal father. By a singular paradox, the princess in question, who, so long as she was at Court, had enjoyed not the least credit, had, since her retirement from the world, become a force to be reckoned with. The King paid her frequent visits, and was reported to be deeply moved by her exhortations to repentance.

Urged on by Chistophe de Beaumont, the Archbishop of Paris, and the Chancellor, who believed that he de-

[*] *Souvenirs de Jeanne Etienne Despréaux*, p. 10, *et seq.*

tected in the King signs of remorse, and had decided that it might be more advisable for him to be on the side of the confessor than on that of the mistress, Madame Louise returned to the project of Louis's marriage with the Archduchess Elizabeth of Austria, which had never been wholly abandoned, and when her father demurred to this, suggested that perhaps the widowed Princesse de Lamballe might serve equally well.

Madame du Barry became seriously alarmed, and one day, when the King was on the point of starting for Saint-Denis to visit his daughter, threw herself at his feet, told him that she knew that her disgrace was decided upon, and that she would prefer to receive her dismissal from his own lips than to suffer the humiliation of receiving it from the base cabal which was conspiring to ruin her.[5]

The project of the King's remarriage came to nothing, but the influence of the royal Carmelite over her father seemed to increase as Louis grew older, and towards the end of the year 1773 rumours of the favourite's approaching fall were rife. They were, however, without foundation, and the King, learning

[5] If we are to believe that amusing work, *Les Fastes de Louis XV.*, Madame du Barry's friends advised her to persuade the Pope to annul her marriage with Guillaume du Barry, in order that she might herself be in a position to marry the King, and Terray drew up for her a petition to the Vatican, which, briefly put, was as follows:

"Madame du Barry represents to his Holiness that, having but little knowledge of canonical rules, she was unaware at the time of the celebration of her marriage with the Comte Guillaume du Barry that it was not permissible to espouse the brother of a man with whom one had lived. She avows, with all the grief of a repentant soul, that she had had a weakness for the Comte Jean du Barry, her husband's brother; that she had been, happily, warned in time of the incest she was about to commit, and that her enlightened conscience did not permit her to live with her new husband; that thus the crime had not yet been committed; and she implores his Holiness to consent to free her from an alliance so scandalous."

what was reported, took an early opportunity of dis-
proving it. On November 16, the marriage of the
Comte d'Artois to Maria Theresa of Savoy, younger
sister of the Comtesse de Provence, was celebrated.
The ceremony was preceded by a banquet, which was
understood to be confined to the Royal Family and
Princes and Princesses of the Blood. To the general
astonishment, however, Madame du Barry appeared,
"radiant as the sun, and wearing five million livres
worth of jewels on her person." A place was reserved
for her immediately opposite the King, and it was remarked that throughout the repast she seemed to have
eyes for no one but his Majesty, who, in return, bent
upon her many affectionate glances, *et lui faisoit des
mines remarquables.*" "It is believed," continues the
chronicler, "that his Majesty was very pleased to
thus give a denial to the rumours concerning the
disgrace of this lady which were going about, while
she evinced no less plainly her gratitude and profound
respect."[6]

At the beginning of the year 1774, the last of her
favour, Madame du Barry, encouraged by the fact that
Marie Antoinette had of late "abstained from morti-
fying remarks" in reference to the countess, made
another attempt to overcome the hostility of the Dauphiness. A jeweller in Paris was offering for sale a
pair of magnificent earrings, "formed of four diamonds of extraordinary size and beauty," and valued
at 700,000 livres. Aware of the princess's passion for
jewellery, the favourite persuaded the Comte de
Noailles to bring these earrings to the notice of Marie
Antoinette and to say that "if her Royal Highness
found them to her taste, she need not trouble herself
about the price or the payment, as means would be

[6] *Nouvelles à la main de la maison d'Harcourt,* cited by M.
Vatel.

found to persuade the King to make her a present of
them."

In vain was the net spread; Marie Antoinette replied simply that she had enough diamonds, and had
no desire to increase her collection.

Madame du Barry, unlike Madame de Pompadour,
was not thin-skinned, and cared little or nothing for
the libels and lampoons wherewith her enemies assailed
her. The story goes that on one occasion the Lieutenant of Police came to her and said: "Madame, we have
just caught a rascal who has composed a scandalous
song about you. What are we to do with him?"
"Make him sing it, and then give him something to
eat," answered the good-natured favourite, laughing.
However, there is a limit even to the patience of the
saintliest monk, as the long-suffering Major of the
Bastille observed when he had that egregious impostor,
M. Latude, under his care; and, in the case of Madame
du Barry, this was reached in the early weeks of 1774.

There happened to be living in London at this time
an adventurer from Burgundy named Théveneau de
Morande, who, having got into trouble in his own
country, had taken refuge in England. Here he found
himself entirely without resources, but, being possessed
of a lively imagination, a facile pen, and boundless
impudence, soon hit upon a highly remunerative mode
of earning a livelihood. This was to compose gross
and scandalous libels about persons of exalted station,
which were printed in England and Holland, and introduced clandestinely into France. Among other
works, he had published, under the title of *Le Gazetier
cuirassé* (The Journalist in Armour), *ou Anecdotes
scandaleuses de la Cour de France,* a collection of the
most atrocious stories, which inspired such consternation among his victims that many, including the Mar-

quis de Marigny, Madame de Pompadour's brother, hastened to send money across the Channel, in order to secure immunity from further attacks.

Encouraged by his success, M. de Morande determined to fly at still higher game. Accordingly, he wrote to Madame du Barry, enclosing the prospectus of a forthcoming work, in four octavo volumes, founded upon her life, and bearing the piquant title of *Mémoires secrets d'une femme publique, ou Essai sur les aventures de madame la comtesse Dub*** depuis son berceau jusqu'au lit d'honneur*. The author intimated that if the subject of his biography preferred that the work should not appear, he would be willing to enter into negotiations for the sale of the copyright.

The unfortunate favourite, who had already been outrageously libelled in *Le Gazetier cuirassé*, wherein it was asserted, among other charges, that she had founded a new Order at Court, to which only those women were to be admitted who had bestowed their favours on at least ten different men, was greatly alarmed, and hurried off to consult the King and d'Aiguillon, who applied to the English Government for Morande's extradition.

The English Government answered that it was impossible for them to comply with such a demand, as Morande's offence was not one which came within the scope of the extradition treaty; but, inasmuch as the person in question was "a pest to society and a plague to mankind," they would offer not the slightest objection to his seizure and removal to France, provided that it could be done secretly and in such a way as not to wound the susceptibilities of the English public.

The French Ministry thereupon sent a brigade of police-agents to London, with orders to capture Morande and restore him to his native land, where the darkest cell and the heaviest irons to be found in Gal-

banon awaited him. But Morande was prepared for
them. He had received timely warning of the expe-
dition against him from a confederate in Paris, and
had denounced it in the London journals, at the same
time giving himself out as a political exile, whom his
persecutors dared to follow even on to the sacred soil
of liberty, thus violating the generous hospitality which
the English people never failed to extend to the unfortunate of all nationalities.

This ingenious appeal for public sympathy was not
made in vain; and when the French police-agents arrived in London, they had no need to search for their
prey; for he was waiting to receive them, at the head
of an infuriated mob, which fell upon them and would
have thrown them into the Thames, had they not prudently sought safety in flight.

After this fiasco, the French Government had recourse to negotiations, and sent over two ambassadors,
named Bellanger and Preaudeau de Chenilly, to treat
with Morande. The latter, however, refused to receive them, posed before the English people in the
character of an avenger of public morality, and hastened on the publication of his work.

Three thousand copies of the book had been printed
and were on the point of being despatched to Holland
and Germany, to be afterwards circulated throughout
France, and Madame du Barry and Louis XV. were in
despair, when La Borde, the King's *valet-de-chambre,*
suggested to his master to send over Beaumarchais,
whose masterly conduct of his lawsuit against Göez-
man had excited general admiration, though it had
ruined him in fortune and credit.

The famous dramatist was ready enough to embrace such an opportunity of reinstating himself in
the good graces of the King, and in March set out for
London, under the name of Ronac, an anagram of

his patronymic of Caron, to treat with the "Journalist in Armour" for the sale and suppression of the *Mémoires secrets*.

More fortunate than MM. Bellanger and de Chenilly, he succeeded in obtaining an interview with Morande, who gave him a copy of his book and the manuscript of another libel, with which he intended to follow it up, and promised to suspend publication while Beaumarchais returned to Versailles to lay his demands before the King.

After a good deal of haggling a bargain was struck, whereby M. Morande was to suppress his work and abstain from further attacks upon the reputation of Madame du Barry, and the French Government was to pay him 20,000 livres in cash and a pension of 4000 livres, half of which sum was to revert to his wife— "a respectable Englishwoman, whom he treated abominably"—in the event of his death.[7]

The manuscript and the 3000 copies of the *Mémoires secrets* were then burned by Beaumarchais and Morande in an oven in the suburbs of London, and the dramatist returned to France to receive the reward of his successful diplomacy. But alas! there was no reward forthcoming, not even poor Beaumarchais's expenses; for when he reached Versailles, Louis XV. lay on his death-bed.[8]

---

[7] Some writers assert that the pension was revoked in the succeeding reign, Louis XVI. refusing to be bound by the acts of his grandfather. This, however, is an error. Morande's pension was an annuity duly secured, and all that the French Government did was to commute a portion of it at the recipient's own request.

[8] Loménie's *Beaumarchais et son temps*, i. 376, *et seq.* Dutens' *Mémoires d'un voyageur qui se repose*, ii. 39.

CHAPTER XVII

LOUIS XV. was growing old; slowly but surely his constitution, undermined by long years of debauchery, was breaking up. He had become obese and unwieldy; to get him on to his horse or into his carriage was now "quite an affair of State"; his digestive organs were impaired; he was compelled to dilute his wine with Vichy water, and his *petits soupers* had become Barmecide feasts, so far as he himself was concerned. "I see that I am no longer young, and that I must put on the drag," said he one day to La Martinière, his First Surgeon. "Sire," was the answer, "it would be wiser for you to unharness the horses."

And with the decline of his physical powers, the King's mental faculties were failing too. His fits of *ennui*—a malady from which nearly all the Bourbons suffered to a greater or less degree—were becoming more frequent and more prolonged, and taxing all the ingenuity of Madame du Barry to combat successfully. In his correspondence with Maria Theresa, Mercy frequently refers to this incurable melancholy of Louis XV.: "The King is growing old, and from time to time seems to have regrets. He finds himself isolated, without aid or consolation from his children, without zeal, attachment, or fidelity from the bizarre assemblage composing his Ministry, his society, his surroundings."[1] And again: "From time to time the King begins to make remarks concerning his age, his health,

[1] Letter of August 14, 1773.

243

and the frightful account that must one day be rendered to the Supreme Being for our employment of
the life He has accorded to us in this world.   These
reflections, occasioned by the death of some persons of
his own age, who died almost before his eyes,[2] have
greatly alarmed those who retain the monarch in his
present errors, and from that moment everybody has
thought it his duty to conceal such events so far as
possible."[3]

The King's conscience, in short, was beginning to
awaken; Holy Week, a period always dreaded by his
mistresses, was becoming each year more dangerous,
and those of 1773 and 1774 had reduced the superstitious monarch to the most abject terror.   Corrupt
and sycophantic as so many of the Court clergy were,
there had, happily, never been wanting honest and
courageous ministers of the Gospel amongst them.
The celebrated Jesuit preacher, Bourdaloue, had not
hesitated to denounce the profligacy of *le Grande
Monarque* in the most scathing terms; and now
Bourdaloue had found two worthy successors in the
persons of the Abbé de Beauvais and the Abbé
Rousseau.   "Yet forty days and Nineveh shall be destroyed!" was the text of one of the former's sermons
in April 1774; and Louis applied the threat of the
prophet to himself and trembled.[4]

[2] In November 1773, at one of the *petits soupers,* the Marquis
de Chauvelin fell dead actually at Louis' feet; shortly afterwards, the Abbé de la Ville, to whom the King was giving audience, was seized with a fatal attack of apoplexy; and the
Genoese Ambassador, Sorba, also died in a terribly sudden
manner.

[3] Letter of February 19, 1774.

[4] In Holy Week of the previous year, the Abbé de Beauvais
had preached a sermon in which the following passage is said
to have occurred: " Solomon, satiated with voluptuousness, tired
of having extinguished, in the endeavour to revive his withered
senses, every sort of pleasure that surrounded the throne, ended
by seeking one of a new kind *in the vile dregs of public corrup-*

Madame du Barry, on her side, was scarcely less uneasy. The *Almanach de Liége* for that year had contained among its predictions one which announced that, in the month of April, "a great lady playing an important rôle at a foreign Court would cease to fill it," and, in dire alarm, she racked her brains to find means to divert the mind of her royal lover from thoughts of death and judgment.

On Tuesday, April 26, Louis XV. left Versailles to spend a few days at the Little Trianon, the pavilion recently constructed by the architect Gabriel. The following morning, on rising, he felt unwell, complaining of pains in the head, shivering-fits, and giddiness. He refused, however, to countermand the hunt arranged for that day, and, in the hope that exercise might prove beneficial, decided to take part in the sport as usual. His calèche was accordingly ordered, and he set out for the meet, but, on arriving there, felt too ill to mount his horse, and followed the chase in his carriage, returning to Trianon about half-past five.

During the day the headache from which Louis had suffered in the morning had become much worse, and Madame du Barry advised that one of his physicians should be summoned. To this, however, he refused to consent, declaring that it was merely a passing indisposition, which a little medicine and a night's rest would cure, and spent the evening in the favourite's apartments, where he took some simple remedy.

But the King passed a restless night, and in the morning was so much worse that Lemonnier, his First Physician, was sent for.

tion." M. Vatel, who discusses this question at some length, with the view, apparently, of vindicating the character of the Jewish monarch, is of opinion that the Abbé de Beauvais never used the words imputed to him, as they are not to be found in his collected sermons. Perhaps, however, as Mr. Douglas suggests, they were omitted by a timid editor.

Lemonnier found his royal patient in a fever, but did not appear to think that there was any cause for alarm; and Madame du Barry, much reassured, decided, after a consultation with the Duc d'Aumont, the First Gentleman of the Bedchamber in attendance on his Majesty, to keep the King at Trianon until he recovered, and to allow no hint of his illness to reach the Royal Family, who had remained at Versailles.

Now it is probable that the favourite and d'Aumont, who was devoted to her interests, acted merely from selfish motives, knowing full well that even the slightest indisposition was enough to arouse qualms of conscience in the superstitious monarch. Nevertheless it is now generally admitted that, had they been allowed to carry out their plan, the life of Louis XV. might have been saved, for, in his light and airy apartments at Trianon, with every one but Lemonnier, Madame du Barry, and his *valet-de-chambre* excluded from his sick-room, he would have had an infinitely better chance of recovery than at Versailles, where unbending etiquette demanded that not only his whole staff of medical advisers, but every one who had the *entrée,* should be admitted to the royal bedchamber, even though its unfortunate occupant were *in extremis.*[5]

However, ill news flies apace, and, in spite of the precautions of Madame du Barry and the duke, the state of the King was soon known at Versailles. The Royal Family did not dare to go to Trianon without a summons from his Majesty; but the Dauphin despatched La Martinière, who had great influence over Louis and was permitted to speak his mind freely.

La Martinière did not love Madame du Barry, and was, therefore, unlike Lemonnier, but little inclined to forego what he conceived to be his duty out of deference to that lady's wishes. He was an honest man,

5 Vatel's *Histoire de Madame du Barry,* ii. 320.

brusque but firm, and he resolved to persuade Louis to
return to Versailles.

Early in the afternoon of the 28th, he reached
Trianon, saw the King at once, and represented to him
that it was absolutely without precedent for a King of
France to allow himself to be nursed anywhere save
in his principal residence and with the whole Faculty
standing round his bed; and, in spite of the entreaties
of the favourite, poor Louis, ever a slave to etiquette,
yielded, and told La Martinière to order his carriage
to be got ready. The King entered it in his *robe-de-
chambre,* and, on arriving at the château, waited in
Madame Adélaïde's apartments while his bed was
being prepared. When, a little later, Marie Antoinette
and the princesses presented themselves at the door of
the royal bedchamber, his Majesty intimated that he
desired to be alone, and they withdrew, leaving the
invalid to the care of Madame du Barry, who entered
by the private staircase; and took her place by his side.

The fever and the pains in the head increased in severity during the night; the King could not sleep,
and at times his mind wandered. In the morning,
Friday, April 29, Lemonnier and La Martinière held
a consultation, and decided that his Majesty must be
bled. They asked that other doctors should be called
in, and Louis, prompted by Madame du Barry, named
Lorry and Bordeu, the physicians of the favourite and
d'Aiguillon, while, at Lemonnier's request, Lassonne,
the Dauphiness's physician, was also summoned.

The bleeding did not produce the effect hoped for;
the fever continued to increase, and there could no
longer be any doubt that the King was seriously ill.
The doctors who had been sent for arrived about noon,
and were followed into the sick-room by all his Majesty's medical advisers—physicians, surgeons, and
apothecaries—and also by a number of people who had

the *entrée,* and whom Madame du Barry and d'Aiguillon had up till then contrived to exclude.

The King called upon each doctor in turn to come and feel his pulse, described his symptoms, and demanded to know what was the nature of his illness; a point upon which none of the learned gentlemen were able to satisfy him. They all looked exceedingly solemn, conferred together in whispers, shook their heads repeatedly, and, finally, decided that his Majesty must be bled again in the course of the afternoon, and a third time at night or the following morning, if the second bleeding failed to give him relief.

This announcement alarmed the King. "I am then seriously ill," he exclaimed. "A third bleeding will leave me very weak. Can it not be avoided?"

The Court was in a ferment of excitement when the decision of the doctors became known, and the enemies of the favourite and d'Aiguillon could not conceal their elation. A third bleeding meant the Sacraments and, with the Sacraments, confession and the solemn renunciation by the King of his mistress, as had been the case with Madame de Châteauroux at Metz, in 1744.[6] It is true that on that occasion, so soon as the monarch recovered, Madame de Châteauroux was taken back into favour; but it was deemed very improbable that, if Madame du Barry were once dismissed, Louis would have the courage to break his word again. At sixty-four a man is less ready to incur the wrath of Heaven than when in the prime of life.

On their side, the Du Barry party, alive to the danger which threatened them, used every effort to prevail upon the doctors to abandon the idea of a third bleeding. They succeeded, but only in a measure,

[6] For a full account of Louis XV.'s illness at Metz, and the dismissal of Madame de Châteauroux, see the author's " Madame de Pompadour," pp. 11-19.

as the Faculty, to satisfy its conscience, made the second bleeding unusually copious, and reduced the wretched King to the last stage of prostration. Nevertheless, the fever continued, and Bordeu went up to the apartments of the favourite, who had retired from the sick-room before the entry of the crowd of doctors and courtiers at midday, and told her that he feared the King was threatened with a long and dangerous illness.

Towards five o'clock, Louis sent for his children and kept them for half an hour round his bed, during which time, however, he never once addressed them. In the evening the Duc d'Aumont wished to introduce Madame du Barry, but the doctors and the grand officers of the Household opposed it energetically, and he was compelled to give way.

The Faculty was composed of fourteen persons—six physicians, five surgeons, and three apothecaries; but the King seemed to derive comfort from their number, and whenever he happened to observe that one of the doctors had left the room, requested that he should be brought back, "as if he imagined that, surrounded by so many satellites, no harm could happen to his Majesty."

That evening the sick man was moved from his great State bed into a smaller one, for the sake of convenience. All at once, some one happening to approach him with a light, observed red specks upon his forehead and cheeks. The doctors looked at one another in amazement; not one among them appears to have entertained the least suspicion that the King's illness could be small-pox, for Louis had had the disease already in 1728, and it was believed that he was proof against further attacks.[7]

[7] Louis was commonly believed to have contracted the disease from a young girl of the neighbourhood, with whom he had had

However, after they had recovered from their astonishment, the doctors seemed much relieved to find that
all uncertainty was at an end, and assured the Royal
Family that there was no cause for alarm, citing instances of persons of the King's age who had recovered from the disease. The Dauphin, the Comte de
Provence, the Comte d'Artois, and their wives, on the
advice of the doctors, decided to keep away from the
sick-room; but *Mesdames,* although none of them had
had small-pox, declared that their place was by their
father's side, and that they intended to remain with
him; a resolution which does them much honour. The
Court seemed to share the opinion of the Faculty that
the chances were greatly in favour of the King's recovery, and retired to rest, "convinced that it was an
affair of eight or nine days and of a little patience."[8]

Bordeu, however, thought otherwise, and when the
Duc de Liancourt reported to him the optimistic feeling
which prevailed, shook his head and remarked that
small-pox to a man of Louis's age and constitution was
a terrible disease.

The event justified his previsions. Next day, it became evident that the disease was developing in its
most virulent form, and the doctors could not conceal
their apprehensions. After much discussion, it had
been decided not to inform the King of the nature of
his illness, and he was accordingly told that he was
suffering from a miliary fever. But, with his knowl-

a *"passade"*: *"une petite vachère,"* according to the Abbé Baudeau; the daughter of the gardener of Louveciennes (*Anecdotes*); the daughter of Montvallier, Madame du Barry's steward
(Métra); "the once so buxom daughter of the gatekeeper"
(Carlyle), and so forth; for the shapes of the damsel are pro-
tean. There is, however, not a shred of evidence to support this
story, and we prefer to believe Voltaire, who says that there was
an epidemic of small-pox in the environs of Versailles, and the
King fell a victim to the scourge in the ordinary way.

[8] *Mémoires du Baron de Besenval,* i. 300.

edge of diseases, of which he had all his life taken a
morbid pleasure in talking, the symptoms surprised
him. "Were it not that I have had the small-pox," he
exclaimed, "I should believe that I was about to
have it."

Mesdames passed the day in the sick-room or in one
of the adjoining cabinets, and assisted at Mass, which
was said at noon, on a portable altar placed before the
King's bed. They, with the Duc de Noailles, the faithful Prince de Soubise, and the banker *valet-de-chambre*
La Borde, were probably the only persons in the room
who cared for Louis for his own sake; the rest, con-
sumed with hatred and jealousy of one another, thought
only of the political changes for which the administration of the Sacraments would be the signal. Decency,
of course, compelled them to dissimulate their feelings;
and many of those who appeared most affected by the
condition of their sovereign were secretly rejoicing at
the prospect of the fulfilment of their hopes.

In Paris, where the affection of the people, so strik-
ingly manifested during Louis's illness at Metz, had
long since changed to hatred and contempt, there was
not even a pretence of sorrow.[9] Public prayers for
the King's recovery were, of course, ordered; but the
churches and chapels were deserted. The shrine of
Sainte-Geneviève was solemnly opened; but hardly a
knee was bent before it.[10] If people were observed to

[9] A striking instance of the steady decline of Louis XV.'s
popularity is afforded by comparing the number of Masses said
on his behalf at Notre Dame, at the expense of private individuals, during his three illnesses in 1744, 1757, and 1774. On
the first occasion, no less than 6000 were said; on the second,
the number had fallen to 600; while in 1774 only three persons
were found willing to pay for a Mass!—Bingham's "Marriages
of the Bourbons," ii. 421.

[10] After the death of Louis XV., the Abbé de Sainte-Geneviève
was rallied by some friends, who said that his saint had lost all
her power. He replied: "Well, Messieurs, what reproach have
you to address to her? Is he not dead?"

whisper anxiously together, if apprehension were remarked on any face, its cause was not the gravity of their sovereign's condition, but lest Death should, after all, be deprived of his prey. Louis *le Bien-aimé,* as he himself had once bitterly remarked, had become Louis *le Bien-haï,* and all hearts waited impatiently for the event which was to open that new *régime* on which so many hopes were founded.

In the evening, La Borde, having on some pretext contrived to get every one out of the room, brought in Madame du Barry and conducted her to the King's bedside; but Louis was in too much pain to show any pleasure at the sight of his mistress, and, after remaining for a short while, she withdrew.[11]

On the Sunday, May 1, the King, who had passed a terrible night, was so weak that it was the general impression that he could not survive more than a couple of days, and the battle between the " Barriens " and "Anti-Barriens " over the question of the Sacraments began in earnest. By a singular inversion of the usual order of things, it was the patrons of the philosophers who cried out against the scandal of allowing the King to remain longer in a state of sin, while the *dévots* declared that confession and absolution would effectually destroy any chance of recovery his Majesty might have, as everything depended on concealing his true condition from him.

In the midst of this unseemly wrangle, the news arrived that Christophe de Beaumont, the Archbishop of Paris, had announced his intention of visiting the King on the following day. No one doubted that the object of the prelate's visit was to exhort his Majesty to repentance and confession, and the Du Barry party, in great alarm, held a council of war, which was at-

[11] *Mémoires du Baron de Besenval* (edit. Berville and Barrière), i. 303.

tended by the favourite, d'Aiguillon, Richelieu, and his son, the Duc de Fronsac. After some discussion, it was decided that, as it was impossible to keep the archbishop away from the King, the only course to adopt was to ensure that the Duc d'Orléans, first prince of the blood, should be in the room all the time; that the visit should be one of courtesy only, and that no mention should be made of the Sacraments. Madame Adélaïde, whom the doctors of the favourite's faction had solemnly assured that the question of Eternity was premature, and that it would be her father's death-blow, joined the conspiracy.

At eleven o'clock the next morning, the archbishop, in his violet robes, presented himself at the door of the King's ante-chamber, where he was met by Richelieu, who led him into the Cabinet du Conseil, made him sit down by his side, and spoke to him "with great vehemence and animated gestures."

Now, the archbishop was an honest and pious, if narrow-minded man, who had suffered exile and persecution for the truth's sake, or rather for that of the Bull *Unigenitus*. He deplored the irregularities of the King, but he was well aware of the services which Madame du Barry had rendered to the party of which he was the ecclesiastical head by the overthrow of Choiseul, the elevation of d'Aiguillon, and the destruction of the Parliaments. He had come to insist on the dismissal of the favourite, as a preliminary to confession and the Sacraments, to the saving of the King's soul; but when Richelieu, with brutal frankness, pointed out to him that the saving of the King's soul meant the return of Choiseul and the old Parliament, the triumph, in fact, of the enemies of the Church, the archbishop began to wonder whether his Most Christian Majesty's salvation was indeed worth so great a sacrifice.

While he hesitated "between his zeal and his con-

science," the Duc d'Aumont came to announce that the
King awaited him. The prelate rose and made his way
into the sick-room, where the first object his eyes rested
upon was a lady perched on the royal bed. The lady
was, of course, Madame du Barry, who, however, fled
at his approach, leaving him alone with the King and
the Duc d'Orléans, charged by Madame Adélaïde to
take care that M. de Beaumont did not say anything
which might alarm her father.

The audience, as might be expected, had no result;
the archbishop remained a few minutes, condoling with
his Majesty on the unfortunate event which had temporarily deprived his loving subjects of the joy of
seeing him amongst them, and then went back to Paris,
without saying a single word about confession;[12] while
the King, inferring from the prelate's avoidance of
this unpleasant subject, that the doctors could not consider him in any danger, sent at once for Madame du
Barry, "wept with joy, and covered her hands with
kisses."

The "Anti-Barriens," highly indignant at the weakness of the archbishop, now fell back upon the Grand
Almoner, the Cardinal de la Roche-Aymon. Incited
by them, the Bishop of Carcassonne, an honest man,
who sincerely desired his sovereign's salvation, brand-
ishing his pectoral cross before the eyes of the cardinal,
summoned him, in the name of that cross, to do his
duty and propose the Sacraments to the King.

The Cardinal de la Roche-Aymon, who was an exceedingly supple and cautious ecclesiastic, felt himself
placed in a most embarrassing position. If he declined
to exhort the King to repentance, and Louis were to
die without having received absolution, he would be
ruined. On the other hand, if he did his duty, and the

---

[12] The archbishop returned the next day, and again saw the
King, but whether he spoke of confession is uncertain.

King were to recover, his disgrace would be equally
certain. He, therefore, determined to steer a middle
course, and replied that, as the doctors were opposed
to anything which might tend to alarm the King, he
could not propose to administer the Sacraments openly,
but that he would avail himself of the first opportunity
of putting his Majesty in the right way. He then went
to visit the King, but conversed with him in so low
a tone that no one else could hear what was said. In
this way, the astute cardinal was able to give his own
version of what passed between Louis and himself.

That day a slight improvement was observed in the
royal patient's condition, in consequence of which a
number of courtiers who, in the belief that his Majesty
was doomed, had for the last day or two abstained
from visiting the favourite, hastened to atone for their
neglect. But during the night the disease took an
alarming turn, and the following morning the doctors,
who had hitherto issued relatively satisfactory reports,
published a bulletin announcing that the King had been
delirious. D'Aiguillon, in a violent passion, rushed
into the ante-chamber and began to upbraid the doctors
with their indiscretion in so loud a tone that Louis
sent to learn what was the matter. When the Minister
went to visit him soon afterwards, he inquired very
tenderly after Madame du Barry, and expressed a desire to see her; and it was arranged that La Borde
should bring the countess to the sick-room in the
evening.

But before the time for the favourite's visit arrived,
an event of great importance had taken place: the
King had ascertained the disease from which he was
suffering. He had, it appeared, questioned La Martinière, and the latter, disgusted with the conduct of
his colleagues, had confirmed his suspicions.

In an agony of terror, the conscience-stricken King

at once resolved to purchase absolution by the dismissal, or rather the apparent dismissal, of his mistress; and when, according to arrangement, La Borde brought in the favourite, he called her to his bedside and said: "Madame, I am very ill; I know what I must do; I do not wish to have a repetition of the scandal that took place at Metz. We must part. Go to Rueil, to the Duc d'Aiguillon's château; await my orders there, and be assured that I shall always entertain for you the most tender affection."[13]

Madame du Barry, who had expected a very different reception, left the room dissolved in tears, consoling herself, however, with the reflection that Rueil was but two leagues from Versailles, and that such a very modified form of exile probably implied a speedy recall in the event of the King's recovery.

At four o'clock the following afternoon, Tuesday, May 5, a carriage stopped under the northern arcade of the château. Madame du Barry entered it, accompanied by her sister-in-law, Mademoiselle "Chon," and the Duchesse d'Aiguillon, and departed from the scene of her triumphs, which she was fated never to revisit.

There was, of course, great excitement at Court when it became known that the favourite had left Versailles; but the joy of the "Anti-Barriens" was somewhat marred by the knowledge that, if the King happened to change his mind, a courier and a pair of fast horses could bring her back within an hour.

It was believed that the Sacraments would be administered that same evening, but the enemies of the favourite were doomed to disappointment. Towards six o'clock, the King called La Borde and bade him fetch Madame du Barry.

[13] There are several versions of Louis's farewell speech to Madame du Barry; we have followed Besenval.

".Sire, she has gone," answered the *valet-de-chambre*.

"Whither has she gone?"

"To Rueil, Sire."

"Ah! already!" And the sick man seemed distressed at finding that he had been so quickly taken at his word.

Shortly afterwards he summoned d'Aiguillon, and inquired if he had been to Rueil; all of which showed plainly that his thoughts were occupied far more by his mistress than by his confessor; that the lady's departure was merely a precautionary measure, and that she would be recalled the moment the illness of her royal lover took a decided turn for the better.[14]

Later in the evening there was a disgraceful scene in the ante-chamber. The curé of Versailles announced his intention of entering the sick-room to exhort the King to place himself in a state of grace without further delay, upon which the Duc de Fronsac threatened to throw him out of the window if he dared even to mention the word "confession" in his Majesty's hearing. "If I am not killed, I shall return by the door," replied the priest, "for it is my duty." However, the attitude of the duke was so threatening that the curé eventually decided to remain silent.

There was no change in Louis' condition the following day, but during the night of the 6th to 7th he had a relapse, and ordered the Duc de Duras to summon his confessor, the Abbé Maudoux, an honest man, who was also the *directeur* of Marie Antoinette. The duke, a bitter enemy of d'Aiguillon, obeyed the order with alacrity, and soon returned with the abbé, who remained with the King a quarter of an hour.

When the confessor left, Louis declared his inten-

[14] *Mémoires inédits du Duc de Croy,* cited by M. de Nolhac in *Marie-Antoinette Dauphine,* p. 323.

tion of receiving the Sacrament on the morrow. Then
he sent for d'Aiguillon, to whom he confided that the
abbé had refused to give him absolution so long as
Madame du Barry was anywhere in the neighbourhood; that he had, therefore, decided to send her to
Richelieu's château at Chinon in Touraine, and desired
that he would convey his commands to the countess.
D'Aiguillon, who, on the principle that while there is
life there is hope, was determined not to abandon the
struggle, assured the King that there must be some
mistake, and, instead of sending Madame du Barry to
Chinon, hurried off to the Cardinal de la Roche-Aymon and the Abbé Maudoux, to endeavour to persuade
them to administer the Sacraments unconditionally.
He met, as might be expected, with a good deal of opposition from the latter; but the cardinal was complacent enough, and, in the end, matters were settled as
the Minister desired.

At six o'clock the next morning, preceded by the
clergy of the parish and the chapel, surrounded by
bishops and followed by the Dauphin and his brothers,
the Princes and Princesses of the Blood, the grand
officers of the Crown, the Ministers and Secretaries of
State, and nearly the whole of the Court, all with
lighted tapers in their hands, the Holy Sacrament is
brought in solemn state to the apartments of the dying
King. The clergy, with *Mesdames* and the princes,
enter the royal bedchamber, the rest of the *cortège* remains in the adjoining cabinets. The Cardinal de la
Roche-Aymon delivers a short exhortation to the King,
which is quite inaudible, and then administers the
Sacrament.

But the ceremony is not yet over. As the cardinal
turns away, the Abbé Maudoux, "with anxious, acid-
ulent face," plucks him by the sleeve and whispers in
his ear; upon which the prelate comes to the door, and

there repeats the formula of repentance drawn up by the Archbishop of Paris, the bishops, and the confessor:

"Messieurs, the King charges me to inform you that he asks pardon of God for having offended Him and for the scandal he has given his people; that if God restores him to health, he will occupy himself with the maintenance of religion and the welfare of his people."

Two voices break the silence which follows: one is old Richelieu's, growling out some uncomplimentary reference to the Grand Almoner, which Besenval, who records the incident, is too modest to repeat; the other is that of the King, who has listened attentively to the declaration of his penitence, and now murmurs: "I should have wished for sufficient strength to say it myself."

From that moment the intrigues ceased; and all, save those whose duties compelled them to remain, fled from the sick-room, the infection from which was so terrible that over fifty persons in the château are said to have contracted the disease and ten to have died. Hour by hour the King grew worse. On May 9, two days after the first religious ceremony, the second, the administration of Extreme Unction, took place, and on the following afternoon, at a quarter-past three, the Duc de Bouillon, the Grand Chamberlain, appeared at the door of the Œil-de-Bœuf and made the announcement which had not been heard for fifty-nine years, and was not to be heard again until the death of Louis XVIII., half a century later:

"Messieurs, le Roi est mort. Vive le Roi!"

The body of the King, which had been hastily enclosed in two leaden coffins, remained in the chamber of death, guarded only by a few priests, until the evening of the 12th, when it was conveyed to Saint-Denis, "the funeral resembling rather the removal of a load one is anxious to get rid of than the last duties rendered to a monarch." The coffin was placed in a large carriage covered with a pall of black velvet, embossed with gold; another carriage contained the Ducs d'Aumont and d'Ayen; a third, the Grand Almoner and the curé of Versailles. All three carriages were those which the King had used to take him to the chase, and it had not been deemed necessary to drape them, according to custom, nor even to caparison the horses in black. The *cortège* was very simple, consisting merely of a score of mounted pages and fifty Gardes-du-Corps.[15] The faithful Soubise also followed the remains of the man from whom he had received so many favours, and was the only genuine mourner present.

The funeral procession left Versailles, at a trot, at half-past seven, and arrived at Saint-Denis soon after eleven. Among his subjects all feeling of respect and affection for the King had long ceased, and coarse laughter and ribald jests greeted the *cortège* as it passed by. In the streets of Versailles, the people cried, *"Taïaut! Taïaut!"* imitating the tone in which the King had been accustomed to pronounce the word, while at Saint-Denis there were shouts of *"Voilà le plaisir des dames! Voilà le plaisir!"*[16]

---

[15] It is not generally known that by his will, bearing date January 6, 1770, Louis XV. had forbidden all great ceremonies at his funeral, and directed that his body might be conveyed to Saint-Denis "in the most simple manner that may be." It is doubtful, however, if, under ordinary circumstances, his wishes would have been so literally observed.

[16] *Chronique de l'Abbé Baudeau, Revue rétrospective,* 1834, vol. iii. p. 42. Too much significance ought not, perhaps, to be attached to these demonstrations, for much the same had been witnessed at the funeral of *le Grand Monarque.* It was the oppres-

The body of the King was received by the Benedictines, accompanied by the clergy of the parish. At the door of the abbey, the Bishop of Senlis presented the body to the prior and pronounced some words in eulogy of the deceased monarch. The prior replied in a similar strain; then the coffin was lowered into the vaults, and the fifteenth Louis was left to sleep with his fathers—until the Revolution.

sive taxation, not the King's moral character, that his subjects resented.

CHAPTER XVIII

UNDER date May 13, 1774, Hardy writes in his *Journal:* "I am informed that the Comtesse du Barry left the village of Rueil last evening, in virtue of a *lettre-de-cachet,* for the Abbey of Pont-aux-Dames . . . under the strictest prohibition either to see or to write to any one. She was seen in a coach drawn by six horses, followed by a second carriage containing two persons, one of whom was an exempt (inspector of police)."

The *lettre-de-cachet* mentioned by Hardy, banishing Madame du Barry to the Abbey of Pont-aux-Dames, in Brie, has been generally attributed to Louis XVI., spurred on by Marie Antoinette; and M. Paul Gaulot, in his interesting work, "Love and Lovers of the Past," severely criticises the conduct of the new King, and declares that it was nothing less than an insult to the memory of his grandfather.

The indefatigable M. Vatel, however, in the course of his researches, had occasion to examine the *Registre des Ordres du Roi,* then preserved in the Archives of the Prefecture of Police, and found there the following entries:

The 9th of the month of May 1774.
Note of the Minister.

The sieur Comte du Barry	To be taken to the Château of Vincennes.
The dame Comtesse du Barry	To be taken to the Abbey of Pont-aux-Dames.

Now, on May 9, Louis XV. was still alive—he did not die till the afternoon of the 10th—and there is no reason to believe that the official who made the entries committed an error in transcribing the date, as the register was made up each day, and the entries in question were preceded and followed by other entries also dated the 9th. Nor is it at all probable that the then Dauphin, foreseeing the death of his grandfather, should have taken upon himself to order the arrest and banishment of the favourite, as, on the advice of Marie Antoinette, he had declined to receive the Ministers or give any orders whatever during Louis XV.'s illness.[1]

It follows, then, that the order must have come from the late King, and this is M. Vatel's explanation:

On the 8th, the day after he had received the *Viaticum,* there was a slight improvement in the King's condition; but on the 9th he was much worse, and Extreme Unction was administered. It was then that he resolved on the complete sacrifice of his mistress, and also of the chief participator in the scandal, "in the belief, perhaps, that he would thereby disarm the wrath of Heaven and escape the death which threatened him."[2]

M. Vatel's explanation is quite consistent with the singular religion of the monarch, who had the most implicit belief in the efficacy of certain devotional practices, prayers of forty hours, the opening of the shrine of Sainte-Geneviève, and so forth, who was accustomed to rise from the side of Madame de Mailly in order to perform his orisons, and who, if Besenval is to be believed, used even to pray with his victims of the Parc-aux-Cerfs that they might preserve their orthodoxy; and the fact that, on the day before his death, Louis had an interview with d'Aiguillon and gave him certain instructions in a low voice removes, we think, all doubt about the matter.

[1] M. de Nolhac's *Marie-Antoinette Dauphine,* p. 315.
[2] *Histoire de Madame du Barry,* ii. 334, *et seq.*

The name of Jean du Barry did not go to swell the roll of distinguished persons who had been incarcerated in the Château of Vincennes.* No sooner did that crafty adventurer learn that his *"frèrot"* (little brother), as he had the impertinence to style Louis XV., was *in extremis,* than he went to a friend named Goys, a famous wit, and asked what he advised him to do. " Valuables and post-horses," was the laconic reply; and when the *"Roué"* inquired if he had no better counsel to give him than that, answered that perhaps it would be wiser to make sure of the post-horses before troubling about the valuables.

The "count" followed his friend's advice, and when the officers of the law came to his house to apprehend him, he was well on his way to the Swiss frontier, leaving his mistresses and his numerous creditors to bewail his departure.

The new King lost no time in sending the other members of the Du Barry family after their chief. "The creature has been placed in a convent," writes Marie Antoinette to her mother on May 14, "and all who bear this scandalous name have been driven from the Court." Such, indeed, had been the case. On May 12, the "Vicomte" Adolphe and his wife each received a *lettre-de-cachet,* informing them that the Court was henceforth forbidden ground. The order sent to the viscountess was couched in the following terms:

"Versailles, 12th of May, 1774.

" I trust, Madame, that you will not doubt all the reluctance that I feel in being obliged to announce to you a prohibition to appear at Court; but I am obliged to execute the orders of the King, who charges me to inform you that his intention is that you do not present yourself there until a fresh order from him. His Majesty, at the same time, is willing to permit you to visit your aunt at the Abbey of Pont-aux-Dames, and I am, in consequence, writing to the abbess, in order that you may experience no difficulty. You will be kind enough to acknowledge the receipt of this letter by the bearer thereof, so that I may be able to justify to his Majesty the execution of his orders.

"I have the honour to be, with respect, Madame, your very humble and very obedient servant,
                    "The DUC DE LAVRILLIERE."[3]

The so-called Marquis du Barry and his consort shared the fate of the viscount and viscountess, the marchioness being likewise accorded permission to visit the favourite at Pont-aux-Dames, though neither of the ladies would appear to have availed themselves of the privilege. Elie and his wife, indeed, were anxious to dissociate themselves from the odium attaching to all who bore the "scandalous name," and, three months later, solicited and obtained permission to drop it and assume that of Conty d'Hargicourt, the uncle of the marchioness.

[3] We give this letter in full, as it has been the subject of a singular misconception. Many years after it was written it fell into the hands of a collector of autographs, a certain M. Leber, who, in his catalogue, described it as "A rare and curious document, being the original *lettre-de-cachet* sent to Madame du Barry," and added the interesting information, culled from the anecdotists, that, on receiving it, the fallen favourite exclaimed, "in the way that was usual with her," "A —— fine reign that commences with a *lettre-de-cachet!*" In course of time, M. Leber's collection passed into the possession of the Municipal Library of Rouen, where the letter was seen by the brothers De Goncourt. These distinguished writers did not, apparently, make the least attempt to verify M. Leber's statement; and, in consequence, we find it repeated in their *Les Maîtresses de Louis XV.*, and again in their *La Du Barry*, wherein they also assert that the aunt of Madame du Barry mentioned in the letter as living in retirement at Pont-aux-Dames "was without doubt Madame de Quantigny, her mother's sister."

Now, as M. Vatel and Mr. Douglas point out, if the Goncourts had exercised any care in reading the letter, they could hardly

The Abbey of Pont-aux-Dames, for which the fallen favourite was now compelled to exchange the gilded salons of Versailles, was a convent of the Benedictine Order, situated some two leagues to the south-west of Meaux. It was a very ancient house, having been founded by Hughes de Châtillon, son of a Comte de Saint-Pol, in the year 1225, and had been famous for a long line of illustrious abbesses. At one time a very wealthy community, it had now fallen on somewhat evil days, and the vast buildings were in a sadly dilapidated state.

The nuns numbered fifty, and wore the costume of the Bernardines—white woolen wimple and gown, black veil, and long scapulary of the same colour descending to the feet. The regulations, though not austere, were strict, and none of the laxity of morals which prevailed in so many convents at this period was to be found at Pont-aux-Dames; for which reason it was occasionally used as a kind of prison for ladies who had been so unfortunate as to incur the royal displeasure.

We may here remark that there was nothing shameful or humiliating in a detention of this kind. For a woman, confinement in a convent was very much the same thing as imprisonment in the towers of the Bastille or Vincennes for one of the opposite sex, and

have failed to notice three clear proofs that this *lettre-de-cachet* could not have been the one sent to the favourite: in the first place, it is addressed to the *viscountess* and not to the *countess;* in the second, there is no evidence that Madame de Quantigny, or any aunt of Madame du Barry, was ever at Pont-aux-Dames; and in the third, the lady's difficulty was not to get to Pont-aux-Dames, but to get away from there.

The error into which the Goncourts fell, however, singular as it is, is not nearly so extraordinary as their confusion of Madame du Barry's lover, the Duc de Cossé-Brissac, with *his father,* the Maréchal de Cossé-Brissac, an old gentleman of some four-score summers, to which we shall have occasion to refer presently.

many of the greatest ladies in the land had at different
times suffered the same fate as Madame du Barry.

We can imagine the impression which the first sight
of this grim old convent, with its crumbling walls,
must have made upon the ex-favourite accustomed to
the splendours of Versailles. "Oh, how *triste!*" she
cried, bursting into tears. " And it is to a place like
this that they send me!"

It is related that on her arrival she was conducted to
the refectory, to wait whilst her room was being prepared; and that the good sisters, impelled by a kind of
morbid fascination, came one by one to peep at her.
They did not dare to look directly upon the face of so
terrible a sinner, but regarded its reflection in a mirror
which was opposite to her, "expecting to see appear
therein the features of a demon." What was their
astonishment, however, to perceive a sweet-faced
young woman, who might well have stood to one of
the great painters of old time as the model for a saint,
and whose woebegone expression and tearful blue
eyes touched every heart with compassion!

The Abbey of Point-aux-Dames was razed to the
ground during the Revolution, and there is not even
a plan of it in existence; but M. Vatel, who visited
the spot some thirty years ago and questioned the vil-
lagers, learned that several of them had heard their
grandparents speak of Madame du Barry, who, it
would appear, was lodged in the inner quadrangle of
the building, in a bare room with whitewashed walls.

At first, the lady's confinement was somewhat rigorous; but her early experiences of conventual life at
Sainte-Aure stood her in good stead, and she soon became reconciled to an existence with which she was
already familiar, and won golden opinions not only
from the abbess, Madame de la Roche-Fontenille, who
had been by no means predisposed in her favour, but

from the whole community. "La Du Barry is very contented in her convent," writes the Abbé Baudeau on May 25; "the nuns are enchanted with her; she loads them with little presents and will, perhaps, end by making them very sprightly."[4] Nor was she altogether out of touch with the outside world, for she was permitted to receive letters on business matters; and Desfontaines,[5] her steward Montvallier's secretary, took advantage of this concession to write long and frequent letters, giving her an account of everything that was likely to interest her.

The contagious nature of the disease to which Louis XV. had fallen a victim had prevented the usual memorial services being held at the time of his death. His successor, however, had no intention of allowing them to be abandoned, and, in due course, every church and chapel from Dunkerque to the Pyrenees resounded with eulogies of the deceased monarch.[6] The Abbey of Pont-aux-Dames conformed to the general practice, and Madame du Barry had, no doubt, the satisfaction of hearing some glib ecclesiastic deliver an eloquent appreciation of the virtues of the Well-beloved in the chapel of the convent. "Strange contrast!" remarks M. Vatel. "Louis XV. elevated to the Pantheon of religion and history, while Jeanne Vaubernier, his last

---

[4] *Chronique de l'Abbé Baudeau: Revue rétrospective,* 1834, vol. iii. p. 56.

[5] François Guillaume Fougues-Deshayes (1733-1825), better known under the name of Desfontaines de la Vallée. In later years, he became a prolific dramatist, author of *La Bergère des Alpes* and other plays.

[6] The higher clergy vied with one another in adulation and baseness. To read their sermons one would imagine Louis XV. to have been an all-conquering monarch, of unblemished virtue, who had died at the height of his glory. " I will not talk," said the Bishop of Arras in his funeral oration, " of the great achievements of this mighty King, his glory, his successes, his victories. *A prince so dear to human hearts must have been according to*

mistress, was undergoing, for the same deeds, the public penance of confinement in a cloister!"

Gradually, the restrictions imposed upon Madame du Barry were relaxed; she was allowed to take walks in the neighbourhood; to send for her chef and several of her servants;[7] and her steward, her banker, and Aubert, the Court jeweller, obtained permission to visit her. Now that the lady no longer had the Treasury to draw upon, her creditors were becoming clamorous, and we, accordingly, find her instructing Aubert to sell her *parure* of diamonds, composed of "a stomacher, epaulettes, four rows for the waist, and a knot to loop up the skirt," and another *parure* of rubies and diamonds: collar, pendant, and earrings. The reserve price placed upon the first was 450,000 livres, and on the second 150,000, and the money was to be devoted to the payment of her debts.

The ex-favourite's financial embarrassments were, indeed, at this period, a constant source of annoyance to her, and she was, moreover, apprehensive that Louis XVI., entirely dominated as he was by Marie Antoinette and *Mesdames,* might take into his head to confiscate the gifts she had received from the late King and reduce her to poverty. She was, therefore, naturally anxious to recover her liberty, *"pour solliciter ses affaires,"* according to the phrase then in vogue,

---

God's heart." There were, however, a few honourable exceptions, and the sale of the Bishop of Alais's sermon, wherein he had spoken of the evil example which the late King had set his people and had besought his successor to regard the laws of God, was forbidden by the Government.

[7] Hardy says that Madame du Barry had twenty servants with her at Pont-aux-Dames, but this is, no doubt, an exaggeration. The same chronicler also reports that her architect, Ledoux, had built for her a new wing to the abbey, "where she might lodge more commodiously." Another absurd rumour credited the Prince de Ligne with having scaled the walls of the convent in order to visit the fair prisoner.

and, in August, wrote to La Vrillière, pleading the convent life was unsuited to her constitution.

La Vrillière returned a courteous answer, expressing his profound regret at learning that her health was not all that could be desired, and informing her that the King had the matter under his consideration, which was equivalent to a refusal; and a similar fate awaited an application from the Abbess of Pont-aux-Dames, on her charge's behalf, some three months later.

However, the countess's detention was now drawing to a close, and, on March 24, 1775, the *Nouvelles à la main* announce: "Madame du Barry has permission to leave the Convent of Pont-aux-Dames. She takes walks in the environs, but returns to the abbey to sleep. There is a rumor that she is about to purchase an estate."

The announcement was correct. Permission to leave Pont-aux-Dames had been accorded the ex-favourite on condition that she did not take up her residence within ten leagues of the Court of Paris; and, on April 9, she purchased, from a certain Sieur Sauvage, the château and estate of Saint-Vrain, situated in what is now the Department of Seine-et-Oise, two leagues from Arpajon, and about twice that distance from Corbeil.

This property had formerly belonged to François Pierre de la Garde, younger son of the old lady with whom its new owner had lived for a short time as *demoiselle de compagnie,* or rather to his wife, a Mademoiselle Duval de Lepinay, and it is probable that the countess had visited it some seventeen years previously. The château was in the style of Henry IV. or Louis XIII., with a turret at each corner, and was surrounded by a moat. The estate comprised about one hundred and fifty acres. The price paid by Madame du Barry was 200,000 livres, and she gave a further 15,000 livres for the furniture of the château. The whole of the countess's immense staff of servants, not one of whom had been discharged, in spite of their mistress's fallen fortunes, was brought to Saint-Vrain; Mademoiselle "Chon" du Barry and her sister followed.

An old inhabitant of Saint-Vrain, interviewed by M. Vatel, gave him some interesting details about Madame du Barry's life there, which, it appears, he had heard from his mother:

"There was a great deal of entertaining at the château; they gave balls, receptions, and evening parties.

"At the same time, Madame du Barry made distributions of bread, meat, and wood to the poor; all the unfortunate received assistance, or rather there were no longer any fortunate. To one she sent something for the pot; to another, if it was a woman lying-in, for example, soup, linen, caps for the child, and so forth. Her waiting-women brought to Saint-Vrain her cast-off clothing, in which she dressed up all the little girls. Often she made the people of the village dance in her park.

"She was much regretted.

"As to her appearance, I can tell you nothing. Every one knows that she was a beautiful woman. I only remember one thing that my mother told me. She had a black paroquet, which always cried out when he caught sight of her: 'Là voilà la belle comtesse!' "[8]

In the following September, Madame du Barry purchased for Madame Rançon, who had left the Couvent de Sainte-Elizabeth about the same time as her daughter was exiled to Pont-aux-Dames, the little country-house at Villiers-sur-Orge, to which reference has already been made, having previously rescued her

[8] Cited in Vatel's *Histoire de Madame du Barry,* ii. 380.

and her husband from a usurer into whose clutches they had fallen. This generosity, combined with the purchase of Saint-Vrain, had apparently made rather severe calls upon the countess's resources, for, six months later, we find her selling her hôtel in the Avenue de Paris at Versailles to *Monsieur* (the Comte de Provence). The Court was then at Fontainebleau, and, in order to facilitate the transfer of the property, Madame du Barry was allowed to revisit Louveciennes and to remain there some days.

On October 28, Malesherbes wrote to the Lieutenant of Police, informing him of the approaching publication of "a very scandalous book about Madame la Comtesse du Barry," and charging him to take every possible precaution to prevent its circulation in France.

This book was the famous *Anecdotes,* the appearance of which must have considerably damped Madame du Barry's pleasure at escaping from her convent. The author was that mendacious scribe, Pidansat de Mairobert, of whose inventive talent we have already had occasion to speak. It was printed in London, and copies were imported into France by way of Holland, the usual channel for such publications.

Acting on the instructions of Malesherbes which were, no doubt, dictated by regard for the memory of the late King rather than for the reputation of his mistress, the police made heroic efforts to cope with the invasion; but, though a number of copies were seized and destroyed, many more escaped their vigilance, and the book, adroitly "puffed" by piquant criticisms in various journals, probably written by the author himself, soon became the talk of Paris.

Although this atrocious libel was probably rated at its true value by the majority of its victim's contemporaries, that large class of French historians who prefer piquancy to probability have chosen to ignore the character of its author—who, it may be mentioned, committed suicide two years later—and to regard it as an authoritative work, with the result that among those unacquainted with the works of the Goncourts, Vatel, and Mr. Douglas the name of Madame du Barry is still regarded "as a synonym for all the depravity, profligacy, and vice of which a woman is capable."

About the same time as the *Anecdotes* were published, a "satirical brochure," entitled *L'Ombre de Louis XV. devant le tribunal de Minos,* appeared at Bordeaux. The police, however, were on the alert, and not only seized some two thousand copies, but arrested a number of persons suspected of being "aiders, abettors, accomplices, and adherents" of the crime of *lèse-majesté*. Although published at Bordeaux, the printing of the libel was traced to Cahors, which led to an acrimonious dispute on the question of jurisdiction between the Parliament of the former city and that of Toulouse. Finally, the matter was referred to the King, who decided in favour of the Parliament of Toulouse, by which time, we may suppose, "the aiders, abettors, accomplices, and adherents" had had enough experience of prison life to last them for the remainder of their days.

The winter of 1775-1776 was an exceptionally severe one; indeed such terrible weather had hardly been known since the never-to-be-forgotten winter of 1709; and Madame du Barry, snowed up at Saint-Vrain, was a prey to the direst *ennui*. She seems, however, to have had company. The inevitable "Chon" was of course there, and with her a M. Fauga, who passed for the lover of that somewhat mature spinster, and also a third person, whose relations with his fair hostess are decidedly amusing.

This was a certain Vicomte de Langle, a veteran of the Seven Years' War, *"fort connu par l'éclat de ses désordres, de ses services militaires, et de ses ouvrages."*[9] In appearance, we are told, he bore a striking resemblance to Mirabeau, and, like that remarkable character, had spent a great part of his youth in various fortresses, where he had been incarcerated by his family to keep him out of mischief. Mr. Douglas attributes to the viscount matrimonial designs upon Madame du Barry, who was still a rich woman;[10] but inasmuch as Comte Guillaume was still in the flesh, the designs, if there were any, must have been of a less legitimate character. However that may be, M. de Langle's presence at Saint-Vrain appears to have afforded material for much illnatured gossip, and in the Archives Nationales is preserved a curious document, entitled *Mémoires du chevalier de Langlès* (*sic*) *pour se justifier d'avoir gagné au jeu* 90,000 *livres à Madame du Barry, et d'avoir cherché à la raccommoder avec le duc de Choiseul.*

In this memoir, the viscount states that three charges have been brought against him in regard to his conduct at Saint-Vrain. The first is that he had demanded from Madame du Barry 90,000 livres which he had won off her at play; the second, that he had been in love with the lady and jealous of her; and the third, that, in order to revenge himself upon her for having

---

[9] *Le voyage de Figaro en Espagne* is his best known—or least forgotten—work.

[10] In addition to her life-tenancy of Louveciennes and *Les Loges de Nantes,* worth 40,000 livres per annum, the ex-favourite had an income of 105,000 livres derived from *rentes* on the Hôtel de Ville, which had been given her by Louis XV., while her jewellery and art treasures were worth a considerable fortune.

rejected his addresses, he had given an account of her conduct to the Duc de Choiseul, who was always anxious to hear anything to the discredit of his old enemy.

All three charges, he declares, are utterly false. He says that on the night before Madame du Barry left Saint-Vrain for Louveciennes, "in a moment of *ennui*," she made a bet of twelve sols that she would "hole" nine balls out of the nineteen at the first throw at *Trou-Madame*,[11] and went on increasing the stakes till she owed him 90,000 livres; but that of this large sum he refused to accept more than fifty louis, for the benefit of a young woman, a *protégée* of his, who was about to enter the countess's service.

On another occasion, the viscount, according to his own showing, was still more generous. This time, his fair hostess, forgetting for the moment apparently that she no longer had the Treasury at her back, staked on the martingale system, with the result that, at one period of the game she was in his debt to the extent of 1,500,000 livres. "But," he adds, "she was the only one who was alarmed. The bystanders were as convinced as I myself was that I should continue playing until she had recovered her losses; and, in fact, that was exactly what happened."

The other charges, namely, that he made love to the lady and was repulsed, and that, out of spite, he betrayed the secrets of her household to M. de Choiseul, are equally without foundation. It is a fact that M. de Choiseul attempted to "draw" him on the subject, but he got nothing for his pains. One day the duke and the viscount met, when the following conversation took place:

"You are a frequent visitor at Madame du Barry's?"

---

[11] *Trou-Madame* was a game somewhat similar to bagatelle; but the balls were thrown with the hand, not pushed by a cue, and the pockets were numbered both for gain and loss.

The viscount admitted that he did occasionally pay his court to the countess. "She has kept all her servants?" "Yes, M. le Duc." "Her servants perform comedies?" "Yes, M. le Duc." "But she must have a considerable fortune to support all this expense?" "I believe so, M. le Duc." "Adieu, M. de Langle." "Your servant, M. le Duc.[12]

The viscount takes great credit to himself for having so skilfully baffled the ex-Minister's curiosity; but, as a matter of fact, there was very little to relate, as life in *"cette abominable campagne,"* as the author of the above amusing memoir designates Saint-Vrain, was singularly uneventful. However, the countess only remained there eighteen months, for, on November 15, 1776, the *Nouvelles à la main* announce that "Madame du Barry comes and goes freely between Paris and Louveciennes." The writer adds that this concession was due to the Comte d'Artois, who was desirous of succeeding his departed grandfather in the good graces of the lady, and had had a tender interview with her at Radix de Sainte-Foy's house at Neuilly; M. de Sainte-Foy receiving, as the price of his complaisance, the post of *surintendant* of his Royal Highness's finances.

The latter part of this paragraph was a gross libel upon the persons mentioned, as Radix de Sainte-Foy had held the post of *surintendant des finances* to the Comte d'Artois for some considerable time; while the prince in question was so hostile to Madame du Barry that, during the last months of the lady's favour, he had forbidden his wife to speak to her. But the first statement was correct: principally, it would appear, through the good offices of Maurepas, d'Aiguillon's uncle, now first Minister to Louis XVI.,[13] the decree of

---

[12] Vatel's *Histoire de Madame du Barry*, ii. 399, *et seq.*
[13] D'Aiguillon had been replaced by Vergennes, Terray by Tur-

exile pronounced against the ex-favourite, except so far as regarded her appearing at Court, had been cancelled, and she had been permitted to return to Louveciennes.

got, and Maupeou by Miromesnil, and all three had been exiled to their estates, though the fall of the duke had been broken by a *gratification* of 500,000 livres. Maurepas, though first Minister, had no portfolio. Paris went wild with joy over the dismissal of Maupeou and Terray; the former was burned and the latter hanged in effigy, and the riots of triumph continued for a whole week. Terray was indeed regarded as the very incarnation of evil. One day, being ill, he sent for Bouvard, the celebrated doctor, and told him he was suffering *" comme un damné."* "What? already, Monsieur!" was the reply, which aptly expressed the popular feeling in regard to the Comptroller-General.

CHAPTER XIX

THE beautiful little château of Louveciennes, with its almost priceless art treasures, had up to that time seen but little of its mistress. Obliged to remain the greater part of the year at Versailles, and to follow the Court in its journeys from one royal residence to another, a few days at considerable intervals had been all that Madame du Barry had been able to spend in her "palace-boudoir." Henceforth, however, she was to reside here continuously, until the doors of Sainte-Pélagie closed upon her, and her name was to become as indissolubly connected with Louveciennes as Madame de Montespan's with Clagny, or Madame de Maintenon's with the old château from which she took her title.

It was, perhaps, fortunate for the ex-favourite that residence at Louveciennes had still for her the charm of novelty, for, during the first year or two, she appears to have led a very quiet life. The memory of courtiers is proverbially short, and few indeed of the many friends she had made in the days of her splendour cared to brave the displeasure of the King and Queen by visiting the fallen sultana.

One visitor, however, she had, who could afford to ignore the opinion of Louis XVI. and Marie Antoinette, and whose arrival must have gone far to console the mistress of Louveciennes for the neglect of those who had once been so loud in their expressions of attachment.

In April 1777, the Emperor Joseph II. arrived in France, on a visit to his sister, travelling under the

name of the Comte de Falckenstein. The bluff, out-
spoken monarch spent some weeks in the capital, and
appears to have greatly pleased the Parisians by the
interest he took in all that he saw around him; but
the impression which he created at Court, where he
took upon himself to animadvert in the strongest terms
on the shameful extravagance which prevailed, and the
indecorous behaviour of the Queen and her unworthy
favourites, was by no means so favourable; and Marie
Antoinette must have been unfeignedly glad when the
time came for him to return to Vienna.

About a month after his arrival in France, his Imperial Majesty announced that he had a great desire to
inspect the celebrated hydraulic machine at Marly,
which, as we have mentioned, was close to Louveciennes. He had previously, it appears, caused inquiries
to be made in order to ascertain if Madame du Barry
was likely to be at home that day; and the lady in
question happened to be taking an unpremeditated
walk in the direction of the machine at the very moment when the Emperor arrived there. His Majesty
requested that the countess might be presented to him,
expressed great admriation for the pavilion which he
saw in the distance, begged that he might be permitted to examine it more closely, and remained in conversation with the fair châtelaine for the space of two
hours.

After Joseph II. had duly admired the Fragonards,
Drouais, and other treasures, he remarked upon the
beauty of the gardens. The countess proposed to
show them to him; the Emperor accepted, and offered
his arm; the lady modestly declined: "Oh, Sire! I am
unworthy of such an honour." To which the monarch
replied gallantly (he was very far from gallant, it
may be remarked, where the Polignacs, Guémenées,
and other harpies whom his foolish sister had gathered

round her were concerned) : "Raise no objection on that score. Beauty is always Queen."[1]

Joseph afterwards expressed the opinion that the countess was not so beautiful as he had expected to find, but that he was very glad to have seen her.

Marie Antoinette was greatly annoyed on learning of her brother's escapade, and her indignation was intensified by the Emperor's refusal to visit the Choiseuls. The ex-Minister's hopes of a speedy return to place and power on the death of Louis XV. had not been realised, for the new King had learned the lessons which La Vauguyon had taught him but too well; and though that intriguing old gentleman had died some years before, his teaching had not been effaced from his former pupil's mind. Choiseul had counted much on the Emperor's visit; but Joseph did not share Marie Antoinette's admiration of the duke, and one day remarked to Louis XVI. that it was fortunate that he had a judicious and even-tempered Minister at the beginning of his reign, adding: "If the Duc de Choiseul had been in office, his restless and turbulent spirit would have plunged the Kingdom into great difficulties."

On February 10, 1778, Voltaire returned to Paris, after an absence of eight-and-twenty years, and was received with the utmost enthusiasm by the Academy, by Society, and by all the more important foreign visitors. He received all Paris in his bedroom at the house of the Marquis and Marquise de la Villette, in the Rue

---

[1] *Mémoires secrets*, May, 21, 1777. Mercy, in a letter to Maria Theresa, says that Joseph met the lady in the garden, tones down the two hours' conversation to one of "a few moments," and states that his Imperial Majesty "found the said countess such as I have depicted her." The Empress replies: "I should have been better pleased if the Emperor had refrained from visiting that despicable Du Barry."

de Beaune. There was an ante-chamber, which from seven o'clock in the morning until half-past ten at night was thronged with worshippers. They were introduced one by one to the Patriarch, whom they found enveloped in an enormous velvet pelisse lined with ermine and braided with gold, and with a nightcap on his head, ostentatiously correcting the proofs of his tragedy of *Irène*. Madame du Barry came to pay her court among the rest, but had considerable difficulty in obtaining an audience. We read in the *Mémoires secrets*, under date February 21 :

"*Friday.*—Voltaire has worked so hard, that he has not allowed his secretary time to dress himself. Madame la Comtesse du Barry presented herself after dinner; but they had great difficulty in persuading the old invalid to see her. His *amour-propre* would not permit him to appear before this beauty without having made his toilette. He yielded at length to her importunity, and repaired by the graces of his mind what he lacked in the matter of outward elegance."[2]

Madame du Barry's visit was marked by an interesting episode. Brissot, the future leader of the Girondins, relates in his *Mémoires* that he was very anxious to submit to Voltaire the first part of his *Théorie des Lois criminelles*. He made his way to the Rue de Beaune, but, on arriving there, his courage failed him,

[2] In reference to this visit, Lebrun wrote to Buffon : " The tears rolled from his (Voltaire's) eyes when speaking of his *Belle et Bonne* Madame de Villette), as he calls her, and comparing her simple grace to Madame du Barry, who had just left him." Five years before, when Louis XV. was still alive, and Madame du Barry all-powerful, the Patriarch had, as we have seen, formed a much higher opinion of the lady's charms. But times had changed, and she could no longer be of any assistance in procuring for him the honours of the Court, which were needed, he thought, to put the *comble* upon his glory. So goes the world !

and he left without attempting to obtain an interview with the great man. On the following day, however, he returned to the charge.

"I had almost reached the ante-chamber," he says, "where there seemed that day less commotion than on the previous evening, when I heard a noise within, and the door opened. Assailed by my foolish timidity, I quickly redescended the stairs, but, ashamed of myself, I retraced my steps. A woman, whom the master of the house had just shown out, was at the foot of the staircase. This woman was beautiful and had a kind face. I did not hesitate to address myself to her, and inquired if she thought that it was possible for me to be introduced to M. de Voltaire, telling her frankly the object of my visit. 'M. de Voltaire has received scarcely any one to-day,' she answered kindly. 'However, it is a favour, Monsieur, which I have just obtained, and I do not doubt that you will obtain it also.' And as if, through my embarrassed air, she had divined my timidity, she herself called the master of the house, who had not yet closed the door upon her, and I was admitted. She left me, after having responded to my profound salutations by a smile full of kindness and which seemed to recommend me.

". . . I ought to mention the name of this amiable woman, whom I met at Voltaire's door; it was Madame du Barry. In recalling to myself her smile so full of sweetness and kindness, I became more indulgent towards the favourite; but I leave to others the task of excusing the weakness and infamy of Louis XV. . . ."

Brissot goes on to tell us that in a conversation with Mirabeau he happened to remark that, bad as Madame du Barry was, she compared very favourably with the Maintenons and Pompadours, since she, at any rate, had never made a despotic use of her power; to which

Rice, who recovered from his wound, was tried for homicide at Taunton Assizes in the following April, and acquitted. He lived for many years, and was eventually killed in the Peninsular War.[4]

The widowed viscountess returned to France, and retired for a few months to a convent. On quitting it, she caused the arms of her husband to be removed from her carriages, changed her servants' liveries, and finally, having succeeded in obtaining permission to return to Court, reappeared there under the title of the Comtesse de Tournon. These insults to the memory of his son, to whom, to do him justice, he seems to have been genuinely attached, greatly exasperated the *"Roué,"* and when, to crown all, the lady petitioned to have the estates she had inherited from her husband formed into a "county of Tournon," he opposed the application. A long and acrimonious lawsuit followed, in which the "Comtesse de Tournon," although she had the best of the compromise eventually arrived at, was made to cut a very sorry figure. In 1782, she married again, her second husband being a relative, the Marquis de Claveyron, but died three years later.

For some years after the death of Louis XV. Madame du Barry appears to have led an exemplary life. We cannot, however, agree with Mr. Douglas that this was attributable to the fact that the image of the late King had not yet been effaced from her heart; it is more likely to have been due to accident, or to the fear that a resumption of her irregularities would have been promptly visited with another and longer period of cloistral seclusion. Towards the year 1780, however, the restraining influence, if one there was,

[4] Dutens's *Mémoires d'un voyageur qui se repose* (edit. 1806), ii. 125, *et seq.* M. Marius Tallon's *La Vicomtesse de Tournon et les Du Barry, passim.*

had evidently been removed, for we find her indulging in a *grande passion*.

About half a league from Louveciennes, and clearly visible from the terrace adjoining the pavilion of Madame du Barry, there stands a villa called Prunay, built or restored by a Madame Le Neveu at the beginning of the eighteenth century, and occupied at the time of which we are writing by a middle-aged Englishman named Henry Seymour.

A good deal of misconception exists among both French and English writers in regard to the identity of this Henry Seymour. The Goncourts refer to him as *Lord* Seymour, and state that he was English Ambassador at the French Court; to M. Vatel he is *"un assez grand personnage,"* and "though neither lord, ambassador, or even barronet (*sic*), a count"; while the late Captain Bingham, in his delightful work, "The Marriages of the Bourbons," calls him *Lord* Henry Seymour.

As a matter of fact, Henry Seymour had no title at all, though M. Vatel is correct in supposing him to be *"un assez grand personnage."* He was the son of Francis Seymour, of Sherborne, Dorset, M. P. for Great Bedwyn, 1732-1734, and for Marlborough, 1734-1741, by Elizabeth, daughter of Alexander Popham of Littlecot, Wiltshire, and widow of Viscount Hinchingbrook. His uncle was Sir Edward Seymour, who, on the death of Algernon, seventh Duke of Somerset, in 1750, succeeded in establishing his claim to the dukedom.

Henry Seymour was born in London in 1729, and educated at New College, Oxford. At the age of twenty-four, he married Lady Caroline Cowper, only daughter of the second Earl Cowper, and during the absence of his brother-in-law, the third earl, at Florence, where he resided for some years, seems to have occupied the family seat, Panshanger, near Hertford. He was himself, however, a considerable landowner. From his father, who died in 1762, he inherited Sherborne; from his uncle, William Seymour, the estate of Knoyle, in Wiltshire; while he also owned Northbrook Lodge, Devon, Redland Court, Bristol, and a property at Norton, near Evesham. His town house was in Charles Street, Berkeley Square.

Following the example of his father and his uncle, the duke, he entered political life, was appointed Groom of the Bedchamber, and successively represented in Parliament the boroughs of Totnes (1763-1768), Huntingdon (1768-1774), and Evesham (1774-1780). He only addressed the House upon one occasion, however, which was on February 29, 1776, in support of Fox's motion for an inquiry into the mismanagement of the American War.

Lady Caroline Cowper died in 1771, after bearing her husband two daughters, Caroline, who married William Danby, of Swinton, Yorkshire, and Georgina, who became the wife of Comte Louis de Durfort, sometime French Ambassador at Venice; and, four years later, Seymour married Anne Louise Thérèse, Comtesse de Panthou, a young widow, twelve years his junior, by whom he had a son, Henry, born in 1776.

In 1778, for reasons which are uncertain, though Mr. J. G. Alger—to whose interesting article in the *Westminster Review* (January 1897) we are indebted for most of our information about Madame Du Barry's English lover—seems to think it was for the sake of economising, Seymour settled in France, rented a house in Paris, Rue de la Planche, Faubourg Saint-Germain, and applied for legal domicile, to protect his property from forfeiture to the Crown as *aubaine,* in the event of his death. About the same time, he pur-

chased Prunay, and appears to have spent a considerable sum on improving the house and grounds.

The only evidence of Seymour's connection with the
ex-favourite, apart from a passing reference in the
Mémoires of the Abbé Georgel, are the lady's letters
to her lover, a number of which, together with a lock
of her hair tied with blue ribbon, were sold by auction
in Paris in 1892.

Only a few of these letters, however, have been published, and it is uncertain into whose possession the
remainder have passed.   As none of the published
letters bear any date, except the day of the week, it
is impossible to say when the *liaison* began.   According to the Abbé Georgel, the attachment was
formed shortly after Madame du Barry's return to
Louveciennes, that is to say, in the early part of the
year 1777; but M. Vatel thinks it was not until 1779
or 1780, as in one of the countess's letters, written
while they were still only friends, she speaks of a little
girl called *Cornichon,* "who talks of you constantly."
This little girl, says M. Vatel, who was the daughter
of the gardener at Louveciennes, and a great pet of the
mistress of the château, was not born until 1775, and,
therefore, must have been at that time three or four
years of age at least.

The *liaison* between Henry Seymour and Madame
du Barry does not appear to have been exempt from
storms, nor was it of long duration.   However, while
it lasted, it was undoubtedly a genuine passion, and
the lady's letters to her lover bear the unmistakable
stamp of sincerity.   "What an unlooked-for tone in
this correspondence!   How different a du Barry is
revealed to you in the shadow, behind the popular du
Barry of pamphlets and romances!   It is no longer the
courtesan, no longer the favourite; it is a woman who

loves."[5] "What a romantic passion, what sensibility, what transport! It was a real love drama, with elegies, pastorals, and eclogues to satisfy the least sentimental man in the world."[6]

In the first letter, we find Madame du Barry inquiring anxiously after the health of Seymour's younger daughter, who is ill, and assuring him of the deep sympathy she feels for him in his trouble:

"I am greatly touched, Monsieur, by the cause which deprives me of the pleasure of seeing you at my house, and I most sincerely pity your daughter in the illness from which she is suffering. I imagine that your heart is undergoing quite as much pain as hers, and I share your sensibility. I can only exhort you to take courage, since the doctor assures you there is no danger. If the interest that I take (*ji prans!*) were able to be of some consolation to you, you would be less agitated.

"Mademoiselle du Barry ('Chon') is as sensible as I am to all that concerns you and begs me to assure you of it.

"Our journey has been very fortunate; *Cornichon*[7] does not forget you and talks of you constantly. I am delighted that the little dog affords your daughter a moment's diversion.

"Accept, Monsieur, the assurance of the sentiments that I have for you.

" *Louveciennes, Saturday, 6 o'clock.*"

In the next, they are still only friends, but the lady is evidently glad to avail herself of any excuse for writing to him:

"It has long been remarked that little attentions preserve friendship, and Monsieur Seymour ought to be

[5] E. and J. de Goncourt's *La Du Barry,* p. 211.
[6] *Nouvelles à la main sur Madame du Barry,* a pretended manuscript published by Emile Cantril in 1761.
[7] See p. 288, *supra.*

well persuaded of the extent to which Louveciennes is
interested in all that can please or satisfy him. He appears to be very anxious to possess a coin squandered
very unsuitably in the little game of loto;[8] it is of the
time of Louis XIV. Monsieur Seymour is a great ad-
mirer of that age, so fertile (*fégont!*) in marvels. Here
is a miniature of it, which the Louveciennes ladies
send you. They part with it with pleasure, because
they know that Monsieur Seymour will appreciate the
sacrifice, and will be well assured that the ladies will
find more essential occasions of proving their friendship for him.

"We have no news here, except of the little dog,
which is well and drinks of its own accord."[9]

In the third letter, friendship has developed into
love—into passion. He has become necessary to her
happiness: she desires to be constantly with him:

"Now that I am deprived of the satisfaction of seeing you, I have a thousand things to tell you, a thousand things to communicate to you. . . . Never have
I felt so much as at this moment how necessary you
are to me. Rest assured that it would be a happiness
to be constantly with you. . . . Adieu, my friend.
What an age between now and Saturday!"

The next letter was, apparently, written later in the
same week. She is all impatience for Saturday to arrive:

"The assurance of your affection, my affectionate
friend, is the happiness of my life. Believe that my

[8] She probably means that the coin had been used as a counter
at loto.
[9] Apparently a puppy which Seymour had given her, in return
for the little dog she had sent his daughter.

Madame Du Barry.

From the painting by Decreuze in the Museum of Versailles.

heart finds these two days very long and that were it in my power to curtail them, it would have no more uneasiness. I await you on Saturday with all the impatience of a soul entirely yours, and I hope that you will desire nothing (*sic*). I mean to be rid of all my ailments by Saturday, and to feel alone the pleasure of proving to you how dear you are to me. Adieu, I am yours.

"*Thursday, 2 o'clock.*"

The letter which follows is in an equally passionate strain:

"My heart is undividedly yours, and, if I have failed to keep my promise, my fingers alone are to blame. I have been very unwell since you left me, and I assure you that I have only strength to think of you. Adieu, my affectionate friend; I love you—I repeat it, and I believe myself happy. I embrace you a thousand times, and am yours. Come early."[10]

From the next it would appear that a little cloud had arisen upon the lover's horizon; Seymour had evidently a suspicion that the lady's heart was no longer undividedly his:

"You will only have a single word, and it would be a reproach if my heart could make you one. I am so tired after four long letters which I have just written that I have only strength to tell that I love you. To-morrow I will tell you what has prevented me giving you tidings of myself, but believe me that, *whatever you say,* you will be the only friend of my heart.

"*Friday, 2 o'clock.*"

[10] Printed in the catalogue at a sale of autographs in February 1755, and published by the Goncourts.

The tone of its successor, however, must have been calculated to reassure him:

"*Mon Dieu!* my affectionate friend, how melancholy are the days which follow those that I have had the pleasure of spending with you, and with what joy I see the moment arrive which is to bring you to me!"

But at the time the next was written the cloud had become larger:

"I shall not go to Paris to-day, because the person I was to go and see came on Tuesday just after you left. His (or her) visit greatly embarrassed me, for I believe that you were the object of it. Adieu; I await you with the impatience of a heart entirely yours and which, in spite of your injustice, feels that it cannot be another's. I think of you; I tell you so and repeat it, and have no other regret than that of not being able to tell you so every moment.

"*Louveciennes, noon.*"

The ambiguities of the French language, as Mr. Alger points out, prevent us from knowing whether *la personne* and *sa visite* mentioned in the aforegoing letter refer to a man or woman. "Was it Mrs. Seymour suspicious of her husband's intimacy with Madame du Barry, or was it the Duc de Brissac, already hovering round his future mistress?" Both he and M. Vatel incline to the opinion that it was the latter; and the lady's complaint of Seymour's "injustice," presumably unjust suspicions, certainly strengthens this supposition. However, all doubt on the matter is set at rest by the next letter, which, together with the four which follow it, is not given in the works of the Goncourts or Vatel, but was published, we believe, for the first time by Mr. Alger:

"I am as much surprised as you, my affectionate friend, at the visit. I assure you that it gave me no pleasure. I am so absorbed with you that I could not be diverted by anything that was not you. How unjust and cruel you are! What pleasure do you take in tormenting a heart which cannot and will not be anybody's but yours!

"Adieu; do not forget *une amie* who loves you. I have no strength to tell you more. I would fain, but cannot, flee from you."

But if Seymour was jealous of Brissac, Madame du Barry was jealous of Mrs. Seymour:

"I wish it were possible for you to live for me alone, just as I would live only for you; but your ties are an invincible obstacle, and every moment of my life, even those I pass with you, is embittered by this cruel idea."

From another letter it would appear that Seymour had proposed to visit Madame du Barry, but that she had had a prior engagement, possibly with his rival:

"I am vexed at having an engagement to-day. I am not much in Society, but as we cannot pass our lives in a *tête-à-tête,* you will understand that I require a few diversions."

The next shows that relations between them were becoming very strained, and that Seymour had reproached her bitterly, and threatened to break off the connection:

"I feel the value of such a friend as you, Monsieur. I form empty plans, which I should not have the strength to carry out. Your letter has rent my soul;

the idea of seeing you no more adds to all my sufferings. Come, my friend, strengthen my still wavering
heart. Your tender and persuasive friendship can
alone assuage the throbbing wound of my soul. Come
back, my affectionate friend; I cannot be happy without you."

She will not, cannot, give him up; he has become
necessary to her very existence:

"Understand my heart and my weakness, my friend.
I would fain renounce and shun you, but I am so ill
that I believe it would be impossible to live without
seeing you."

But the rupture comes none the less, and it is her
own hand which severs the chain:

"It is needless to speak to you of my affection and
sensibility; you know it; but what you do not know are
my sufferings. You have not condescended to reassure
me as to what disturbs my mind. Therefore I think
that my tranquillity and happiness are immaterial to
you. It is with regret that I speak to you of this, but
it is for the last time. My head is well, my heart is
what suffers; but with much resolution and courage I
shall succeed in subduing it. The task is hard and
grievous, but it is necessary. It is the last sacrifice
that remains for me to make. My heart has made all
the others; it is for my reason to make this. Adieu;
be assured that you alone fill my heart.

" *Wednesday, midnight.*"

Seymour does not appear to have been altogether an
amiable person. He had an illegitimate son, with
whom his relations were strained, and he was on very

bad terms with his wife. In January 1781 they separated, having for some months previously communicated only in writing, though living in the same house; but, according to Mr. Alger, it is doubtful whether the husband's attentions to Madame du Barry were responsible for their disagreement.[11]

Seymour continued to reside at Prunay down to August 1792, when, alarmed at the progress of the Revolution, he fled to England, leaving all his papers behind him. He was registered as an *émigré*, and his property appears to have been confiscated and sold. "Madame du Barry's letters," says Mr. Alger, "must have been included in the seizure, and Seymour's preservation of them, coupled with his continued residence at Prunay, seems to show that, parting in sorrow not in anger, they remained acquaintances, if not friends; but the letters either never reached the Archives or were abstracted. They are said to have been purchased by Barrière, the editor of "Memoirs of the Eighteenth Century and of the Revolution," at a sale of autographs in 1837, perhaps the Baillot sale of October 25, 1837. But Barrière, who was a clerk at the Prefecture of Police, may have found them there, or have come by them in some clandestine way. We know what collectors are capable of, and Barrière appears to have made a mystery of them. In 1838 he communicated six of them to the brothers Goncourt for publication in their *Portraits Intimes,* and, twenty years, later he produced a seventh, which appeared in their *Maîtresses de Louis XV.* He evidently gave them the impression that he had no others, but Vatel, Madame du Barry's latest biographer, was presented by him with an eighth, which he bequeathed to a Versailles publisher. Yet

[11] See Mr. Alger's article on Henry Seymour in the *Westminster Review,* January 1897, in which he gives some interesting details about Mrs. Seymour.

Barrière was all along in possession of thirty others, which, together with the lock of hair, were not disposed of till 1892. Though the whole collection is doubtless in safe keeping, I have been unable to ascertain its whereabouts."[12]

Seymour spent the rest of his life at his Wiltshire seat, Knoyle, where he died in 1805. His heirs after Waterloo claimed £8000 out of the compensation paid by France for losses of British subjects, and Mr. Alger thinks that the claim was allowed. His son, Henry, who lived till the age of seventy-three, also resided at Knoyle, and was High Sheriff of Wiltshire in 1835. He married a Miss Hopkinson, of Bath, but his marriage vows, like those of his father, seem to have been but lightly regarded, for after Waterloo he revisited France, and formed a connection with a lady of the Bourbon-Conti family. Of this intrigue a daughter was born, who married Sir James Tichborne, and became the mother of the young man personated by "the Claimant."

[12] *Westminster Review,* January 1897.

CHAPTER XX

MADAME du Barry would not appear to have experienced much difficulty in finding consolation for the loss of her English lover, for not long afterwards she formed what the Goncourts call *"une liaison tendrement maritale"* with the Duc de Brissac,[1] whose attentions to her, if M. Vatel's and Mr. Alger's suppositions are correct, had been responsible for her breach with the jealous Seymour.

The Duc de Brissac,[2] who until the death of his father, the Maréchal Duc de Brissac, in December 1780, was known as the Duc de Cossé, was a very great personage indeed. He was Governor of Paris, Captain of the Hundred Swiss, and Grand Pantler,[3] and was, in addition, a man of considerable wealth. His friendship with Madame du Barry was of many years stand-

---

[1] The Goncourts confound the Duc de Brissac with his father, the Maréchal de Brissac, who died in December 1780: " Enfant gâtée de l'amour, elle (Madame du Barry) finit par l'adoration d'un chevalier, du dernier preux de France! . . . Ce héros d'un autre temps, dont l'âme est, comme l'habit, à la mode de Louis XIV., l'héritier des mâles vertus de la vieille France; ce beau vieillard, le dernier courtisan des femmes, élevé dans le monde et presque dans la langue des grands sentiments et des raffinements de tendresse de Clélie et de l'Astrée," &c. &c. The absurdity of this error will be appreciated when we mention that at the time of Louis XV.'s death the Maréchal de Brissac was already seventy-six and had been *paralysed* for more than twenty years!

[2] He was the eighth holder of the title, the dukedom dating from 1620. The family of Cossé-Brissac came originally from Anjou, and had had several distinguished members, including four *Maréchals de France*.

[3] This office appears to have been hereditary in the family.

ing, and it will be remembered that on the death of the
Duchesse de Villars, in 1772, the then favourite had
succeeded in procuring for the duke's wife the post of
dame d'atours to Marie Antoinette.[4]

At what date the friendship between Brissac and
Madame du Barry developed into intimacy is uncertain.   Some writers place it as early as 1780; but in
December of that year Hardy speaks of the duke attending his father's funeral at Saint-Sulpice, and
"ogling with misplaced affectation every member of the
sex who crossed his path," conduct which greatly
scandalised the worthy bookseller, and which M. Vatel
considers entirely inconsistent with the possession of a
grande passion. On the other hand, in the summer of
1783, the *Mémoires secrets* give publicity to an un-
founded rumour that the quondam favourite had had
a child by Brissac;[5] while Hardy reports that Madame
du Barry was fast ruining her noble lover,[6] and both
express their belief that the affair would end in the lady
being relegated a second time to Pont-aux-Dames.
From this it would appear that the *liaison* was not a
new one, and the probability is that it began about
1782.

However that may be, by the middle of the following year, as we have seen, the connection between the
two was a matter of common knowledge. The duke
passed a great part of his time at Louveciennes, while
Madame du Barry often came to Paris, "enveloped in

[4] The duchess did not share her husband's admiration for
Madame du Barry. In the autumn of 1772 she declined to attend
a supper given by the Duc de La Vrillière to the favourite, and
when Brissac wrote her a harsh letter, demanding that she should
show her regard for the Comtesse du Barry and never refuse
to do anything that might please her, replied that "she would
rather resign her post than do anything which might expose her
to being put on a level with the favourite."

[5] *Mémoires secrets*, June 5, 1783.

[6] *Journal*, July 13, 1783.

the strictest incognito," to spend a day or two with her lover at his hôtel in the Rue de Grenelle Saint-Germain, and even had letters addressed to her there. What the poor, neglected Duchesse de Brissac, who, Creutz tells us, was "beloved and revered for her virtues and her charm of mind," had to say to these arrangements history does not record; presumably she accepted the situation, as the majority of wives similarly circumstanced did in those days.

The affair seems to have been regarded with an indulgence remarkable even in that age of easy morality. "The love for M. de Brissac," writes d'Allonville, as a rule, by no means inclined to be over-tender towards the ex-favourite, "did Madame du Barry the greatest honour. It would have been equivalent to the purification of her past life, had it not been illegitimate and doubly adulterous from a moral point of view,"[7] and this was the general opinion of their contemporaries.

The duke wrote a number of love-letters to his mistress, some of which have fortunately been preserved, and "show the depth, and, if we may be excused the expression, the purity of his affection."[8]

THE DUC DE BRISSAC *to* MADAME DU BARRY.
" Sunday, 2.0 P. M.

'A thousand loves, a thousand thanks, dear heart. This evening I shall be with you. Yes, I find my happiness in being loved by you. I have this evening, at eight o'clock, an appointment with Madame Lascases. I do not know what she wants with me. I shall go to her house, as I will not give her the trouble to come to mine, although no one can touch my heart but you.

"Adieu; I love you and for ever. I am waiting for my visitors, who, I think, will be many."

[7] *Mémoires,* i. 154.
[8] Bingham's " Marriages of the Bourbons," ii. 428.

THE DUC DE BRISSAC *to* MADAME DU BARRY.
"La Flèche, August 26, 1786, 10 A. M.

"I arrived here yesterday at one o'clock, and all the people who were to travel by post passed before me, so that, dear heart, I am waiting here for horses. I shall have to take a cross road, along which one can only go at a walking pace, and shall thus be delayed one day. I am none the less impatient to join you. Yes, dear heart, the moment for our reunion, not in spirit—for my thoughts are ever with you—but bodily, is a violent desire that nothing can appease. . . . Adieu, dear heart; I kiss you thousands and thousands of times with all my heart. Expect me Tuesday or Wednesday early."

THE DUC DE BRISSAC *to* MADAME DU BARRY.
"Vensdosme (sic), August 16, 1789.

"I should have wished, dear heart, that you could have informed me of your complete recovery, and that you had recovered your plumpness; but you say nothing about either. Nevertheless, dear heart, I must rejoice at your new fit of laziness, which is a strange thing for you, since it makes me hope that you will not be so much away from me. . . . Dear friend, I must now go and inspect my troops and leave you. I must tell you that I love you and how happy I shall be to see you again in as good health as I wish you to be."

THE DUC DE BRISSAC *to* MADAME DU BARRY.
"Angers, August 29, Noon.

" . . . What a wise and philosophic letter is yours of the 22nd, Madame la Comtesse! yes, indeed, it is necessary to speak of hope and philosophy and of patience also when far from you, and when the States-General work so slowly on the truly important matters which all France awaits, and which ought to tranquillise her . . .

"I wish I could share with you the splendid crop of fruit that the beautiful Angevin Ceres has procured us this year; but it would be neither wise nor possible to attempt to send you any, for the municipalities are afraid of the people, who, not content with the necessaries of life, wish to appropriate the luxuries.

"But adieu, adieu, Madame la Comtesse; it is nearly noon, and I intend going to dine at Brissac. I offer you my respects, and my thanks for the punctuality with which you write to me. My only joys are the reception of your letters, the thought of you, and the everlasting affection I have for you, and which I offer you with my whole heart.

"I might have received a letter from you yesterday, but I did not."

The Duc de Brissac *to* Madame du Barry.
"The Tuileries, Wednesday, November 11, 1789.

"I am going to remain in bed, dear heart, so that my cold may be better to-morrow, and that I may be a more pleasant companion for you than I should be if I were as ill as I am now. This cold is the consequence of biliousness, which comes from the stagnation of a too long stay in Paris, to which I am unaccustomed, and will end in killing me or sending me mad, if I am not soon allowed to change my residence. I hope that I shall; but I do not speak to you of it for fear that premature rejoicing may retard it.

"Adieu, dear friend. I love you and kiss you a thousand times from the heart which is the most tender, of our two—I mean mine—but I will not erase what my pen has written, for I love to think that our hearts are one for ever. Adieu till to-morrow. Everything that happens appears to me mysterious and foolish, and the only wisdom is for us to be together. Adieu, affectionate friend; adieu, dear heart. I love you and kiss you.'"[9]

The affection of the devoted Brissac does not appear to have altogether consoled Madame du Barry for all that she had lost by the death of Louis XV. In 1783, Belleval, "her *chevau-léger*," paid her a visit at Louveciennes, and found her as beautiful as ever; "indeed her beauty seemed more remarkable and more perfect." On the other hand, she gave him the impression of being sad and lonely. "Instead of the laughter of former days, the tears welled from her eyes. She harped always on the past, in which I saw, with pity, she took refuge as much as possible, for it was worth more to her than the present. When I left her, she gave me her hand and said adieu to me in a voice full of feeling.'"[10]

In the spring of that same year, Madame du Barry commuted 50,000 livres per annum which had been secured to her by Louis XV. on the *rentes* of the Hôtel de Ville for a sum of 1,200,000 livres. Even that zealous champion of the lady, M. Vatel, feels bound to protest against this "senseless munificence" on the part of the Government, and declares that she received at least half a million francs more than her claim was worth. If such were the case, however, her good fortune could not have benefited her very much, as the news that she was in possession of a large sum of money brought down upon her a whole horde of clamorous creditors. Amongst others, the Marquis de Claveyron, the second husband of Sophie de Tournon, poor Adolphe du Barry's widow, put in a claim for his wife's dot, and compelled the countess to give

[9] Vatel's *Histoire de Madame du Barry*, iii. *passim*.
[10] *Souvenirs d'un Chevau-léger*, p. 136.

security for the payment of the interest thereon. This demand must have been particularly annoying to Madame du Barry, for not only does the interest in question appear to have been regularly paid up to that date, but one of the reasons given by her niece for dropping her first husband's name in 1780 had been the desire to dissociate herself from a family which had caused so much scandal. She had been, she declared, at the time of her marriage to the "viscount" in entire ignorance of the position of the Comtesse du Barry; but, having ascertained the truth, her virtue would no longer permit her to bear the same name! She was ready enough, it appeared, to acknowledge the relationship when there was anything to be gained by so doing.

One day in the year 1782 a very pretty young woman had called at Louveciennes, informed Madame du Barry that she was a descendant of an illegitimate branch of the House of Valois, and, apparently unaware that the lady before her was no longer a *persona grata* at Court, had begged her to present a petition on her behalf to Louis XVI., begging for the restoration of certain estates which had been granted to her family by Henri I., but had subsequently reverted to the Crown. This young woman was none other than the notorious Comtesse de la Motte, the adventuress whose machinations got the poor Cardinal de Rohan into such terrible hot water; and when the famous Diamond Necklace affair came on for trial, in 1786, before the Parliament of Paris, the ex-favourite was one of the witnesses examined.

Madame du Barry's evidence does not appear to have been of much importance, and the only interesting part of it was her statement that on hearing that the order sent by La Motte to the jeweller Böhmer was signed "Marie Antoinette de France," she had exclaimed. "Why, there is no forgery there; that is her signature!" as she had remembered that the petition which she had been requested to present to the King bore the signature, "Marie Antoinette de France, de Saint-Remy de Valois." However, the evidence against the adventuress was too overwhelming for this testimony in her favour to carry any weight.[11]

In her *Mémoires justificatifs,* published in London shortly before her death, La Motte violently attacked Madame du Barry and asserted that the forged letters had been fabricated at the ex-favourite's house; but the statements of so worthless a woman are, of course, utterly undeserving of credence.

Apart from the above-mentioned incidents, and a visit which she received from the ambassadors whom Tippoo Sahib sent to France in 1788 to seek assistance against the English, and who came to Louveciennes to pay their court to its fair owner, in the belief that she was the mistress of the reigning and not of the late King, there is little in Madame du Barry's life to call for remark until the Revolution. She lived entirely at Louveciennes, visited occasionally by some stranger of distinction, "who came to see her as the most curious relic of the last reign," and by a few intimate friends. The Marquise de Brunoy, wife of the spendthrift son of the famous financier, Paris de Montmartel, Madame de Souza, the Portuguese Ambassadress, and Madame Vigée Lebrun, the painter, were almost the only friends of her own sex whom she saw; and these, with the Duc de Brissac and a M. Monville, "an amiable and very elegant person," who lived in a château modelled on a Chinese padoga in the midst of an estate which he called "The Desert," seem to have formed her circle.

In the *Souvenirs* of Madame Lebrun we find some

[11] Vatel's *Histoire de Madame du Barry,* iii. 70.

interesting information about life at Louveciennes during these years. The magnificence of the little château, the writer tells us, which, with its busts, vases, columns, rare marbles, and other precious objects, "gave you the impression that you were in the house of the mistress of several sovereigns, who had all enriched her with their gifts," contrasted oddly with the simplicity observed by the countess both in her toilette and manner of living. Both in summer and winter Madame du Barry wore only white muslin or cotton-cambric *peignoirs,* and every day, no matter how severe the weather, she walked in the park and sometimes beyond it, "without feeling any ill effects, so much strengthened was she by her country life."

In the evenings, when Madame Lebrun and her hostess were alone, they would sit by the fire, and the latter would occasionally speak of Louis XV. and his Court, "always with the greatest respect for the one and very cautiously about the other." But, as she avoided all details, and it was evident that she preferred not to mention the subject, her conversation struck the disappointed auditor as rather uninteresting.

Madame Lebrun expresses her conviction that Madame du Barry was "a good woman both in words and actions," and says that she was most benevolent and assisted all the poor people at Louveciennes. On one occasion, they went to visit a woman in the village who had just given birth to a child and was in great want. "'What!' cried Madame du Barry, 'you have had neither linen, wine, nor soup?' 'Alas! neither, madame.' As soon as she returned to the château, Madame du Barry sent for her housekeeper and the other servants who had not executed her orders. I cannot describe to you the indignation she was in, and she ordered them to make up a parcel of linen in her presence and take it at once to the poor woman, with soup and Bordeaux wine."

Every day after dinner they adjourned to the famous pavilion for coffee. The first time Madame Lebrun entered it, the ex-favourite said: "It was in this room that Louis XV. did me the honour to dine with me. There was a tribune above for the musicians who played during the meal." When the Duc de Brissac happened to be at Louveciennes, which appears to have been pretty frequently, he accompanied them; but it was his habit, as soon as he had finished his coffee, to throw himself on one of the luxurious couches in the salon and indulge in a siesta, leaving the ladies to stroll about the grounds. Madame Lebrun, however, is careful to tell us that "nothing either in his manner or in that of Madame du Barry would have caused any one to suppose that he was anything more than a friend of the mistress of the château."[12]

The favourable opinion which Madame Lebrun formed of Madame du Barry was shared by another person who saw her for the first time about the same period, and whose impressions of the lady are of considerable interest, as from 1751-1764 he had occupied the post of *"introducteur des ambassadeurs,"* and would, therefore, hardly have failed to remark upon the fact, had he observed in the ex-favourite any of that vulgarity and bad taste with which so many historians have charged her.

This was the Comte Dufort de Cheverny, who met Madame du Barry, in 1785, at the house of a certain Don Olivadez de Pilos, a wealthy Spanish gentleman, who had fled to France to escape the vengeance of the Inquisition,[13] and had settled in Paris, where, according

[12] *Souvenirs de Madame Vigée Lebrun,* i. 109, *et seq.*
[13] Don Olavidez had been condemned as a heretic to the follow-

to Grimm, he speedily forgot his misfortunes "amidst our theatres, our philosophers, our Aspasias, and sometimes our Phrynes." Madame du Barry, Cheverny tells us, had "a marked veneration" for this victim of priestly intolerance, and was "so to speak at his orders," and when, therefore, Don Olivadez informed her that he had some friends who were extremely anxious to be presented to her, she readily agreed to gratify their desire.

"It was freezing hard enough to freeze a stone," the chronicler continues. "She arrived alone in a carriage drawn by six horses. She was tall, extremely well made, and, in short, a very pretty woman in every respect. At the end of a quarter of an hour she was as much at her ease with us as we were with her. My wife was the only other lady present. Madame du Barry paid marked attention to my wife and the master of the house, but was pleasant and amiable to all. Président de Salaberry[14] and his nephew, the Chevalier de Pontgibault,[15] were there, and several others. She bore the brunt of the conversation, spoke of Louveciennes, and invited us to come and see it and dine with

ing penalties: (1) To make a public recantation of his errors, " without prejudice to the confiscation of all his goods." (2) To be confined eight years in a monastery and subjected to the most rigorous discipline. (3) To be afterwards exiled twenty leagues from any royal palace or important town. (4) Never to ride on horseback or in a coach. (5) Never to hold any office or enjoy any title. (6) Never to wear cloth, silk, or velvet, but to dress always in yellow serge.

[14] Charles Victor François d'Irumberry de Salaberry, Président of the *Chambre des Comptes.* He perished on the scaffold in 1794. He was the father of Charles Maurice d'Irumberry, Comte de Salaberry, who fought in the wars in La Vendée and took a prominent part in politics after the Restoration, in which he distinguished himself by his reactionary tendencies.

[15] The Chevalier de Pontgibault, or Pontgibaud, as the name is commonly spelt, had accompanied La Fayette to America. His *Mémoires,* wherein he relates his experiences during the War of Independence, are of considerable interest.

her. We accepted the invitation, but without naming
any particular day.

"Her pretty face was slightly flushed; she told us
that she took a cold bath every day. She showed
us that under her long furred pelisse she had only
her chemise and a very thin *manteau de lit*. Everything she wore was of such costly material, relics
of her former splendour, that I have never seen
finer batiste. She insisted that we should feel her
petticoats, to prove to us how little she cared for
the cold.

"The dinner was delightful; she told us a hundred
anecdotes about Versailles, all in her own style, and
she was very interesting to listen to. Seeing that Pontgibault wore the Cross of Cincinnatus, she related to
us the following story: 'When I was at Versailles my
name made a great impression, and I had six lackeys
called footmen, the finest men that could be found;
but they were the noisiest and most unruly rascals in
all the world. The ringleader of them gave me so
much trouble that he saw plainly that I should be
obliged to dismiss him. It was at the beginning of the
war in America, and he came to me and asked for
letters of recommendation. I gave them to him, and
he left me with a well-filled purse, and I was only too
glad to get rid of him. A year ago he came to see me,
and he was wearing the Cross of Cincinnatus.' We
all laughed at the story, except the Chevalier de Pontgibault.

"The conversation after dinner took a more serious
turn. She spoke with a charming frankness about the
Duc de Choiseul, and expressed regret for not having
been on friendly terms with him; she told us of all the
trouble she had taken to bring about a better understanding, and said that, had it not been for his sister,
the Duchesse de Gramont, she would have succeeded

in the end; she did not complain of any one and said nothing spiteful."

Cheverny happening to mention that once, during her favour, he had made an unsuccessful atempt to obtain a post at Court for one of his friends, Madame du Barry exclaimed: "Why did you not come to me? I wanted to oblige everybody. Ah! if M. de Choiseul had but known me, instead of yielding to the counsels of interested persons, he would have kept his place and have given me some good advice, instead of which I was forced to fall into the hands of people whose interest is was to ruin us, and the King was no better off."

When she had gone, Cheverny and his friends were unanimous in praise of the good humour with which she accepted her changed fortunes, and all agreed that they no longer felt any surprise at the influence she had exercised over a *blasé* old man of sixty-four, "as she must have been a charming mistress."[16]

[16]*Mémoires de Cheverny*, ii. 22, *et seq.*

CHAPTER XXI

THE year 1789 arrived. Posing for her portrait to Madame Lebrun in the gardens of Louveciennes, Madame du Barry was startled by the distant boom of the cannon which announced the taking of the Bastille and the end of the old *régime*, and which so frightened poor Madame Lebrun that she rushed off home the same day and never returned to finish the picture.[1]

However, the former favourite continued to live quietly at Louveciennes, and except that she was made the heroine of a satirical and somewhat licentious poem by Saint-Just, the future colleague of Robespierre, and was attacked in an obscure newspaper called *Le Petit Journal du Palais-Royal, ou Affiches, Annonces, et Avis divers*, which only survived for six numbers, no notice appears to have been taken of her during the first year of the Revolution.[2]

[1] The head, however, had already been painted and the bust and arms traced out, and some years after the death of Madame du Barry the artist completed it. Madame Lebrun tells us that she painted two other portraits of her friend—the first, at half-length, " in a peignoir and straw hat "; the other, representing the countess " robed in white satin, with a wreath in one hand, and one of her arms resting on a pedestal." Both of these pictures had been commissioned by Brissac.

[2] *Organt, poème en vingt chants, au Vatican*, 1789, was the title of Saint-Just's production. Madame du Barry, who figures under the name of Adelinde, is thus described:

> " Ces yeux errants sous leur *paupière brune,*
> Ces bras d'ivoire étendus mollement,
> Ce sein de lait que le soupir agite
> Et sur lequel deux fraises surnageaient,
> Et cette bouche et vermeille et petite,
> Où le corail et les perles brillaient,
> Au dieu d'amour les baisers demandaient."

Her lover, the Duc de Brissac, in spite of the fact that he was, to a certain extent, in sympathy with the new ideas, was not so fortunate. A fortnight after the fall of the Bastille, while on his way to visit his estates in Anjou, he was arrested at Durtal, near La Flèche, and a courier despatched, by the local authorities, to Paris to ascertain if his "patriotism" was under suspicion, and whether he was to be imprisoned there or sent back to the capital. After a short detention, he was released, or contrived to effect his escape, and no further attempt was made to molest him for some time; but the incident foreshadowed the terrible fate which awaited him three years later.

In the *Notices historiques* appended to his *Mémoires de la Reine de France,* by Laffont d'Aussonne, the following passage occurs:

"When the Revolution broke out, the house of Madame du Barry became the rendezvous of all the friends of Louis XVI. and the Queen. The *Gardes-du-corps* who escaped the massacre of October 6 dragged themselves from Versailles to Louveciennes, and the countess nursed them in her château as their own relatives would have done. The Queen, informed at Paris of this amiable and generous conduct on the part of the countess, charged some nobles in her confidence to go to Louveciennes and carry thither her sincere thanks. Upon this, Madame du Barry had the honour to address to the Queen the words I am about to transcribe. I had them from one of her relatives:

" 'MADAME.—The young men who were wounded only regret that they did not die along with their comrades for a princess so perfect and so worthy of all respect as Your Majesty assuredly is. What I am doing for these brave soldiers is much less than they

deserve. Had I had no waiting-women or other servants, I would have attended to your guards myself.
I console, I honour them for the wounds they have received, when I reflect that, but for their devotion and
their wounds, Your Majesty might be no longer alive.

" 'Luciennes is at your disposal, Madame. Is it not
to your favour and kindness that I owe it?' All that I
possess is derived from the Royal Family, and I have
too much good feeling and gratitude ever to forget
that. The late King, by a sort of presentiment, made
me accept a number of valuable presents before sending me away from his person. I had the honour to
offer you this treasure at the time of the meeting of
the Notables.' I offer it you again, Madame, with
eagerness and in all sincerity; you have so many expenses to bear and benefits without number to bestow.
Permit me, I beg, to render unto Cæsar the things that
are Cæsar's.

" 'Your Majesty's most faithful subject and servant,
            " 'COMTESSE DU BARRY.' "

Laffont d'Aussonne is not a chronicler in whom
very much confidence is reposed, and this, combined
with the fact that the style and orthography of the
above letter are much superior to those of Madame du
Barry's which we possess, has caused its authenticity
to be doubted. M. Vatel, however, discovered that
two of the wounded *Gardes-du-corps* did take refuge

---

³ She means that it was due to the magnanimity of the King
and Queen that she had been allowed to retain Louveciennes
after the death of Louis XV.
⁴ In February 1787, Calonne, the Comptroller-General, called
together an extraordinary council or assembly of notables,
nominated by the King, and proposed to them the reform of the
entire system of administration and taxation. This assembly,
however, composed almost entirely of privileged persons, was
unfavourable to the proposed reforms, and Calonne soon afterwards resigned.

at Louveciennes after the events of October 6, and that their names were Marion de Barghon-Monteil and Lefebvre de Lubersac, and his conclusion is that the circumstances as stated by Laffont d'Aussonne are correct, though the letter is probably a paraphrase of the one written by the ex-favourite. There was certainly nothing surprising in Marie Antoinette sending to thank Madame du Barry for her care of the soldiers wounded by her defence, while it was but natural that the favourite should acknowledge the Queen's condescension.

With regard to the offer made at the time of the meeting of the Notables, M. Vatel professes himself unable to discover any proof of this "in spite of persevering researches"; but it is certain that the King received a number of offers of this kind, both from private individuals and corporations.[5]

Every day the situation became more serious; every day it became more and more apparent that for the despotism of the Crown France was substituting the infinitely worse despotism of the mob. Most of the great nobles followed the example of the Comte d'Artois and took refuge across the frontier; but Brissac, though well aware of the fate which awaited him were the enemies of the Monarchy to triumph, courageously refused to desert his sovereign and remained at his post.

And Madame du Barry remained too. Love, and possibly also the knowledge that her departure would almost inevitably entail the confiscation of her property, kept her at Louveciennes—that beautiful spot from whose terrace she could perceive the spires of the great city so soon to run red with blood. Nor at first did she have any reason to regret her decision, for the year 1790, so fruitful in great events, was for her as

[5] Vatel's *Histoire de Madame du Barry*, iii. 132.

uneventful as had been its predecessor;[6] and it is quite
possible that the storms of the Revolution might have
passed her by unscathed had it not been for an unfortunate incident, which served to draw public attention to her ill-gotten wealth, and was ultimately the
means of bringing her to the scaffold.

On January 10, 1791, Madame du Barry attended a
fête given by the Duc de Brissac at his hôtel in the
Rue de Grenelle Saint-Germain.   The countess had, it
appears, intended to return to Louveciennes that evening, but, at the duke's suggestion, changed her mind
and slept at the Hôtel de Brissac, where a suite of
rooms was always reserved for her use.   Well indeed
would it have been for her had she carried out her
original intention, as, early on the morrow, a mes-
senger arrived in hot haste from Louveciennes with the
news that the previous night a gang of burglars had
broken into the château and made off with the greater
part of the countess's jewellery.[7]

In great agitation, Madame du Barry at once returned home, gave information of the robbery to the
local authorities, and then sent for her jeweller, Rouen,
to consult him as to the best means of recovering her
stolen treasures.

---

[6] She was, however, the object of an attack in Marat's journal,
L'Ami du Peuple, which, in its issue of Thursday, November 11,
1790, informed its readers that the National Assembly cost only
a quarter of the money which "that old sinner," Louis XV., had
squandered on his favourite wanton, and added that the writer
of the article had seen the Du Barry, twenty years before,
"covered with diamonds and giving away the louis d'or of the
nation by the basketful to her thieves of relations."
[7] Madame du Barry's jewel-cases were kept in the ante-
chamber leading to her bedroom.   A soldier belonging to the
Suisses rouges, quartered at Courbevoie, was on guard outside
the château during the night; and, before leaving home, the
countess had given orders that, in the event of her not returning
till the morrow, the gardener was to sleep in the ante-chamber.
As, however, it was not easy to put up a bed in this room,

Now, Rouen was a very capable craftsman and an honest man; but he appears to have been singularly wanting in discretion; for no sooner was he acquainted with the extent of the disaster than he hastened back to Paris, and, without giving a thought to the delicate position occupied by his patroness in the face of the Revolution, caused a handbill to be circulated through the city bearing this sensational title:

"Two Thousand Louis Reward."
"Diamonds and Jewels lost."

Then follows a portentously long list of the stolen treasures: diamonds, rubies, sapphires, and emeralds in every shape and form; rings, pendants, earrings, watches, and bracelets; "a pair of shoe-buckles composed of eighty-four brilliants, weighing seventy-seven carats and a quarter"; "a cross of sixteen brilliants, weighing eight to ten grains each"; "a beautiful pair of sprigs composed of large brilliants, valued at 120,000 livres"; "a string of four hundred pearls, weighing four to five grains each"; "a pair of sleeve-buttons consisting of an emerald, a sapphire, a yellow diamond, and a ruby, the whole encircled by rose diamonds, weighing thirty-six to forty grains"; a pair of bracelets of six rows of pearls weighing four to five grains each; at the bottom of the bracelet is an emerald surmounted by a cipher in diamonds, an L on one and a D and B on the other, and two padlocks of four bril-

Morin, her head *valet-de-chambre,* had taken upon himself to dispense with the attendance of the gardener; while the robbers had taken the precaution to entertain the Swiss at a neighbouring *cabaret,* with the result that he became temporarily unfit for duty. Then, with the aid of a ladder which had been left near the house, they mounted to the window of the ante-chamber, broke the outside shutters, cut out a pane of glass, opened the window, and ransacked the room at their leisure.

liants, weighing eight to ten grains." It was a veritable
inventory of Golconda.[8]

The effect of this ill-judged production on the minds
of the exited, half-starved "patriots" who perused it
can well be imagined. Instantly, the revolutionary
Press, ever on the alert to fan the flame of popular resentment, rang with denunciations of the ex-mistress.
Prudhomme's journal, *Les Révolutions de Paris,* led
the way and published an article in which it accused
Madame du Barry of inventing the robbery: "It is
thought that the lady, fearing that her income would
be cut short, wanted to excite pity by representing
herself as the victim of a regrettable incident and
gaining thereby the indulgence of the inflexible National Assembly."

Elsewhere the same journal made a violent attack on
the countess, who, it is alleged, had, on discovering the
robbery, driven off to Courbevoie in a coach and four,
and obtained from the commanding officer of the
Gardes Suisses a body of fifty men to arrest the
drunken sentry, "a young man eighteen years of age,
of an amiable appearance and very honest." "The
theft of all the diamonds of Golconda," continued the
indignant writer, "would not justify such a violation
of the rights of man and of the citizen, and, moreover,
is it a sufficiently grave offence to deserve the punishment of being placed in irons, on the simple suspicion
of a woman, still proud of having been for a moment
the first courtesan of the empire?"

Madame du Barry appears to have been too much
occupied in endeavouring to trace her lost property to
pay much attention to the attacks of Prudhomme and
his *confrères,* which, however, were to bear fruit in due

[8] See the list of the stolen jewellery published by the Goncourts in *La Du Barry,* p. 373, *et seq.*

season. But, though she engaged the services of Bar-
thélemy Piles, one of the most skilful police-agents of
the day, nothing was heard of the stolen jewels for upwards of a month, when a courier arrived from England, with the information that the thieves had been
arrested in London. The gang consisted of five persons: three German Jews, a Frenchman, who called
himself a broker and wore the uniform of the National
Guard, and an Englishman named Harris, who acted
as interpreter, and who, according to the *Public Ad-
vertiser* (February 17, 1791), had already undergone
a term of penal servitude.

On arriving in London, they had gone to an inn and
engaged a single room, from which it is to be presumed
that the old proverb which tells us that there is honour
among thieves did not hold good in their case, and that
each of them was fearful of letting his confederates
out of his sight. They had no money, but quieted the
landlord's objections by telling him that by the morrow
they would be in possession of a considerable sum.
They then went out and called upon a rich jeweller,
named Simon, to whom they offered a portion of their
booty at about one-sixth of its value. Simon paid
them £1,500, and then inquired if they had any more
to sell. They replied in the affirmative, whereupon, his
suspicions aroused, the jeweller laid information
against them before the Lord Mayor, who immediately
issued a warrant for their arrest.

The day after receiving the news of the apprehension of the burglars, Madame du Barry set out for
England, accompanied by one of Brissac's aides-de-
camp, the Chevalier d'Escourre, the jeweller Rouen, a
waiting-woman, and two menservants, and arrived in
London on February 20. "Madame du Barry," writes
Horace Walpole to the Berrys on February 26, "is
come over to recover her jewels, of which she has been

robbed—not by the National Assembly, but by four
Jews, who have been seized here and committed to
Newgate. Though the late Lord Barrymore acknowledged her husband to be of his noble blood, will she
own the present Earl as a relation when she finds him
turned strolling player?[9] If she regains her diamonds,
perhaps Mrs. Hastings may carry her to Court."[10]

Two days later he returns to the subject:

"Madame du Barry was to go and swear to her
jewels before the Lord Mayor. Boydell, who is a little
better bred than Monsieur Bailly,[11] made excuses for
being obliged to administer the oath *chez lui,* but
begged she would name her hour, and when she did, he
fetched her himself in the state-coach and had a Mayor-
Royal banquet ready for her. She has got most of her
jewels again. I want the King to send her four Jews
to the National Assembly and tell them it is the change
or *la monnaie* of Lord George Gordon, the Israelite."[12]

In a subsequent letter (March 5) Walpole writes:
"I have not a tittle to add—but that the Lord Mayor
did not fetch Madame du Barry in the City-Royal
coach, but kept her to dinner. She is gone, but returns in April."

The lady had, in fact, left England on March 1.
During her stay she had been confronted with the
thieves, but had stated that she had never seen any of
them before. On the other hand, Rouen had identified

[9] For an account of the theatrical undertakings of Richard,
Earl of Barrymore, see Mr. J. B. Robinson's interesting work,
"The last Earls of Barrymore."

[10] "Mrs. Hastings was supposed, by the party violence of the
day, to have received immense bribes of diamonds."—*Note of
Wright.*

[11] Jean Sylvain Bailly, Mayor of Paris, the celebrated astron-
omer.

[12] Lord George Gordon, who was then undergoing a sentence
of five years' imprisonment for libel, had appealed to the National Assembly to intercede for his release.

the jewels, in spite of the fact that several of them had been defaced, and had declared them to be "the result of his laborious toil."

The expenses of this first journey, which the Duc de Brissac, who looked upon himself as the involuntary cause of the robbery, had insisted on defraying, amounted to 6193 livres.

At the end of a month, Madame du Barry was obliged to return to London, where a serious legal difficulty had arisen. As the robbery had been committed in a foreign country, the delinquents could not be brought to trial in England, nor, unless a special application was made for the purpose by the French Government, could they be even detained in custody or sent to France for trial. The utmost satisfaction that Madame du Barry could obtain would be to have her property restored to her, but before she could hope for this, many legal formalities must be complied with.[13]

The countess left Louveciennes on April 4 and arrived in London five days later. She was again accompanied by d'Escourre and Rouen, and was furnished by her bankers, the Vandengyers, with a letter of credit on Simmonds and Hankey, of London. She had also taken the precaution—a very necessary one at a time when everybody leaving France ran the risk of being promptly registered as an *émigré* and having their property confiscated—of procuring a passport from the Minister Montmorin.[14]

---

[13] *St. James's Chronicle,* February 24, 1791.

[14] Here is the passport:

"De Par Le Roy,

" *A tous officiers civils et militaires chargés* de surveiller et maintenir l'ordre public dans les différens départemens du royaume et à tous autres qu'il appartiendra; salut. Nous vous mandons et ordonnons que vous ayiez à laisser passer librement *la dame du Barry allant à Londres avec le S. d'Escours, chevalier*

We have very little information about Madame du Barry's movements during this visit, the expenses of which amounted to over 15,000 livres, inclusive of the purchase of two English horses. She appears, however, to have found a welcome in very exclusive circles indeed, for, on April 17, Walpole writes to Miss Berry that the previous day the countess had dined with the Duke of Queensberry, and that among the guests was the Prince of Wales. It would be interesting to know what the First Gentleman in Europe and she who, for a brief period, had been the first lady in France thought of one another; but, unfortunately, Walpole does not tell us.

Madame du Barry reached Louceviennes on Saturday, May 21, but during the night of the 23rd a courier arrived to inform her that her presence in London was indispensable, and, on the following day, she set out for England for the third time. In spite, however, of the powerful influences that she was able to enlist in her favour and the expenditure of a great deal of money, the affair dragged on—it seems to have been begun in a very careless manner and to have been conducted still more carelessly—and it was not until towards the end of August that it was finally decided that, as the robbery had not taken place within English jurisdiction, the burglars must be acquitted, and that Madame du Barry must obtain from the French courts a condemnation of the culprits and a declaration that the property was really hers. Pending the proof of her claim to their possession, the jewels were placed

de S. Louis, le S. Rouen, jouaillier, deux femmes et un valet de chambre et deux couriers.

" Sans *lui* donner ni souffrir qu'il *lui* soit donné aucun empêchement; le présent passe-port valable *pour trois semaines seulement.*

"Donné à Paris, le 3 Avril 1791.
Par Le Roy

" Louis."

in a sealed box and deposited with Messrs. Ransom, Morley, and Hammersley, bankers, of Pall Mall.

During this, her third visit to England, Madame du Barry rented a house in Bruton Street, Berkeley Square, and, notwithstanding her anxiety to regain possession of her beloved diamonds, seems to have had a very pleasant time. She mixed freely in English society, and we hear of her at several celebrated houses, notably at the Duke of Queensberry's, where Horace Walpole made her acquaintance and "had a good deal of frank conversation with her about Monsieur de Choiseul."[15] She also visited some of the French *émigrés* who had found refuge in London—a very unwise proceeding, as it subsequently proved—went to St. Paul's, the Tower, and Ranelagh, gave away a considerable sum in charity, and made numerous purchases: a portrait of the Prince of Wales and another of the Duchess of Rutland, "two English books," for the Prince de Beauvau, with whom she was now on very friendly terms, and Thomas Paine's "Rights of Man," and a Shakespeare in parts, for herself.

Perhaps, however, the most interesting incident of her stay was her visit to the studio of the celebrated painter Cosway, to whom she sat for the charming miniature portrait which Condé's fine engraving has perpetuated for us, and which is certainly the most pleasing of all the portraits of Madame du Barry.

The former favourite is represented in a white gown with a high waist, a toilette which seems to anticipate the fashion of the Directory. Her head is turned slightly aside, a string of pearls encircles her throat, her hair is loose and falls in luxuriant curls over her shoulders, her eyes sparkle with merriment through their half-closed lids, a half-smile plays round her mouth. It is indeed hard to believe that this exquisite

[15] Letter to the Berrys, August 23, 1791.

miniature, "in which one seems to see the portrait of the Voluptuousness of the eighteenth century: a Bacchante of Greuze,"[16] is that of a woman in her forty-eighth year.

Madame du Barry landed in France on August 25, 1791, and proceeded to Louveciennes, where she remained until October 14, 1792, that is to say, for more than thirteen months.

[16] E. and J. de Goncourt's *La Du Barry*, p. 215.

CHAPTER XXII

DURING Madame du Barry's absence in England, important changes had taken place in France. Since the flight to Varennes, in the previous June, it was impossible for the country to have any further confidence in its King, and although the unhappy monarch continued to reign, his authority was reduced to the merest shadow. He was still, however, permitted to retain most of the outward and visible signs of sovereignty; and one of the first acts of the Legislative Assembly, when it met on October 1, 1791, was to appoint a *Garde constitutionelle,* to take the place of his disbanded bodyguard.

This *Garde constitutionelle,* which consisted of 600 cavalry and 1,200 infantry chosen from the troops of the line or the National Guards, was recruited very differently from the old *Maison du Roi,* and no one was allowed to be enrolled unless he had given "proofs of citizenship." The choice, however, of its commander and one-third of the officers was left to the King; and Louis, in spite of the remonstrances of Marie Antoinette, who still regarded with disfavour all who continued on terms of intimacy with Madame du Barry, offered the command to Brissac,[1] trusting, in his secret heart, that the latter would give a very

---

[1] According to Gabriel, Duc de Choiseul, when the flight of the Royal Family was first contemplated, Brissac was suggested as the man best qualified to carry out the scheme; but the proposal was rejected, as it was feared that he might confide the secret to Madame du Barry, and that she might reveal it.

liberal interpretation to the intentions of the Assembly
with regard to the proofs of citizenship.

The duke accepted the appointment, though with
many misgivings, for the dangers attending his new
office were obvious. Nor were his fears groundless,
as, before many weeks had passed, hostile criticisms
of the manner in which he was discharging his
duties began to appear in the Press. These soon
changed to violent denunciations, and, finally, the Legislative Assembly intervened, and on the nights of May
30-31, 1792, after a lengthy and acrimonious debate,
that body decreed that the *Garde constitutionelle*
should be disbanded, and its commander be forthwith
arrested and arraigned on a charge of treason before
the High Court, then sitting at Orléans.

It was one o'clock on the morning of the 31st when
the decree was passed, and Gabriel de Choiseul, who
was present, hurried to the Tuileries to inform the
King and Queen. Louis at once sent a message to
Brissac's apartments in the palace, urging him to make
his escape without a moment's delay. Brissac, however, was not the man to desert his post, and answered
that he would remain and abide by the consequences.
He then rose, and spent the rest of the night in writing
a long letter to his mistress, which he despatched to
Louveciennes by Mussabré, one of his aides-de-camp.

It would appear to have been on the previous evening, while the debate in the Assembly was proceeding,
that Madame du Barry wrote to the duke as follows:

MADAME DU BARRY *to* THE DUC DE BRISSAC.
" Wednesday, 11 *o'clock.*[2]

"I was seized with a mortal fear, M. le Duc, when
M. de Maussabré was announced. He assured me that

[2] M. Vatel is of opinion that this letter was written on July 6,
that is to say, some days *after* the arrest of the duke and his

you were in good health, and that you had the tranquillity of a good conscience. But this is not enough for my interest in you; I am far from you; I know not what you intend to do. Of course you will answer that you yourself do not know, and I am sending the abbé[3] to find out what is happening and what you are doing. Oh! why am I not near you? You would receive the consolation of tender and faithful friendship. I know that you would have nothing to fear did reason and honesty reign in the Assembly.

"Adieu! I have no time to say more. The abbé is in my room, and I want to send him off as quickly as possible. I shall not rest until I know what has become of you. I am well assured that you have done your duty with regard to the formation of the King's Guard, and on this point I have no fear for you. Your conduct has been so open ever since you have resided at the Tuileries that they will find no charge against you. Your 'patriotic actions' have been so numerous that indeed I wonder what they can impute to you.

"Adieu. Let me hear from you, and never doubt my affection for you."[4]

At six o'clock that morning Brissac was arrested and conducted the same day to Orléans. The popular exasperation against him was such that special precautions had to be taken to guard him against attack; but the

departure for Orléans, which took place on May 31. But, in her examination on the 9th Brumaire (October 19, 1793), Madame du Barry, when questioned as to the date, answered that she wrote the letter "on the same day that he (Brissac) started for Orléans, *or the evening before.*" She added that it was never sent, "as she had news of him from one of his people."

[3] The Abbé Billiardi, of the Foreign Office, a great friend of the lovers.

[4] *Tribunaux révolutionnaires, dossier de Madame du Barry, Archives nationales.* E. and J. de Goncourt's *La du Barry,* p. 225.

journey was uneventful, and, a few days later, Madame du Barry received, though Maussabré, a letter from the duke announcing his safe arrival.   Although Brissac would not appear to have shown much anxiety at his position, probably from a desire not to alarm his friends, the latter were fully alive to the grave dangers which threatened him; and his daughter, the Duchesse de Mortemart, who had emigrated, with her husband, at the beginning of the Revolution and was now at Aix-la-Chapelle, wrote to Madame du Barry begging for information concerning her father.

THE DUCHESSE DE MORTEMART *to* MADAME DU BARRY.

" June 5.

"Will you recognise my handwriting, Madame?   It is three years since you saw it, and at a sad moment.[5] This is sadder still for your affection and mine.   Ah! how I have suffered for the last two days!   His courage, his firmness, the praises which are showered upon him, the regrets which are expressed, his innocence, nothing can quiet my agitated mind.   M. de . . .[6] and myself wished to start the day before yesterday; but several powerful persons dissuaded us from doing so, pointing out that it would be dangerous for my husband and be of no advantage to my father, and adding

[5] On leaving France, in 1789, Madame de Mortemart had written to Madame du Barry: " Madame,—I beg that you will accept my best thanks for the kindness you have always shown me, and believe that I deeply regret not being able to see you before leaving.   I feel very sad at the thought that I shall be so long without seeing my father, and that I cannot even take leave of him before I set out.   But there is nothing left for me, except to submit to my fate.   I beg that you will kindly accept the assurance of my affection for you."

From the above letter it would appear that the duchess regarded her father's passion for Madame du Barry with complacence, and was on very friendly terms with the latter.

[6] Mortemart, without doubt.

that the fact of his being an *émigré* would injure him. But I, Madame, could not I be of some service to him? might it not be possible for me to see him? Can it be imputed as a crime to a woman in delicate health to have gone to take the waters, and must it be visited on my father? I cannot believe it, and it is the only thing of which I am afraid. If you think that I could be of any use to him either at Paris or Orléans, have the kindness to let me know, and I will fly thither. Is there any means of hearing from him or communicating with him? Send me word, I entreat you, and I will hasten to take advantage of it. I learned, through a man who is, perhaps, unknown to you" (the name, written between parentheses, is erased) "that you had gone to Orléans. Let me tell you that such token of attachment for one who is dear to me gives you an eternal claim on my gratitude. Accept, I beg of you, the assurance of the affection which I have for you for life.

"Allow me to curtail the usual compliments at the end of letters, and give me the same mark of friendship. I send this letter through a reliable person at Paris, who, I trust, will be able to forward it to you without inconvenience. Pardon my scribble."[7]

Whether Madame du Barry went to Orléans, as the duchess's informant stated, is doubtful. According to one writer, she not only did so, but took with her a considerable sum of money, in the hope of bribing Brissac's gaolers to connive at his escape. But it seems very difficult to believe that the duke, who, as we have seen, had made no attempt to escape on the night when his arrest was decreed by the Legislative Assembly, when he could have done so with the certainty of success, would have consented to a plan

[7] Cited in Vatel's *Histoire de Madame du Barry,* iii. 163.

which must have presented many obstacles, and which, in case of failure, must have gravely compromised his mistress; while, on the other hand, the ex-favourite's presence in Orléans, by awakening memories of the scandalous past, would have undoubtedly injured the prisoner.

Brissac was incarcerated in an old convent in the Rue Illiers. He was examined on June 15, but hardly attempted to justify himself. When charged with admitting royalists into the *Garde constitutionelle,* he merely denied it: "I have admitted into the King's Guard no one but citizens who fulfilled all the conditions contained in the decree of formation."

He was taken back to prison, but does not seem to have been kept in very close custody, and was permitted to communicate with his friends; for on June 20 Madame de Mortemart informs Madame du Barry that she had had a letter from her father.

THE DUCHESSE DE MORTEMART *to* MADAME DU BARRY.
"June 20.

"A million thanks, Madame, for the news which you have so kindly sent me. Your letter has been delayed, and I only received it together with one from my father, which has afforded me great pleasure. Since then I have heard that he has been examined, and is no longer in close confinement. He is now as comfortable as a prisoner can be. Although he is known to be innocent, I fear that the proceedings will last a long while. I should have rejoiced had I been able to have been of any use to him or given him any pleasure in his confinement. Adieu, Madame. Pardon my scribble. Be assured of my love for life."[8]

But neither daughter nor mistress were ever to be-

[8] Cited in Vatel's *Histoire de Madame du Barry,* iii. 167.

hold the prisoner at Orléans again. The ill-advised manifesto of the Duke of Brunswick, the declaration that the country was in danger, the arrival in Paris of the Marseillais and thousands of enthusiastic volunteers on their way to the frontier, roused the excited populace to madness; and a few weeks after Madame de Mortemart's letter was written, the storm which had so long been gathering burst in all its fury.

After the storming of the Tuileries and the massacres which followed, Brissac and his fellow prisoners could no longer disguise from themselves the terrible danger which menaced them; and on the very day on which the news of the events of August 10 reached him, the duke asked for writing materials, and, with his own hand, drew up his will.

Having appointed the Duchesse de Mortemart his residuary legatee and made provision for various relatives and dependents, the testator recommended very earnestly to his daughter "a lady who was very dear to him, and whom the evils of the time might plunge into the greatest distress," and then added the following codicil:

"I give and bequeath to Madame du Barry, of Louveciennes, above and beyond what I owe her, a yearly income for life of 24,000 livres, free from all conditions; or, again, the use and enjoyment for life of my estate of la Rambaudière and la Graffinière, in Poitou, and the movables belonging to it; or, yet again, a lump sum of 300,000 livres payable in cash; whichever she may prefer. When once she has accepted either of the three legacies mentioned, the other two will become void. I beg her to accept this small token of my gratitude, I being so much the more her debtor in that *I was the involuntary cause of the loss of her diamonds,* and that if ever she succeeds in regaining them from England, those which will be lost, added to the expenses incurred in the various journeys which their recovery has rendered necessary, will amount to a total equivalent to the value of this legacy. I request my daughter to prevail upon her to accept it. My knowledge of her (his daughter's) heart assures me that she will punctually disburse whatever sums she may be called upon to pay in order to fulfil my will and codicil. My wish is that none of the other legacies be paid over until this one has been discharged in full.

"Written and signed with my own hand at Orléans, this August 11, 1792.

"LOUIS-HERCULE-TIMOLEON DE COSSE-BRISSAC."[9]

The same day, the duke wrote the following letter to Madame du Barry, the only one, unfortunately, of those sent from Orléans which has been preserved:

THE DUC DE BRISSAC *to* MADAME DU BARRY.
" Saturday, August 11, Orléans, 6 P. M.

"I received this morning the most amiable of letters, and one which has gladdened my heart more than any which I have received for a long while. I kiss you thousands and thousands of times; yes, you will be my last thought.

"We are in ignorance of all particulars" (of the events of August 10); "I groan and shudder. Ah! dear heart, would that I could be with you in a wilderness rather than in Orléans, which is a very wearisome place to be in."[10]

[9] Le Roi's *Curiosités historiques,* p. 287. The legacy of the duke to Madame du Barry was almost entirely absorbed by the creditors of the lady, and by a lawsuit between the Bécus and the Gomards—both of which families claimed to be her heirs—which lasted from 1814 to 1830.

[10] *Tribunaux révolutionnaires, dossier de Madame du Barry, Archives nationales.* On this letter is written: *" Un mois avant sa mort."*

"You will be my last thought." These words must have seemed to Madame du Barry a presentiment of approaching disaster, and an event which occurred a few days after she received her lover's letter increased her fears for his safety.

The duke's aide-de-camp, Maussabré, happened to be at the Tuileries when the palace was attacked by the mob on the morning of August 10, and had taken part in its defence. He was wounded, and, like the *Gardes-du-Corps* three years earlier, took refuge at Louveciennes, where Madame du Barry concealed him in a room in the pavilion. He imagined himself in safety, but his hopes were vain, for a band of local Jacobins, eager to emulate the deeds of their Paris brethren, came to search the house, and the wretched lad—he was but eighteen—was torn from his hiding-place and dragged away to Paris, prison, and death.[11]

The invasion of her house showed but too plainly that the unpopularity of Brissac was gradually enveloping his mistress, and that she was regarded as his accomplice; and the *Courrier français,* in its issue of September 2, announced the countess's arrest, no doubt with the intention of still further inflaming public opinion against her:

"Madame du Barry has been arrested at Louveciennes, and has been brought to Paris. It was ascertained that the old heroine of the late Government was constantly sending emissaries to Orléans. M. de Brissac's aide-de-camp had been arrested at her house. It was thought—and there was good reason for doing so—that these frequent messages had some other purpose than love, which Madame du Barry must now forget. As the mistress and confidential friend of the Duc de Brissac, she shared his wealth and his pleas-

[11] He was murdered during the September massacres: see p. 345, *infra.*

ures; who knows if she does not, at the same time, share his anti-revolutionary ambition?

"It will be piquant reading for our descendants when they learn that Madame du Barry was arrested almost simultaneously with the pulling down of the statue of the Maid of Orléans. She was arrested during the night of the 30th-31st, about 2 A.M."

On the same day on which this article appeared began the frightful massacres which deluged the prisons with blood; and while these atrocities still continued, Madame du Barry received intelligence that Brissac and the rest of the Orléans prisoners were to be transferred to Paris. It appeared that several of those confined in the convent in the Rue Illiers had contrived to effect their escape, while four others, who had been tried by the High Court, had been acquitted. The fear that yet more of their destined victims might succeed in evading their doom roused the indignation of the more sanguinary of the Paris revolutionists, and petitions from the sections and the clubs demanding that the remaining prisoners should be immediately brought to Paris for trial poured in upon the Assembly.[12] The Assembly, dismayed at the scenes of bloodshed which were being enacted around it, and well aware what would be the result of compliance with such a demand, could not bring itself to consent, until its hand was forced by a body of volunteers from Marseilles, who set out for Orléans, with the intention of bringing back the prisoners; whereupon Fournier[13] was

[12] At the same time, a pamphlet, entitled *Têtes à prix*, was being circulated in Paris, the writer of which offered 12,000 livres—he did not say by whom the money was to be paid—to the man who should "make a little Saint-Denis of M. Timoléon Cossé-Brissac."

[13] Surnamed *l'Américain*, as he had spent some years of his life in San Domingo. He was one of the most violent of Jacobins, and had taken a prominent part in the attack on the Bastille, the affair in the Champ de Mars, and the events of August 10.

despatched at the head of 1800 of the National Guard, with instructions to conduct the prisoners not to the capital but to the Château of Saumur. Fournier, however, misunderstood, or, more probably, deliberately disobeyed, his orders, and, when Brissac and his companions had been handed over to him, took the road to Paris.

Madame du Barry learned of the duke's removal from Orléans from a letter which is supposed to have been written by the Chevalier d'Escourre, the tone of which was far from calculated to reassure her:

THE CHEVALIER D'ESCOURRE (?) *to* MADAME DU BARRY.

" Paris, September 6.

"The Orléans prisoners are to arrive to-morrow at Versailles. It is to be hoped that they will arrive safe and sound, and that, by gaining time, their lives will be saved. Besides, the Assembly is tired of so much bloodshed and proposes to grant an amnesty. The sacrifice is not a very great one, seeing that none of them are guilty.

"I have been to see the editor of the *Courrier français,* who will to-morrow retract the false article about you. I promised him a reward, if the article was satisfactory.

"I have received from Orléans ten letters for the deputies, imploring them to avert the terrible fate which awaits the prisoners. At Orléans, it is believed that as soon as they arrive, they will be murdered.

"I had the letters delivered at once. Madame de Maurepas, when she heard of the duke's transfer, wished to go at once to the Assembly, but was dissuaded from doing so. She then wrote to Danton and the Abbé Fauchet. Madame de Flammarens and I took the letters, and the Abbé Fauchet was much interested in them.

"Poor Maussabré would have been spared, had he not lost his head. He tried to hide in a chimney; they lighted straw to stifle him and force him to come down; he fell, and they shot him without listening to his appeals for mercy.

"I am cast down body and soul; I shall only be at rest when I know the duke is at Versailles. If it is possible to get through, I will send some one, if I cannot go myself. Do you also send some one, but above all be careful and avoid taking any steps which might be made public and be injurious to you both."[14]

Brissac and his fellow captives, to the number of fifty-three, left Orléans on September 3, in tumbrils supplied by a force of artillery stationed in the neighbourhood, escorted by the National Guards and the Marseillais. The authorities saw them depart with considerable misgivings, though Fournier swore that he would sacrifice "even his life" in their defence, and the force under his command was certainly strong enough to overawe any number of fanatical *sansculottes*. On the 6th they reached Etampes, half-way between Orléans and Paris, and halted there till the following day, the prisoners taking advantage of the delay to write letters to their friends, which they handed to Fournier for transmission, and which that worthy subsequently sent to the Convention.

The terrible scenes which were taking place in Paris had thrown the whole of the surrounding country into a ferment of excitement, and as the cortège neared Versailles, the cries of *"A bas les seigneurs! à bas les seigneurs!"* grew more frequent and more threatening,

[14] Cited in Vatel's *Histoire de Madame du Barry*, iii. 177.

Brissac being in particular the object of hostile demonstrations.

The general council of the Commune of Versailles,
fearing that an attack would be made upon the prisoners, had sent orders that they should not be conducted through the more populous part of the town,
and should be confined for the night in the cages of
the Menagerie, "which would have the advantage of
satisfying the popular resentment and lessening the
sentiment of hatred, by giving rise to feelings of contempt."[15] This precaution, however, was quite useless;
the rabble of Versailles was determined to follow in
the footsteps of the murderers of the Faubourg Saint-
Antoine, and was not to be baulked of its prey.

On Sunday, the 9th, about one o'clock in the afternoon, the cortège entered the town by the Petit-Mon-
treuil Gate, passed along the Rue de la Surintendance
(now the Rue de la Bibliothèque) and the Place
d'Armes, and began to descend the Rue de l'Orangerie.
Up to that moment, the people who lined the way had
contented themselves with shouting *"Vive la Nation!"*
and hooting the prisoners; but opposite the Ministry of
War the procession was stopped by a raging mob
armed with spikes, sabres, and other weapons. The
Mayor of Versailles endeavoured to pacify them, but
to no purpose, although the leaders announced that if
Brissac and Lessart, the former Minister for Foreign
Affairs, were given up, the others would be spared.
Meanwhile, the Orangery Gate, for which the tumbrils
were making, had been shut, and the escape of the
prisoners cut off.

As to remain stationary was to court certain disaster, orders were given to turn back and ascend the
street. The mob allowed the procession to get as far
as the corner of the Rue Satory, and then, sweeping

[15] Vatel's *Histoire de Madame du Barry,* iii. 175.

the escort. which made not the slightest attempt at resistance,[16] aside, cut the traces of the horses, and fell savagely upon the hapless prisoners.[17]

Snatching a knife from one of his assailants, Brissac defended himself bravely, but he was soon overpowered by numbers, dragged from his tumbril, and despatched. His body was horribly mutilated, and his head, having been cut off, was fixed upon a pike, with a label bearing his name on the forehead, and carried through the streets in triumph. Later in the day, it was taken to Louveciennes and thrown into the garden, or, according to one account, into the salon of Madame du Barry.[18]

The grief and horror which the terrible death of her lover occasioned Madame du Barry may be judged from the following letter which the countess wrote, a few days after the tragic event, to Madame de Mortemart:

MADAME DU BARRY *to* THE DUCHESSE DE MORTE-MART.

"No one has felt more than myself, Madame, the extent of the loss which you have just sustained, and I trust that you will not be under a misapprehension as to the motive which has prevented me from paying you the sad compliment of mingling my tears with yours before this. The fear of augmenting your justi-

[16] Fournier afterwards declared that he was himself attacked and dragged from his horse, and would have been killed, had it not been for the intervention of his men. But there can be no possible doubt that he was in collusion with the assassins.

[17] Statements of Antoine and Pierre Baudin made before a notary in Paris, September 12, 1792, cited by Vatel.

[18] "We are assured that the head of M. de Brissac was taken to Louveciennes and left in the salon of Madame du Barry."— *Courrier français*, September 15, 1792.

fiable grief prevents me from speaking to you of it.
Mine is complete; a life which ought to have been so
great, so glorious! What an end! *Grand Dieu!*

"The last wish of your unhappy father, Madame,
was that I should love you as a sister. This wish is too
much in conformity with my heart for me not to fulfil it. Accept the assurance of it, and never doubt the
affection which attaches me to you for the rest of my
life."

To which the duchess replied:

THE DUCHESSE DE MORTEMART *to* MADAME DU
BARRY.

"*September* 30.

"I received your letter this morning. Accept my
thanks for the good you have done me. You have
lessened my anguish and brought tears to my eyes.
Many times I have been ready to write to you and
speak of my grief; my heart is rent, broken. Ever
since the fatal day on which my father left Paris I
have suffered, and I still suffer more than I can express. But I judged it wiser to wait until I could
contain some of my feelings. I must open my heart
to you, who alone are able to realise my grief.

"I am eager to fulfil the last wish of him whose
memory I cherish, and whom I shall mourn for ever;
I will indeed love you as a sister, and my attachment
to you will end only with my life. The least of my
father's wishes is a command sacred to me. If I could
only obey every one of the desires he had, or must have
had, in his last moments, I would spare nothing to do so.

"Pardon my scribble. My head aches so that I
cannot see. Deign to accept, Madame, the expression
of my everlasting affection."[19]

[19] *Tribunaux révolutionnaires, dossier de Madame du Barry,
Archives nationales.* E. and J. de Goncourt's *La Du Barry*, p.
230.

CHAPTER XXIII

EARLY in the following month Madame du Barry prepared for a fourth journey to England. On February 6, 1792, the French courts had duly condemned the authors of the robbery at Louveciennes, and declared the jewels found in their possession to be the property of the mistress of the château; but since then a fresh difficulty had arisen.

The unfortunate handbill in which Rouen had advertised the loss of the jewels had been framed in very ambiguous terms. It had offered two thousand louis reward, "and a fair and proportionate reward for the objects which might be recovered." Madame du Barry maintained that the payment of the two thousand louis ought to be accepted in full satisfaction of all claims against her, and such, without doubt, had been Rouen's intention when he drew up the bill. But Simon, the London jeweller whose information had led to the apprehension of the thieves, protested that he was entitled not only to the above-mentioned sum, but to a commission on the value of the property recovered, and brought an action to enforce his claim, which necessitated the lady's return to England.

Aware that she was now an object of suspicion and dislike to the more violent partisans of the Revolution, Madame du Barry, ere leaving France, took every possible precaution to guard against the risk of being denounced as an *émigrée* during her absence. She applied to Lebrun, the Minister of Foreign Affairs, for a passport; and when he advised her to procure one from the municipality of Louveciennes, was careful to have it *visé* both by the *directoire* of Versailles and the administration of her department (Seine-et-Oise). Not content with this, she gave a formal undertaking to the municipal authorities that she would return to France as soon as her lawsuit should be concluded, and wrote to Thuriot, the President of the Convention, to the same effect:

MADAME DU BARRY *to* THE PRESIDENT OF THE CONVENTION.

"MONSIEUR LE PRESIDENT,—A robbery which deprived me, twenty-one months since, of the most valuable portion of my property and the only security that my creditors possess, necessitated a lawsuit in England, on account of which I have already been obliged to make two[1] very expensive journeys. I am advised that the suit will be definitely decided this month, and that it is absolutely necessary for me to go to London, on pain of being condemned in default and losing the considerable expenses to which I have already been put. I have the honour to assure you, Monsieur le Président, that I have not the least intention of deserting my country, where I am leaving all the remainder of my property, but that, on the contrary, I am entering into a most solemn engagement to return to my residence of Louveciennes as soon as my suit is decided. I am placing an undertaking to that effect in the hands of my municipality, from which I am well assured that I have nothing but favourable testimony to expect.

"I am, with respect..."[2]

Thus protected at all points, as she fondly imagined,

[1] She had, of course, made three journeys.
[2] *Dossier de Madame du Barry, Archives nationales.* E. and J. de Goncourt's *La Du Barry*, p. 248.

Madame du Barry set out for England on October 14, accompanied by a M. Labondie, a nephew of the Chevalier d'Escourre. Her case, however, so far from being concluded in a few weeks, dragged on for more than four months, and it was not until February 27 that the court gave a verdict in Simon's favour for one thousand louis, and decided that the jewels were to be handed over to the countess on her paying that sum and the costs of the proceedings. What these amounted to we are not told, but they would appear to have been very considerable, as, when Madame du Barry was arrested in the following September, the jewels were still lying in Ransom's Bank, waiting for their owner to redeem them.

Owing, no doubt, to her grief at the tragic death of poor Brissac, Madame du Barry seems to have gone but little into English society during this visit, and we find no mention of her movements in Walpole's letters. She dined, however, on one occasion at the house of Thellusson, the banker, and there met the young Duc de Choiseul, her old enemy's nephew and successor. "I was placed next to her at table," says the duke, "and during dinner, at which she endeavoured to be very amiable, she spoke to me much about my uncle, deplored the counsels which she had followed, and gave me to understand that she had had for him a *coquetterie réele,* but that she had found him cold and reserved."[3]

The news of the execution of Louis XVI. on January 21, 1793, created a profound impression in England. Court mourning was ordered and worn by persons of all ranks in the metropolis, and Requiem Masses were said in all the Catholic churches. Madame du Barry not only wore mourning, but attended the service in the chapel of the Spanish Embassy; in-

[3] *Revue de Paris,* 1829, vol. iv. p. 48.

discretions which, together with several visits which
she paid to the houses of the Comte de Narbonne,
Calonne, Talleyrand, and other *émigrés,* were duly
noted by the spies of the Republic with whom London
swarmed, and were not forgotten when the poor
woman appeared before the Revolutionary Tribunal.

The countess left for France on March 1,[4] but as
war had broken out between England and France a
month previously, she was compelled to remain some
time at Calais before she could procure a passport.[5]
At length, on the 17th, she was permitted to set out for
Louveciennes, where a most unpleasant surprise
awaited her.

Soon after Madame du Barry quitted Louveciennes
on her last journey to England, a person named

[4] Very much against the advice of her friends, who implored
her to remain. According to Madame Guénard, shortly before
her departure Madame du Barry had an interview with Pitt, who
presented her with a medal bearing his portrait, and warned
her that if she returned to France she would meet the fate of
Regulus. This story is probably apocryphal; but Madame du
Barry does seem to have been acquainted with Pitt, and also
possessed a medal of the kind described; for "living habitually
with Pitt and wearing a medal bearing the effigy of the monster"
was one of the charges against her at her trial.

[5] Here is the passport:

République Française

Au nom de la loi

Département du Pas-de-Calais, district et municipalité de Calais
No. 4829
Laissez passer la citoyenne Devaubergnier Dubarri, Française,
domicile à Louveciennes, municipalité de Louveciennes, district
de Versailles, département de Seine-et-Oise

Agée de quarante ans (!)
Taille de cinq pieds un pouce
Cheveux blond (*sic*)
Sourcils châtain
Yeux bleux (*sic*)
Nez bien fait
Bouche moyenne
Menton rond
Visage ovale et plein

Et prêtez-lui aide et assistance, &c.

George Grieve, or Greive, as he wrote his name in later years, came to the village and took up his quarters at the inn. This Grieve was an Englishman, a member of a respectable family at Alnwick, in Northumberland. His father, Richard Grieve, was an attorney, and his brother, Richardson David Grieve, had been high-sheriff of Northumberland in 1788. The Grieves, however, had always been ardent politicians, and of a particularly turbulent kind. Both the grandfather, Ralph Grieve, and Richard Grieve had been expelled from the Common Council at Alnwick for riotous conduct during elections, and George seems to have inherited the family weakness in a very marked degree. In 1774, he took an active part in defeating the Duke of Northumberland's attempt to nominate both members for the county, and, four years later, headed a mob which levelled the fences of a part of the moor wrongly presented by the corporation to the duke's agent. About 1780, having got into pecuniary difficulties, Grieve left England and went to America, where he became acquainted with Washington and other founders of the Republic, and appears to have supported himself by his pen. From America he proceeded to Holland, it is said, on some political mission, and about 1783 took up his abode in Paris.[6]

Until the arrival of Grieve in their midst, the inhabitants of Louveciennes had been, comparatively speaking, unaffected by the disturbances which were going on around them; but Grieve, who had acquired a thorough mastery of the French language, and seems to

Delivré en la maison commune de Calais, le 17 mars 1793 L'An II. de la République et ont signés (*sic*) Reisenthal, officier municipal; Tellier; Roullier secrétaire commis greffier, qui a signé pour le présent et Devaubergnier Dubarri.—Vatel's *Histoire de Madame du Barry*, iii. 189.

[6] Mr. J. G. Alger's "Englishmen in the French Revolution," p. 187, *et seq.*

have been a fluent and persuasive speaker, soon succeeded in working a complete transformation in that peaceful spot; and by the time Madame du Barry returned it would have been difficult to find a nest of more rabid Jacobins in all France.

But it was against the mistress of the château herself that the agitator's machinations were mainly directed, though what motive he could have had for the implacable hatred he evinced towards her has never been satisfactorily explained, and must, we fear, always remain a matter of conjecture. Some writers think that he was prompted by Marat, with whom he was on intimate terms, and who, as we have seen, had already attacked Madame du Barry in his journal; others, that he intended to terrify her into purchasing his silence; while others, again, incline to the belief that he was enamoured of the lady and persecuted her either out of revenge for her having rejected his addresses or in the hope of compelling her to accept them. The most probable solution of the mystery, however, is that he was merely a fanatic possessed with a mania for delation[7]—he subsequently boasted of having brought no less than seventeen persons to the guillotine—and imagined that the ruin of so prominent a representative of the old *régime* as the former mistress of Louis XV. would add lustre to his sanguinary reputation.

However that may be, Grieve appears to have left no stone unturned to compass the destruction of the unhappy lady. By bribes or threats, he won over two of her servants, Salanave and the Hindoo, Zamor; wormed all their mistress's secrets out of them; organised a club, which had the impudence to meet in her salon and pass resolutions against her; contrived to

[7] He denounced one unfortunate person merely because he had observed him "look furious" when visiting Marat.

persuade the authorities at Versailles that the countess's prolonged absence meant that she had become an *émigrée;* and, finally, on February 16, obtained an order for seals to be placed on her property.

When Madame du Barry returned and found what had been done, she was highly indignant and addressed a vigorous remonstrance to the administrators of her district:

MADAME DU BARRY *to* THE DIRECTORY OF THE
DISTRICT OF VERSAILLES.

"CITIZEN ADMINISTRATORS,—The Citoyenne de Vaubernier du Barry is very astonished that after all the reasons for her being compelled to visit England with which she has furnished you, you have treated her as an *émigrée.* Before her departure, she communicated to you the declaration that she had made to her municipality; you have registered it at your offices, and you are aware that this is the fourth journey that she has been obliged to undertake, always for the same object. She hopes that you will be willing to remove the seals which have been imposed at her house, against all justice, since the law has never prohibited those persons whom private and urgent affairs call to foreign countries leaving the realm. All France is aware of the robbery which took place on the night of January 10-11; that the robbers were apprehended in London, and that a trial followed, in which the final decision was not arrived at until February 28 last, as the enclosed certificate bears witness.[8]

" Louveciennes, March 27, 1793."

This remonstrance had the desired effect, and the seals were promptly removed; but Grieve was not dis-

[8] Cited by the Goncourts, *La Du Barry,* p. 251.

couraged, and, after spending some three months in
maturing his plans, in company with Salanave[9] and a
spy named Blache, who had had Madame du Barry
under observation during her stay in England, where
he had been masquerading as a teacher of French,
returned to the attack.   Profiting by the terrible decree of June 2, 1793, which directed the authorities
throughout the Republic to seize and place under arrest
all persons *"notoirement suspectes d'aristocratie et
d'incivisme,"* he drew up an address to the authorities
of the Department of Seine-et-Oise, signed by thirty-
six of the inhabitants of Louveciennes, complaining
of the presence in their midst of many aristocrats and
suspected persons of both sexes, and demanding the
publication of the decree of June 2.   This request having been granted, Grieve at once made out a list of
"suspects," placed the name of Madame du Barry at
the head of it, and proceeded to the château to arrest
her.   However, the countess had been advised of his
proceedings, and had sent her *valet-de-chambre,*
Morin, and Labondie, to plead her cause with the
members of the superior administrations; and just as
Grieve and the officials of the municipality reached
the house, Boileau, member for the district, arrived
on the scene, reprimanded them for making improper
use of a law which was only intended to be used with
great caution, and suspended the arrest.

Nothing daunted, Grieve lost no time in drawing up
another address, and, on July 3, presented himself at
the bar of the Convention, accompanied by some of
"the brave *sans-culottes* of Louveciennes"; and there
proceeded to read his petition, which contained a ve-
hement denunciation of Madame du Barry, "who had
made her château the centre of liberticide projects,

[9] Salanave had been detected by Madame du Barry, soon after
her return, stealing her porcelain, and had been dismissed.

commenced by Brissac and continued by the aristocrats of every shade with whom she was in constant correspondence; who insulted by her luxury the sufferings of the unfortunate people whose husbands, fathers, brothers, and children were shedding their blood for the cause of equality in our armies, and whose arrest was indispensable in order to destroy the vestiges of a false grandeur, which dazzled the eyes of the good and simple inhabitants of the surrounding country, and put into practice the misunderstood principles of equality."[10]

To this the President of the Convention replied:

"The National Convention applauds the new proofs which the commune of Louveciennes has just given of its patriotism, recognised from the commencement of the Revolution, and which it manifests at the present moment by putting into execution the law of June 2 against a woman too long celebrated for the misfortune of France. The facts that you have just alleged against her are very grave; be assured that, if they are proved, her head shall fall on the scaffold."[11]

He then gave orders that Madame du Barry was to be placed under arrest in her own house, guarded by a gendarme, to be kept there at the lady's expense, and sent the petition to the Committee of General Security,[12] which body ordered the Department of Seine-et-Oise to hold an inquiry into the alleged "incivism" of the Citoyenne du Barry.

[10] *L'Egalité controuvée, ou Petite Histoire de la Protection, contenant les pièces relatives à la arrestation de la du Barry.* (Paris: 1793.) [11] *Ibid.*

[12] The Committee of General Security must not be confounded with the Committee of Public Safety. On special occasions they consulted together, but the former always occupied a subordinate position. The Committee of General Security superintended the measures taken for the detection of political crime. Originally the Girondists possessed a majority in it, but it was now composed of twelve Montagnards.

The inquiry was held a few days later, and the signatories of Grieve's petition were called upon to make good their allegations. This they entirely failed to do; some, whom Grieve had probably intimidated into signing the address, declared that they had done so under a misapprehension as to its contents, while the rest could only adduce rambling statements and vague rumours, which even a revolutionary court was reluctant to admit as evidence. On the other hand, a number of the inhabitants of Louveciennes who looked with disapproval on Grieve's proceedings, and had declined to join the club which he had organised, drew up a counter-petition, in which they spoke in high terms of the Citoyenne du Barry, declaring that she was the benefactress of the village; that they had seen her in all weathers taking food and money to the sick and poor; that she readily paid all taxes that were levied, and had proven her patriotism by lending a room in her house for a meeting of the local committee. The address concluded with a complaint of the conduct of certain persons (Grieve and his friends) who had recently established themselves in their midst and set themselves to disturb the harmony and good-feeling which had hitherto existed.

This petition they sent to the Committee of General Security, who, after having deliberated upon it, decided that there was no evidence to convict the Citoyenne du Barry, and directed the authorities of Seine-et-Oise to set her at liberty.

Thus the countess was saved a second time, and a severe rebuff administered to the malignant Grieve; but the latter was not the man to allow his victim to escape him. On July 31 he published and circulated a violent pamphlet, under the title of "Sham Equality (*L'Egalité controuvée*); or Short Account of the Protection (*i.e.*, that given by Boileau and the authorities of Seine-et-Oise to the ex-favourite), containing the documents relating to the arrest of the Du Barry, former mistress of Louis XV., to serve as an example to those over-zealous patriots who wish to save the Republic and those moderates who understand marvellously well how to ruin it." The author signed himself "Grieve, *défenseur officieux* of the brave *sans-culottes* of Louveciennes, friend of Franklin and Marat, factious (*factieux*) and anarchist of the first water, and disorganiser of despotism for twenty years in both hemispheres," denounced the interference of departments and committees with the course of justice, and called loudly for the death of "the courtesan of Louveciennes, the Bacchante crowned with ivy and roses."[13]

This pamphlet was, in due course, brought to the notice of Madame du Barry, who was astonished to find that it contained a number of intimate details regarding her private life, which could only have been furnished the writer by a member of her household. Her suspicions fell upon Zamor, who had been the only one of her servants who had not been placed under arrest after Grieve's petition to the Convention, and she promptly ordered the treacherous and ungrateful Hindoo to leave the house. She doubtless imagined that she had got rid of him for good and all; but she was mistaken; for Zamor was to reappear to give evidence against his benefactress before the Revolutionary Tribunal.

As the days went by the attitude of Grieve and his confederates towards the mistress of the château became more and more menacing, and at length Madame du Barry was forced to appeal for protection to the administration of the department.

The administrators of Seine-et-Oise were favour-

[13] A copy of this pamphlet, now very rare, is in the possession of the British Museum.

ably disposed towards the ex-favourite; indeed, one of their number, named Lavallery, is commonly believed to have been in love with her; and, in answer to her appeal, Lavallery came to Louveciennes and urged her to remove to Versailles and place herself under the protection of himself and his colleagues. Madame du Barry, however, explained to him that all her jewellery which the burglars had overlooked, her plate, and a very large sum in cash were concealed in various parts of the house and grounds; that the traitors Salanave and Zamor were acquainted with her arrangements, and that her departure would probably be the signal for a raid, which might deprive her of a great part of her fortune.

The visit of Lavallery to Louveciennes did not pass unnoticed by the watchful Grieve, who, the very next day, called a meeting of his club and decided to send a deputation to Versailles, to denounce Madame du Barry to the revolutionary committee of the commune of the town, and to draw up, in concert with that body, a petition to the Committee of General Security, demanding the arrest of her protector and two of his colleagues.[14]

Solicitude for the safety of her hidden treasures was not the only reason which made Madame du Barry reluctant to quit Louveciennes at that moment; from the following letter, which was among the papers seized at her house, at the time of her arrest, it would appear that she had given, or was about to give, a third successor to Louis XV.:

"Saturday, September 7, 1793.

"I send you, my dear and affectionate friend, the picture that you wished for, sad and funereal present,[15]

[14] E. and J. de Goncourt's *La Du Barry,* p. 261.
[15] Without doubt a portrait of Brissac.

but I feel as much as you yourself that you ought to desire it. In such a situation as ours, with so many subjects of pain and grief, it is food for our melancholy that we seek and which becomes us beyond everything.

"I have sent to fetch the three portraits of you which were at his house; they are here. I have kept one of the small ones; it is the original of that in which you are wearing a chemise or white peignoir and a hat with a plume.[16] The second is a copy of that in which the head is finished, but where the attire is only traced out;[17] neither of them are framed. The large one, by Madame Lebrun, is delicious and a ravishing likeness: it is a speaking portrait and infinitely pleasing; but indeed I should have thought myself too indiscreet in selecting it, and the one I am keeping is so pleasing, so excellent a likeness, and so piquant, that I am extremely content with it and transported with happiness at possessing it. The one begun by Letellier is only sketched out, and the head is scarcely anything but a rough draft, which may become a good likeness. I have had it sent back to the painter.

"With regard to your large portrait and the one which I am keeping, tell me, dear friend, if you wish me to send them to you or if I ought to have them taken back to where they came from; in short, what destination you intend for them. I desire nothing more than to have one which I may carry with me and which may never leave me. Come then, dear love, to pass sweet days here; come and dine with me, with whomever you may choose; come and procure me a few moments of happiness; I have none save with you; let me have an answer to all my questions; come to see a mortal who loves you beyond all and above all

[16] See p. 320 note *supra*.
[17] *Ibid.*

until the last moment of his life. I kiss a thousand
times the portrait of the most charming woman in the
world, and whose heart, so good and so noble, merits
an eternal devotion."

This letter, now in the National Archives, is un-
signed, and there is considerable doubt as to the identity of its writer. M. Vatel is of opinion that it was
penned by the Duc de Rohan-Chabot, a young man
some twenty years Madame du Barry's junior, to
whom the ex-favourite had, a few months previously,
advanced a large sum of money, an act which, as we
shall presently see, both she and her unfortunate bankers, the Vandenyvers, who had negotiated the transaction, were to have good cause to rue. But the nobleman in question was certainly not in a position to invite the lady to dine with him just then, or even to
spend "a few moments of happiness" with her, as he
appears to have taken up arms against the Republic,
and had he ventured within a dozen leagues of Paris,
would most certainly have paid for his rashness with
his head. We are, therefore, inclined to think that the
Goncourts, who attribute the letter to another member
of the Rohan family, the Prince de Rohan-Rochefort,
may be nearer the mark, as the princess of that name
was an intimate friend of Madame du Barry. However, as they do not give us any reason for the conclusion at which they have arrived, it is probably
merely a supposition on their part.

CHAPTER XXIV

IN THE second week in September 1793, several members of the Committee of General Security retired, and were replaced by some of the most fanatical and sanguinary members of the "Mountain": Vadier, "that odious mixture of pride, barbarity, and cowardice," as Louis Blanc designates him; Amar, who had voted for the execution of Louis XVI. *"sans appel ni sursis";* and Panis, Santerre's brother-in-law. The implacable Grieve was not slow to perceive his opportunity, and hardly had the new members taken their seats when he presented himself before them with a new petition against Madame du Barry, signed by the revolutionary committee of the commune of Versailles.

On this occasion, his efforts were crowned with success, and, on September 21, the Committee of General Security issued the following decree:

"WARRANT FOR ARREST.
"COMMITTEE OF GENERAL SECURITY,
"*Sitting September* 21, 1793.

"The Committee decrees that the woman named Dubarry, residing at Louveciennes, shall be arrested and conducted to the prison of Sainte-Pélagie, to be there detained, as a measure of general security, as a person suspected of incivism and aristocracy. The seals shall be placed on her effects, and perquisition made of her papers. Those which appear suspicious shall be brought to the Committee of General Security. The Committee delegates the Citizen Grieve to execute

the present decree, and authorises him to requisition
such civil officers of justice as he may find; armed force
if need be. Moreover, the Citizen Grieve will cause
to be arrested and conducted to Paris, to be confined
as a measure of general security in the prison of La
Force, all persons found at the house of the said Dubarry at Louveciennes at the moment of the execution
of the present decree.

"Signed: BOUCHER-SAINT-SAUVEUR,
"AMAR, VADIER, PANIS"[1]

The following day, accompanied by the mayor—
who, poor man! must have been shaking in his shoes,
as he was one of those who had signed the pro-Du
Barry petition of the previous summer—the *juge de
paix* of Marly, several officers of the municipality, and
two gendarmes, Grieve proceeded to Louveciennes, exhibited his warrant to the ill-fated mistress of the
château, directed the *juge de paix* to place the seals on
the doors of the house, ordered the lady to enter a carriage in company with the gendarmes, and set out for
Paris.

As they were passing the hydraulic machine at Marly,
they perceived a cabriolet approaching, in which sat
the Chevalier d'Escourre, who was on his way to
pay Madame du Barry a visit. Although Grieve had
no authority to apprehend any one save the ex-favourite and those found on her premises, he was not the
man to stick at trifles, and immediately ordered the
gendarmes to arrest the chevalier, whom he subsequently declared to have been "at the du Barry's
door," at the moment when her arrest took place. He

---

[1] Cited in Vatel's *Histoire de Madame du Barry,* iii. 451.

[2] " D'Estcourt had already arrived in a cabriolet, with a servant,
at the Dubarry's door, the day of her arrest; but having learned
what was passing in the house, fled at full speed. Our brave
sans-culottes pursued him, and, with difficulty, caught him at the

then removed the lady to the cabriolet, took the reins himself, and drove her the rest of the way to the city.

It would indeed be interesting to know what passed between the Englishman and the woman whose fate he held in his hands during that drive. Did he offer her life? as several writers seem to suppose. If he did, the price was one which she declined to pay, for Grieve never turned aside for a moment from his fell purpose until the guillotine had claimed its victim.

At Sainte-Pélagie, Madame du Barry found herself in the company of many of her own sex: the celebrated Madame Roland, who had been shut up there since September 2; the wives of two other Girondin leaders, Mesdames Brissot and Pétion; Mesdames de Créquy-Montmorency and de Gouy; the Mesdemoiselles de Moncrif and several actresses of the Français, now the Théâtre de la Nation, among them Mademoiselle Raucourt, to whom, in the days of her favour, the countess had presented a magnificent dress.

Madame du Barry was very far from being disposed to follow the example of calm fortitude which the Girondin ladies set her, and on October 2 she wrote a letter to the Administration of Seine-et-Oise, complaining of the treatment she had received at the hands of the Committee of General Security, who, after declaring her innocent of the charges brought against her, had, only a few weeks later, decreed her arrest. She pointed out that, had she desired, she could easily have removed the most valuable part of her property to England during her several journeys thither, and that the fact that she had not done so was a convinc-

foot of the mountain of Bougival."—Note in Grieve's handwriting on the back of d'Escourre's *acte d'accusation,* cited by the Goncourts.

ing proof of her attachment to her country; and she begged the Administration to prevent Grieve from plundering her house.

The letter was without effect, for her enemy, anticipating her appeal to the departmental authorities, had, a few days before obtaining the warrant for the ex-favourite's arrest, denounced Lavallery and his two brother-administrators to the committee of General Security, who had ordered their apprehension; and, on the very day on which Madame du Barry's letter was written, the body of her protector was found floating in the Seine above Paris. Some writers have asserted that he was so madly enamoured of Madame du Barry that he drowned himself on learning of her arrest; but it would appear more probable that his death was due to a desire to escape the ignominy of a public execution, as the warrant for his own arrest had been issued before any steps had been taken against the lady. However, there can be little doubt that his admiration for the mistress of Louveciennes cost him his life.

Finding that she had nothing to hope for from the Department, Madame du Barry appealed directly to the Committee of General Security, to whom her friends at Louveciennes now addressed a second petition, praying for the release of their benefactress. This seems to have alarmed Grieve, who thereupon went to Héron, a member of the Committee, who had a long-standing feud with the Vandenyvers, Madame du Barry's bankers, and urged him to denounce them to his colleagues as accomplices of the ex-favourite in her dealings with aristocrats and *émigrés,* by which move, he perceived, the case against the poor woman would be greatly strengthened. Héron needed very little persuasion to induce him to undertake so congenial a task; and the unfortunate bankers were arrested and removed to Sainte-Pélagie.

While Héron was drawing up his report against the
Vandenyvers, Grieve had received permission to make
investigations at Louveciennes, where he busied himself in going through all the letters and papers he
could find in the château and affixing to them annota-
tions for the guidance of the prosecution. Although
the majority of these letters are of the most trivial
nature, and many anterior to the Revolution, there is
hardly one from which the malice of the scoundrel
does not succeed in extracting something to compromise his victim.

Thus, on a note in which mention is made of the
Abbé Billiardi, he writes: *"This Abbé Billiardi was
one of her most frequent visitors since the Revolution,
as was also the Abbé de Fontenille, ex-vicar of Agen,
guillotined the other day in Paris. Billiardi is dead.
These abbés were inseparable friends, and Billiardi
was also an anti-revolutionist. Behold the friends of
the Dubarry!"* On a letter from Madame Vigée Lebrun, dated from Naples, in which she begs to be remembered to Brissac, Madame de Souza, the Portuguese Ambassadress, and the Marquise de Brunoi:
*"Letter of the woman Lebrun, painter and mistress of
Calonne."*

On a letter from Thellusson, the banker: *"One of
the greatest London bankers, nephew of Thellusson,
former partner of Necker and great enemy of the
Revolution."*

On a letter from Forth, a London dectective whom
Madame du Barry had employed for the recovery of
her jewels: *"Proof of her connection with Forth, the
famous English spy, who has not ceased to intrigue
against France since 1777, and particularly since the
time of Franklin. It is he and Béthune Charost who
have been the most active emissaries of the Courts of
London, Berlin, and the Hague, and it is this Forth*

*who, one may presume, has plotted with her at Louve-
ciennes the pretended robbery of her diamonds."*

On a letter from Lord Hawkesbury,[3] who presents
his compliments to Madame du Barry and will be
charmed to render her any service in his power in regard to her lawsuit: *"Letter which proves her intrigues with the courtiers of George III. Lord
Hawkesbury is the privy councillor of the tyrant, who
governs Pitt himself and who, for twenty years, has
really held the reins of government, although now and
again apparently in disgrace; his son[4] is to-day the
great political courier between London and the allied
Powers in the Netherlands."*

"He forces the letters to say what they do not
say, he connects certain passages with events with
which they have no connection. He imagines, he
supposes, he lies, he tortures, in short, phrases and
words to extract from them a culpability necessary for the furtherance of his schemes and his
hatred."

On a letter from the Duc de Rohan-Chabot referring to the loan of 200,000 livres which Madame du
Barry had made him, he suggests that the money was
to be used to subsidise the insurgents in La Vendée,
where the duke's estates were. A memorandum of
the expenses incurred by the countess during her stay
in London in November 1792 is endorsed with an inquiry if the money were not given to *émigrés*. And a
letter from an old lady to Madame du Barry, dated La
Meilleraie, April 9, 1793, bears the annotation:
*"Remark the time when this letter was written; it is
that of the treason of Dumouriez."*

He details the "liberticide" books, journals, pam-

---

[3] Charles Jenkinson, afterwards first Earl of Liverpool. He
had been created Baron Hawkesbury in 1786.
[4] Robert Banks Jenkinson, afterwards second Earl of Liverpool.

phlets, engravings, and so forth, which he has found, among which he cites the *Histoire des caricatures de la révolte des Français* of Boyer de Nismes; twelve copies of Peltier's *Dernier Tableau de Paris;* a translation of Burke's work on Marie Antoinette; *Epitaphe du Varicourt, tué à la porte de la Reine,* which he declares to have been written by the Abbé Dellile, "poet-in-ordinary of the Dubarry," and a portrait of the Comte d'Artois.[5] Assisted by Salanave and Zamor, he also collected all the jewellery, cash, and securities he could discover, and made an exact inventory of them; after which he drew up a list of twenty-seven witnesses, with himself at their head, and forwarded this, together with a long memorandum of the various facts to which they were prepared to depose, to Fouquier-Tinville, the Public Prosecutor.

On October 30 the Committee of General Security deputed two of their number, Voulland and Jagot, to proceed to Sainte-Pélagie and interrogate the Citoyenne du Barry. This interrogatory, a verbatim account of which will be found in M. Vatel's interesting work, was a very lengthy one, but we shall confine ourselves to the more important points of the examination.

Q. From whom did you receive while in London the money you required for your expenses and the conduct of your lawsuit?

A. From the Citizen Vandenyver, banker of Paris, Rue Vivienne, who gave me a letter of credit on Thellusson; it was during my last journey that I made use of that.

Q. Is your lawsuit concluded?

[5] *Tribunaux révolutionnaires, dossier de la nommée Jeanne Vaubernier du Barry . . . et des Vendenyver, prévenus d'intelligences et correspondances contre-révolutionnaires aves les émigrés: Archives nationales.* E. and J. de Goncourt's *La Du Barry,* pp. 273-278.

A. My lawsuit was concluded on February 27, the last day of term.

Q. Was not the time you were to spend in London specified in your passport?

A. No date was specified, and could not reasonably be, as a lawsuit had to be concluded.

Q. During the time you were in London, decrees were issued by the National Convention ordering all French who had left the Republic within a certain time to return, under pain of being regarded as *émigrés* and treated as such. Were you aware of this?

A. I was aware of these decrees, but did not consider that they concerned me, as I had left for a definite reason and was provided with a passport.

Q. During your stay in London, war was declared between the French Republic and the King of Great Britain. Why, under these circumstances, did you not quit the enemy's territory?

A. War was declared such a short time before my departure,[6] and my case was on the point of being decided. I therefore prolonged my stay, in order to avoid a fresh journey.

She was then questioned about her loan of 200,000 livres to the Duc de Rohan-Chabot, which she admitted, but stoutly denied that she had advanced a similar sum to the Bishop of Rouen, and persisted in denying all knowledge of such a transaction, though shown a letter from the Vandenyvers referring to a proposed loan to that prelate.[7]

[6] Exactly a month. War was declared on February 1, 1793, and Madame du Barry left England on March 1.

[7] This was an important point, as Cardinal de la Rochefoucauld, Bishop of Rouen, was a bitter opponent of the Revolution. He had signed the protest of September 21, 1791, against the innovations in religion made by the National Assembly, incited his clergy to resistance, and, after the events of August 10, had emigrated.

The letters seized at Louveciennes and annotated by Grieve were next produced, and the prisoner taken through them, with a twofold purpose: to make her incriminate herself, and to ascertain particulars about her correspondents which might be used against them hereafter. In the latter object the questioners were but too successful, as Madame du Barry admitted that the writer of a letter which contained an innocent remark about Marie Antoinette was the Princess Lubomirska, a member of an old Polish family, who had come to Paris the previous year with her little daughter; and the unhappy lady was arrested on a charge of "conspiring to effect the escape of the widow Capet," condemned, and executed. It also transpired that the detective Forth—Grieve's "famous English spy"—who had been employed by Madame du Barry to recover her diamonds, had, before the outbreak of war, been in the habit of conveying letters from *émigrés* in London to their friends in France, and that the lady, in her turn, had been requested by a gentleman who had since lost his head to take charge of a letter for Madame Calonne, which, however, she declared she had not delivered.

The commissioners then proceeded to interrogate her in regard to her relations with *émigrés* while in England. She admitted that she had received visits from a few whom she had known previously, "as it was difficult for her to close her doors to them," and had visited them, but denied having given them money, except small sums in two instances, and only as loans. Shown a memorandum of her expenses during her last visit to London and asked to explain, amongst others, payments made to Frondeville, ex-President of the Parliament of Rouen, and a person named Fortuné, she answered that the money had been given them "to gamble for her," and had been repaid.

The jewel robbery at Louveciennes was the next point raised.

Q. Was the list of the diamonds which you had printed correct? Did it not contain a description of other stones besides those stolen?

A. The description was perfectly correct, with the exception of a chain of emeralds and diamonds, which was stolen, and which was brought to M. de Brissac during my third visit to England. M. de Brissac gave a hundred louis to the person who brought it to him.

Q. Did you ever entertain the idea of selling your diamonds, and did you not take steps for that purpose and send them abroad? If so, when?

A. In 1789 or 1790. I applied to Vandenyver, who sent part of them to Holland; but the price offered not being sufficient, I withdrew the jewels from Vandenyver and gave him a receipt cancelling the one he had given me.

After some further questions she was asked what money she had in her house, and replied that she had given instructions to her servants to conceal "eleven bags, each containing 1200 livres, 1531 louis d'or (which she had borrowed from the Duc de Brissac to pay the reward for her diamonds), 40 double louis, and some English half-guineas. She was, however, in ignorance where her people had hidden the money.

The last question put to her was in reference to the shelter she had given to the Abbé de la Roche-Fontenille, nephew of the Abbess of Pont-aux-Dames. She admitted that she had given the abbé a room at Louveciennes, "as a return for the kindness which his aunt had shown her," but she had not seen him since September 1792, and did not know what had become of him.

At this the inquisitors must have smiled grimly, for the poor Abbé de la Roche-Fontenille had been des-

patched to another world, by way of the Place de la
Révolution, three days previously.

Two days later (Brumaire 11), the elder Vandenyver was examined, and questioned very closely as to
the money he had furnished to Madame du Barry
while in England, and particularly in regard to the
supposed loan of 200,000 livres to the Bishop of
Rouen. He admitted paying the sum in question, on
his client's instructions, to a person who had called at
the bank for the money, but declared that he had never
seen the man before, and could not say "positively" if
it was intended for the bishop.[8]

On Brumaire 29 (November 19) the Committee of
General Security issued the following decree:

"*29 Brumaire Year II. of the French Republic one and
indivisible.*

"The Committee of General Security having taken
cognisance of the various documents found at the
house of the Du Barry, placed under arrest as a measure of general security as a suspected person, by the
terms of the decree of September 17 last,[9] and being
of opinion that the said documents show that the
woman Du Barry has been guilty of emigration and of
having, during the sojourn which she made in London
from the month of October 1792 to the month of
March last, furnished to *émigrés* who have sought
refuge there pecuniary assistance, and carried on with
them a suspicious correspondence, decrees that the said
Du Barry shall be transferred to the Revolutionary
Court, to be there prosecuted and judged by the Public Prosecutor."[10]

---

[8] Vatel's *Histoire de Madame du Barry,* iii. 221, *et seq.*
[9] Evidently an error. The warrant for her arrest was issued
September 21.
[10] *Dossier du Barry: Archives nationales.* E. and J. de Goncourt's *La Du Barry,* p. 280.

Three days later, Madame du Barry was brought from Sainte-Pélagie, where she had already spent two weary months, to the Palais de Justice, and interrogated by Robespierre's henchman, the brutal Dumas, vice-president of the Revolutionary Court, in the presence of the Public Prosecutor and the clerk to the court. Dumas asked her a great many questions about the sums she had squandered during her favour, the extent of her influence over Louis XV., the *gratifications* and pensions she had obtained for her friends, and so forth. He then declared his belief that the jewel robbery and the lawsuit were only pretexts to conceal a political secret, and that she had "conspired against the Republic."[11] Madame du Barry contented herself with a simple denial, and was then taken back to Sainte-Pélagie, whence she addressed the following letter to the Public Prosecutor:

MADAME DU BARRY *to* FOUQUIER-TINVILLE.

"CITIZEN PUBLIC PROSECUTOR,—I hope that thou, in the impartial examination of this unhappy affair that Grieve and his confederates have brought against me, wilt see that I am the victim of a plot to ruin me.

"I never emigrated, and I never intended to.

"The use that I made of the two hundred thousand livres that d'Escourre placed for me with the Citizen Rohan[12] should prove this to the most prejudiced eyes.

"I never furnished money to the *émigrés,* and I never carried on any criminal correspondence with them; and if circumstances compelled me to see, either in London or in France, courtiers or persons who were

[11] Vatel's *Histoire de Madame du Barry,* iii. 241.
[12] The Duc de Rohan-Chabot.

not in sympathy with the Revolution, I hope, Citizen
Public Prosecutor, that thou wilt, in the justice and
equity of thine heart, take into consideration the circumstances in which I found myself, and my known
and forced *liaison* with the Citizen Brissac,[13] whose
correspondence is before thine eyes.

"I rely on thy justice: thou canst rely on the eternal
gratitude of thy *consitoyenne* (*sic*)."[14]

The estimable Fouquier was not quite so well known
at this period as he became in the following spring,
when the star of Robespierre was in the ascendant and
the guillotine was mowing down Royalists and Hébert-
ists and Dantonists at the rate of a hundred a week, or
poor Madame du Barry would have been aware that
she had no mercy to expect at his hands. He threw
her appeal unread into a portfolio in which he kept
the letters and papers he did not wish to attend to, and,
harassed as he was by the importunities of Grieve,
hurried on the trial. On December 4, the ex-favourite

[13] It is not clear what Madame du Barry meant by her *forced
liaison* with Brissac, and M. Vatel is of opinion that, in her hurry
and agitation, she must have omitted several words.

[14] Cited in *Mémoires de Favrolle*, iv. 122.

[15] In his *Mémoires,* Dutens relates the following anecdote, *à
propos* of Madame du Barry's imprisonment at the Conciergerie:

"Shortly before the Comtesse du Barry was guillotined, on
December 8, 1793, an Irish priest found means to visit her at the
Conciergerie and offered to save her, provided she could give
him the amount which would be required for bribing the gaolers
and paying the expenses connected with the journey. She inquired if he could save two persons; but he replied that his plan
would only permit him to save one. 'In that case,' said Madame
du Barry, 'I am willing to give you an order on my banker
which will enable you to obtain the necessary amount; but I prefer you to save the Duchesse de Mortemart rather than myself.
She is hidden in a garret of such and such a house in Calais;
here is an order on my banker; fly to her help.' The priest entreated her to allow him to rescue her from the prison; but, on
perceiving that she was resolved to save the duchess, took the
order, obtained the money, went to Calais, and brought the

was transferred from Sainte-Pélagie to the Conciergerie, "the threshold of the scaffold," the walls of
which were still stained with the blood of the victims
of the September Massacres," and, at nine o'clock on
the morning of the 6th, she and the three Vandenyvers were brought before the Revolutionary Court.

duchess out of her hiding place. Then, having disguised her as
a common woman, he gave her his arm, and travelled with
her on foot, saying that he was a good constitutional priest
and married to this woman. Every one cried 'Bravo,' and allowed him to pass. He then crossed the French lines at Ostend,
and embarked for England with Madame de Mortemart, whom
I have since seen in London."—*Mémoires d'un voyageur qui se
repose,* iii. 115.

M. Forneron, in his *Histoire générale des Emigrés,* and the
Goncourts, in their *La Du Barry,* accept this story; but M. Vatel,
in spite of his strong predilection for Madame du Barry, declines
to place any faith in it, at least in its original form. In the first
place, he points out, the lady's banker was, like herself, under
lock and key, and, in the second, escape from the Conciergerie
was absolutely impossible. On the other hand, a Madame de
Mortemart—not the duchess, but her sister-in-law—does appear to
have been in hiding at Calais at this time, and he therefore thinks
that what really happened was that the priest in question having,
like a gallant Irishman, offered to attempt the impossible on
behalf of the poor lady, she replied: "You cannot save me; try
to save Madame de Mortemart." Even in this modified form,
however, the anecdote still reflects credit on Madame du Barry.

CHAPTER XXV

THE Revolutionary Court, which had been created in the previous March, in spite of the strenuous opposition of the Girondins, to judge without appeal conspirators against the State, still retained all the forms of justice—it was not until June 1794 that the hearing of counsel and calling of witnesses were dispensed with—but its proceedings were, in the great majority of cases, a hollow farce. The judges were appointed from the ranks of the most ruthless Terrorists, the jurymen, nominated by the Convention, were all *"gens d'expédition,"* while, as to give evidence on behalf of an accused person was to incur the danger of sharing his fate, witnesses for the defence could with difficulty be induced to come forward. Appalling indeed is the record of the Revolutionary Court. From the time of its institution in March 1793 to its reorganisation on June 10 of the following year it condemned to death 1259 persons, and after June 18, 1794, in seven weeks it sent 1368 persons to the guillotine.[1]

Such was the tribunal before which Madame du Barry and the Vandenyvers appeared that dark December morning. Dumas occupied the president's seat, assisted in his deliberations by three other judges, David, Denisot, and Bravet; the infamous Fouquier, of course, prosecuted; while upon the jury were Topino-Lebrun, the painter, Robespierre's satellite,

[1] For a full account of this famous—or rather infamous—court, see M. Henri Wallon's fine work, *Histoire du Tribunal révolutionnaire* (Paris: 1880-1882, 6 volumes).

Payan, and Sambat and Trinchard, who had been members of the jury which had condemned Marie Antoinette. Chauveau-Lagarde, who had defended Brissot, Charlotte Corday, and the Queen, represented the Vandenyvers; Lafleuterie, Madame du Barry.

The *Bulletin du Tribunal révolutionnaire* contains no account of the trial, but we have, in its place, a document of incontestable value in the shape of the notes taken by Fouquier-Tinville, who wrote with extraordinary rapidity, and jotted down all the answers given—he did not trouble to transcribe the questions—and has also left us a verbatim copy of his own speeches for the prosecution.

The jury having been sworn, the president turned to the accused and demanded their names, ages, professions, and places of birth and residence, to which they gave the following answers:

"Jeanne Vaubernier, separated wife of Du Barry, aged forty-two years,[2] born at Vaucouleurs, residing at Louveciennes."

"Jean Baptiste Vandenyver, aged sixty-six, banker, born at Amsterdam, residing at Paris, Rue Vivienne."

"Edme Jean Baptiste Vandenyver, aged twenty-nine, banker, born at Paris, residing in the same street."

"Antoine Auguste Vandenyver, aged thirty-two, banker, born at Paris, residing here, also in the Rue Vivienne."

The *greffier* then read the indictment, and Fouquier rose to open the attack.

After detailing the various steps which had been taken against the accused, the seizure of their papers, their interrogatories, and so forth, and a piquant account of the career of Madame du Barry at the Court of Louis XV., the prosecutor declared that the examination of the documents found at Louveciennes proved

---

[2] She was, of course, fifty, having been born August 29, 1743.

that "the Aspasia of the French Sardanapalus" had
been the instrument and accomplice of *émigrés,* and
the support and protector of those aristocrats who had
remained in France; and he mentioned the unfortunate Abbé de la Roche-Fontenille as having found an
asylum with her. He declared that, in her desire to
render assistance to the *émigrés,* she had *invented* a
robbery of diamonds in the night of January 10-11,
1791;[3] that this pretended robbery was a pretext con-
cocted with Forth, an English agent, to place her in
communication with all the anti-Revolutionary agents
in London; that during her four visits to London she
had lived only with *émigrés* and English aristocrats
hostile to the Revolution, particularly with "the infamous Pitt, that implacable enemy of the human
race," and that she had brought back with her "a
medal bearing the effigy of the monster." He declared
that her purse was at the disposal of all the rebels in
France; that she had advanced a sum of 200,000 livres
to Rohan-Chabot, possessor of large estates in La
Vendée, "the present centre of rebellion"; 200,000
livres to La Rochefoucauld, former Bishop of Rouen,
and large amounts to the Chevalier d'Escourre, his
nephew, Labondie, and other disaffected persons. He
declared that it had been her intention to make her
house into "a little stronghold," which was proved by
the fact that several guns had been found upon the
premises. He spoke of the treasures which she had
concealed and of the collection of anti-revolutionary
pamphlets and engravings discovered at Louveciennes;
declared that she had worn mourning in London for

[3] When Fouquier said this, he lied deliberately, as he had before
him all the proofs of the robbery, and, in particular, a deposition
of the spy Blache, admitting that he had seen the stolen jewels
at the Lord Mayor's Court in London, no doubt when the jeweller Rouen was identifying them. This fact, needless to say,
was not disclosed at the trial.

the late King, and had carried on a constant correspondence with the most bitter enemies of the Republic: Calonne, Brissac, Maussabré, Mortemart, Narbonne, and many others.

Passing to the Vandenyvers, he described them as
the intermediaries between the Du Barry and the
émigrés. He accused them of having sent the diamonds of the Du Barry to Holland; of having provided her during her visits to England with several letters of credit, one for £50,000 and another "for an
unlimited amount"; of having advanced the loans for
Rohan-Chabot and La Rochefoucauld, and all the
money wherewith their client had provided the *émigrés.*
He declared that they had been "at all times the enemies of France," and in 1782 had been concerned in
a vast plot to ruin the credit of the country and "perpetuate the slavery of the French," and ended by ac-
cusing them of being *"chevaliers du poignard,"* and
of having co-operated "in the massacre of the people."[*]

He then proceeded to call his witnesses, beginning
with Grieve, who deposed that he had found, hidden in
various parts of the château and grounds at Louveciennes, a quantity of precious stones, gold and silver,
portraits of Louis XV. (as a Carmelite friar), Anne
of Austria, and the Regent d'Orléans, and a medal
bearing the likeness of Pitt. He added that an English spy, named Forth, made frequent journeys between London and Louveciennes, previous to the outbreak of war; that the general opinion in the village
was that the robbery had never taken place; and that
the accused had obtained her passports under false
pretences, as so far from her jewels being the only

---

[*] Apparently, the only foundation for this last charge was a
statement of Héron that the elder Vandenyver had fired at him
with a gun during the disturbances which followed the storming
of the Tuileries on August 10, 1792.

security of her creditors, as she had stated in her letter to the President of the Convention,[5] she was possessed of "immense treasures, valued at ten to twelve million livres," lived in most luxurious style, and kept forty servants. He also stated that she had placed obstacles in the way of recruiting at Louveciennes, and gave evidence concerning the papers found at her house.

Xavier Audouin, attached to the Ministry of War, deposed that some days after the events of August 10, 1792, while patrolling with an armed force the environs of Saint-Germain-en-Laye, information was brought him that the Château de Louveciennes was "full of *ci-devant* noblemen of the Court"; that he had repaired thither and questioned the mistress of the house, who offered him refreshments and denied that there was any person concealed on her premises; that, her manner appearing to him suspicious, he had broken into a room, which she had assured him was a linencloset, and found there Maussabré, Brissac's aide-de-camp, whom he arrested and removed to prison.

Jean Baptiste Blache, commissary of the Committee of General Security, stated that he formerly resided in London, where he had seen the accused in the company of various *émigrés* and the supposed English spy, Forth. After the death of "Capet," the Du Barry wore mourning, *"avec le plus grand faste anglais,"* and attended all the memorial services.

Dumas, vice-president: "What answer have you to make to the evidence of this witness?"

Madame du Barry: "I wish to say that I certainly saw in London Mesdames de Calonne and Mortemart, but that our relations were merely those of friendship."

Dumas: "Did you wear mourning in London for Capet?"

[5] See p. 339, *supra.*

Madame du Barry: "I wore a black dress, because I had brought dresses of no other colour with me."[6]

The next witness was a friend, the Chevalier d'Escourre, who was brought up from La Force, and courageously endeavoured to take upon himself the responsibility of the loan to Rohan-Chabot, stating that, being aware that Madame du Barry was desirous of finding an investment for the money, he had suggested the mortgage in question.[7]

When the chevalier had concluded his evidence, Fouquier-Tinville rose and demanded that the witness should be at once removed from La Force to the Conciergerie and brought to trial. His request was granted, and poor d'Escourre, condemned for "practising machinations against the Republic," was executed on December 11.

Then commenced the evidence of the treacherous servants and the other witnesses whom Grieve had recommended.

The thievish Salanave, now a member of the revolutionary committee of Versailles, spoke to the visits of Brissac, Labondie, d'Escourre, the Marquise de Brunoy, and other aristocrats to Louveciennes, and added that, "in his quality of patriot," he had been badly treated by his fellow servants, and, finally, dismissed by his mistress.

Madame du Barry, when asked if she had anything to say to the evidence just given, informed the court that the dismissal of Salanave was due, not to his political opinions, but to his unfortunate weakness for her porcelain, "which disappeared daily."

[6] This was no doubt true, as she was in mourning for Brissac.

[7] It should be mentioned that the loan to Rohan-Chabot was a duly executed mortgage on the duke's estates in Brittany, bearing interest at four and a half per cent., and that the court had the deed in its possession.

Louis-Benoît Zamor, native of Bengal, stated that he had been brought up by the accused since the age of eleven; that her house was frequented by aristocrats, who rejoiced openly over the checks which the armies of the Republic sustained; that he had remonstrated with the accused on the folly and wickedness of her conduct; but that, so far from following his sage counsels, she had, on learning of his connection with Grieve, Blache, and other patriots, "informed him, in an imperious tone, that she gave him three days to leave her house."[8]

Jean Thenot, schoolmaster at Louveciennes, formerly in the service of Madame du Barry, deposed that, in 1789, at the time of the murder of Foulon, he had heard the accused declare that the people were "a pack of wretches and villains."

The Accused, interrupting the witness: "Where did you hear me make such a remark?"

The Witness: "It was while going to your melon-house."

The Accused: The charge is false; it is an atrocious lie."

Two of Madame du Barry's *femmes-de-chambre* were the next witnesses, one of whom stated that she had accompanied her mistress on her visits to London, and that while there she was frequently visited by French *émigrés;* while the other declared that the night after the arrest of Brissac was spent by the accused in burning papers.

Madame du Barry gave a flat denial to this last allegation, after which the court adjourned till the following day.

---

[8] Zamor's treachery did not benefit him much. Soon after the trial he was arrested as an accomplice of the woman he had denounced, and, though released, appears to have led a wretched existence. He died in great poverty in 1820.

MADAME DU BARRY 373

On December 7 (Frimaire 17), further witnesses
for the prosecution were called, the most important of
whom was one Nicholas Fournier, surveyor of buildings, and formerly *juge de paix* for the canton of
Marly, who deposed that he had examined the articles
found by Grieve in various parts of the grounds of
the accused, and that amongst them were a watch-
chain, an opera-glass, and a pencil-case, all of which
objects had been advertised as forming part of the
property stolen on the night of January 10, 1791.

This evidence, of course, went to strengthen the contention of the prosecution that the robbery had never
taken place; but Madame du Barry explained to the
court that the objects in question had been sold by the
thieves ere leaving France, and subsequently restored
to her.

Of evidence for the defence there was none. Two
important witnesses had been summoned: Boileau,
who had suspended Madame du Barry's arrest in the
previous June, and Chaillau, a member of the administration of Versailles; but both, by a curious coincidence, were confined to their beds by severe illness,
and sent certificates of their inability to attend, much,
we may presume, to the chagrin of the amiable Fouquier, who had no doubt hoped to make them incriminate themselves.[9] Lafleuterie for Madame du Barry,
and Chauveau-Lagarde for the Vandenyvers[10] "com-
bated vigorously" (according to the latter advocate's
account) the charges against their clients, and then
Fouquier rose to reply, and in the grotesque jargon

[9] E. and J. de Goncourt's *La Du Barry,* p. 309.
[10] In the course of some questions put to the elder Vandenyver
by Dumas, it transpired that the letter of credit " for an unlimited amount " mentioned by Fouquier in his opening speech, was
a request to Thellusson to furnish Madame du Barry with "any
small sums " which she might happen to require. The letter of
credit for £50,000 had no existence, save in the imagination of
the Public Prosecutor.

which at this period passed for eloquence proceeded to harangue the admiring jury as follows:

"Citizen Jurors,—You have passed sentence on the wife of the last tyrant of the French; you have now to pass sentence on the courtesan of his infamous predecessor. You see before you this Laïs celebrated by the deprivation of her morals, the publicity and the scandal of her debaucheries, whom libertinage alone enabled to share the destinies of the despot who sacrificed the blood and treasure of his people to his shameful pleasures. The scandal and opprobrium of her elevation, the turpitude and disgrace of her infamous prostitution, are not, however, matters to which you must now give your attention. You have to decide if this Messalina,[11] born among the people, enriched by the spoils of the people, who paid for the opprobrium of her morals, fallen by the death of the tyrant from the position in which crime alone had placed her, has conspired against the liberty and the sovereignty of the people; if, after being the accomplice and the instrument of the libertinage of kings, she has become the agent of tyrants, nobles, and priests against the French Republic. The trial, citizen jurors, has already thrown the clearest light on this conspiracy. You know what revelations the depositions of the witnesses and the documents have furnished concerning this execrable conspiracy, to which the annals of nations can afford no parallel; and assuredly never has an affair of more importance been presented for your decision, since it offers you, in a fashion, the principal link in the plots of Pitt and his accomplices against France.

" . . . Such, citizen jurors, is the result of the trial which has taken place. It is for you, in your wisdom,

[11] Fouquier had at first written *"femme"*; but he struck it out and substituted the name of the Roman Empress. He had already compared Madame du Barry to both Aspasia and Laïs!

to weigh the evidence. You see that royalists, feder-
alists, all the factions, though divided among themselves in appearance, have all the same centre, the
same object, the same end. The war abroad, that in
La Vendée, the troubles in the South, the insurrection
in the Department of Calvados, all have the same principle and the same head . . . all march under the
orders of Pitt. But the veil which covered so many
iniquities has been, in some degree, lifted—one may
say to-day that it has been rent asunder—and nothing
remains for the conspirators, save disgrace and the
punishment of their infamous plots. Yes, Frenchmen,
we swear it; the traitors shall perish, and liberty alone
survive. She has resisted and will resist all the efforts ·
of the allied despots, their slaves, their priests, and
their infamous courtesans. . . . The vile *conspiratrice*
who stands before you was able to live in the lap of
luxury, acquired by her shameful debauchery, in the
midst of a country which appeared to have buried,
with the tyrant whose companion she had been, the
remembrance of her prostitution and the scandal of
her elevation. But the liberty of the people was a
crime in her eyes; she required it to be enslaved, to
cringe to its masters, and the best of the substance of
the people was consecrated to her pleasures. This
example, joined to many others, proves more and
more that libertinage and evil morals are the greatest
enemies of liberty and the happiness of peoples. In
striking with the sword of the Law a Messalina
guilty of a conspiracy against the country, not only
will you avenge the Republic for her outrages upon
it, but you will uproot a public scandal and strengthen
the empire of that morality which is the chief foundation of the liberty of peoples."

Fouquier, unfortunately, did not think it worth
while to take down Dumas's summing-up; but, from

a memorandum left by Chauveau-Lagarde, we learn that the charges against Madame du Barry which the jury were called upon to consider, were as follows:

"Accused of conspiring against the French Republic and having favoured the success of the arms of the enemies in its territory by procuring for them exorbitant sums in her journeys to England, where she herself emigrated.

"Wearing, in London, mourning for the late King.

"Living habitually with Pitt, whose effigy she wore on a silver medal.

"Having caused to be buried at Louveciennes the letters of nobility of an *émigré* and also the busts of the former Court.

"And, finally, having wasted the treasures of the State by the unbridled extravagance in which she had indulged before the Revolution, during her commerce with Louis XV."

The Vandenyvers were charged with being "the accomplices of her machinations."

It was a quarter to ten at night when the jury retired to consider their verdict.

They were absent from court an hour and a quarter —fifteen minutes longer than they had required to decide upon the fate of Marie Antoinette—and, on their re-entry, returned "an affirmative answer" on all counts of the indictment against the former favourite, and the same in regard to the charge against the bankers.

Fouquier at once demanded the full penalty of the law; and "the court condemned Jeanne Vaubernier, wife of Du Barry, *ci-devant* courtesan; Jean Baptiste Vandenyver, Edme Jean Baptiste Vandenyver, and Antoine Auguste Vandenyver to the penalty of death, and ordered that the present sentence should be exe-

cuted within twenty-four hours on the Place de la
Révolution of this town.''[12]

The wretched woman heard the terrible sentence
with cries of despair, and was carried back to the
Conciergerie in a half-conscious condition. It has
been stated that, in the hope of obtaining a respite,
perhaps even a commutation of her sentence, she denounced at random a great number of persons; and
Louis Blanc, in his *Histoire de la Révolution française,*
has gone so far as to give us the exact total of her victims, which he places at two hundred and forty![13]
Such an assertion, we need hardly observe, is a mere
fable, and quite unworthy to find a place in an authoritative work. What poor Madame du Barry actually
did was to purchase a few short hours of life by revealing to Denisot and Claude Roger, the deputy-
Public Prosecutor, the whereabouts of a considerable
quantity of gold and silver plate and jewellery, which
she had concealed in her garden, and which had hitherto escaped the prying eyes of Grieve[14] and his confederates. In so doing, she, unfortunately, admitted that
in concealing certain articles she had been assisted by
her faithful *valet-de-chambre,* Morin, and a woman
called Deliant; and the former was subsequently

[12] Of the judicial murderers of Madame du Barry, four per-
ished by the guillotine within eighteen months, Dumas and Payan
sharing the fate of Robespierre, in the folowing July, while the
Public Prosecutor and another member of the jury, named
Vilate, followed them to the scaffold in May 1795. Topino-
Lebrun, who took notes of the evidence which are preserved in
the Archives, was involved in a conspiracy against the life of
Napoleon, and executed on January 7, 1801.

[13] Vol. x. p. 236.

[14] This miscreant appears to have continued his denunciations
until some months after the fall of Robespierre, when he was
arrested at Amiens and twenty-two depositions taken against him.
He was, however, acquitted, and in 1796 returned to America,
where he published a translation of the Marquis de Châtellux's
Travels. Eventually, he settled in Brussels, and died in that
city on February 22, 1809.

brought to trial and executed, while the latter, whose husband, arrested with her, had died in prison, committed suicide. Morin, however, was already in custody, and would, very probably, have shared his unhappy mistress's fate in any case.

For three hours a clerk was occupied in taking down the inventory of the hidden treasure, for every word she spoke added a second to her life; and the declaration terminated with an offer to write to London for her jewels, if such were the desire of the Court, "as she could without difficulty recover the property of which she had been robbed, on payment of the costs of the action."[15]

But those men, "drunk with the blood of a King," were pitiless; she who had been so merciful to others could obtain none herself—in this world at least—and scarcely had the poor lady, with trembling fingers, affixed her signature to the declaration than a gaoler entered to cut her hair and inform her that the tumbril —"the bier of the living," as Barrère cynically called it —was at the door.

On the way to the scaffold, whither she was accompanied by the Vandenyvers and Jean Noël, the brave and upright deputy for the Vosges, whose opposition to the Terrorists had cost him his life,[16] Madame du Barry displayed, we are told, great cowardice, though authorities differ as to the form which this cowardice took. According to the sensational account given by

[15] Madame du Barry's jewels remained in Ransom's bank until the end of the following year, when they were sold by order of the Court of Chancery. The proceeds of the sale, which realised 13,300 guineas, appear to have been paid over to her niece, Madame de Boissaisson, and some of the countess's creditors.

[16] It was Jean Noël who declined to vote at the trial of Louis XVI., on the ground that, as his son had fallen in a war for which he regarded the King as being directly responsible, he could not hope to be an impartial judge.

the Goncourts, which is based on some *Souvenirs* of
the Revolution published in *La Nouvelle Minerva,* she
uttered heartrending cries, offered to give all her
wealth to the nation in return for her life—it had already been confiscated by decree of the Revolutionary
Court—implored the bystanders to save her, and struggled so violently that the executioner and his two as-
sistants had the greatest difficulty in preventing her
springing from the cart.   On the other hand, the
account given in *The Gentleman's Magazine* for 1793
represents her as having been in a state of such prostration that "the executioner was under the necessity
of supporting her in his arms the whole way;" while
it is to be remarked that the Terrorist journals, *Le
Glaive vengeur, Les Révolutions de Paris,* and the rest,
though ever ready to gloat over the sufferings of the
condemned, make no mention of any such scene as the
one described by the Goncourts.

About her behaviour when actually upon the scaffold
there is more unanimity of opinion.   Then she is described as resisting the executioners with all her feeble
strength, and when overcome and forced on to the
plank, entreating them not to hurt her, and begging
for "one moment more." [17]

[17] Here is an account of the tragedy, which, though second-
hand evidence, bears the unmistakable stamp of truth:

" I was well acquainted with a French gentleman, recently dead,
who was an involuntary witness of the execution [of Madame
du Barry], and who has often given me details of it.   He
was then a lad of about seventeen, and had been riding with
a friend of his in the environs of Paris.   On their return through
the Champs Elysées, they found themselves in the Place Louis
XV. [Place de la Révolution, *ci-devant* Louis XV.] surrounded
by a dense mob and the guillotine in full operation.   His first
impulse was to spur his horse and avoid the horrid sight, but
he was checked by his friend, who was more prudent and alive
to the danger, for the crowd had already begun to grumble and
to cry *'Gare aux aristocrats!'*   So they were forced to pull up
their horses and remain silent spectators of the horrid tragedy.
He said her shrieks were dreadful to hear; she struggled with

But the fall of the fatal knife put an end to her anguish, and to the long line of left-hand queens of France.²⁶

the executioners, and they were near enough to hear her exclaim, '*Ah, Monsieur, ne faites pas du mal,*' or '*Vous allez me faire du mal*'—he was not sure which. The scene over, they were forced to take off their hats and shout with the rest, '*Vive la République!*' It was not without difficulty that they got safe to their homes. He soon afterwards entered the army and so escaped; he told me he had often since dreamt of the cries. He had no vivid recollection of her person."—Manuscript of John Riddell, cited by Cunningham in his edition of Horace Walpole's Letters.

²⁸ About five weeks after Madame du Barry had been guillotined in Paris, the "*Roué*" was executed at Toulouse. After his flight from Paris, in May 1774, Jean du Barry had resided at Toulouse, where Arthur Young, the celebrated traveller, found him living in opulence, and was so charmed with a portrait of his sister-in-law which he saw at his house that he felt he could pardon Louis XV. his infatuation for such a beauty. When the Revolution came, the "*Roué*" embraced the new ideas and raised and equipped an armed force, of which he was appointed second colonel. Having got into debt, however, he was obliged to hide from his creditors, and was denounced as an intended *émigré*. At his trial, he refused to plead, remarking that the few years left him to live—he was then about seventy—were not worth arguing about. He died with courage and resignation.